Yasmin Alibhai-Brown has a weekly column in the *Independent* and was recently nominated as Journalist of the Year by the BBC Asian Personality of the Year Awards. She has won the EMMA, CRE and Windrush Awards and is the author of *The Colour of Love*, *No Place Like Home*, *True Colours*, *Who Do We Think We Are!* and *After Multiculturalism*.

Books by Yasmin Alibhai-Brown:

The Colour of Love
No Place Like Home
True Colours
Who Do We Think We Are?
After Multiculturalism

MIXED FEELINGS

The Complex Lives of
Mixed-Race Britons

YASMIN ALIBHAI-BROWN

First published by The Women's Press Ltd, 2001
A member of the Namara Group
34 Great Sutton Street, London EC1V OLQ
www.the-womens-press.com

Reprinted 2007

British Library Cataloguing-in-Publication Data
A catalogue record for this book is available from the British Library.

ISBN 978 07043 47069

Typeset by FiSH Books, London WC1
Printed and bound in Great Britain by
TJ International Ltd, Padstow, Cornwall

For my lovely Leila who is Indian, African, Pakistani, English,
British and a born Londoner.
And for my son Ari, a young man of many places too,
including his beloved Edinburgh.

'The presence of racially mixed persons defies the social order predicated upon race, blurs racial and ethnic group boundaries, and challenges generally accepted prescriptions and proscriptions regarding inter-group relations. Furthermore, and perhaps most threatening, the existence of racially mixed persons challenges long-held notions about the biological, moral, and social meaning of race.'

Maria Root, *Within, Between and Beyond Race*

Acknowledgements

I am obliged to the Joseph Rowntree Foundation for awarding me a Journalist's Fellowship to research this subject in depth. My thanks to my agent Sarah Molloy of A. M. Heath and my editor Elsbeth Lindner who helped to improve this book immeasurably. I owe much to my English husband Colin, whom I met one fortunate day at a railway station

A number of other individuals have provided important insights and information on mixed-race Britons and, like many others interested in the subject, I am indebted to them. I would, in particular, like to thank the following:

Anne Montague (co-author of *The Colour of Love*), Ravinder Barn, Anne Phoenix, Barbara Tizzard, Nick Banks, Ian Katz, Val Hoskins, Jill Olumide, Madeleine Ashtiani and others from People in Harmony, Anne Wilson, Paul Gilroy, Stuart Hall, Sian Peer, Jayne Ifekwunigwe, Charlie Owen, David Olusoga, Rabbi Jonathan Romain, David Dabydeen, Gary Younge, Inspector June Webb of the Leicestershire Police Force, Asher and Martin Hoyle and Brenda M, the only social worker I met who understood this issue.

I could not have written this book without the following immensely useful published works which I list in the order in which they appear in the book:

Susan Benson, *Ambiguous Ethnicity: Interracial Families in London*

Beth Day, *Sexual Life Between Blacks and Whites*

Fernando Henriques, *Children of Conflict: A Study of Interracial Sex and Marriage*

Z Sardar, Ashish Nandy and Merryl Wyn Davies, *Barbaric Others: A Manifesto of Western Racism*

Kenneth Ballhatchet, *Race, Sex and Class Under the Raj*

R C Boxer, *Race Relations in the Portuguese Colonial Empire*

Eldred Jones, *Othello's Countrymen*

Peter Fryer, *Staying Power*

Rozina Visram, *Ayahs, Lascars and Princes*

Rana Kabbani, *Imperial Fictions: Europe's Myth of the Orient*

R G Ragatz, *The Fall of the Planter Class in the British Caribbean*

W E B Dubois, *The Souls of Black Folk*

E Stonequist, *The Marginal Man: A Study of Personality and Culture*

J A Rogers, *Sex and Race*

Eldridge Cleaver, *Soul on Ice*

Frantz Fanon, *Black Skins, White Masks*
Paul B Rich, *Race and Empire in British Politics*
Muriel Fletcher, *An Investigation into the Colour Problem in Liverpool and Other Ports*
David Omissi, *Voices from the Great War*
S Patterson, *Dark Strangers*
Christine Chambers, Sue Fenge, Gail Harris and Cynthia Williams, *Celebrating Identity*
Lisa Jones, *Bulletproof Diva*
Tariq Modood, Richard Berthoud et al, *Diversity and Disadvantage, Ethnic Minorities in Britain*
Valerie Smith, *Split Affinities: The Case of Interracial Rape*
Amin Maalouf, *On Identity*
Peter Akinti, *Untold Magazine*
Maria Root, *Racially Mixed People in America*
James Jacobs, *Identity Development in Biracial Children*
The Early Years Anti-Racist Network, *The Best of Both Worlds, Celebrating Mixed Parentage*
Kenneth Clark, *Prejudice and Your Child*
David Milner, *Children and Race*
Jewelle Taylor Gibbs and Alice M Hines, *Negotiating Identity, Issues for Black-White Biracial Adolescents*
Jacques Janssen, *Mixed Divorce*
John McCarthy, Introduction to *Jack and Zena*
Adhaf Souief, *The Map of Love*
Abdulrazak Gurnah, *Admiring Silence*
Danzy Senna, *From Caucasia With Love*
Ravinder Bam, Ruth Sinclair and Dionne Ferdinand, *Acting on Principle: An Examination of Race and Ethnicity in Social Services Provision for Children and Families*
Lynda Ince, *Making It Alone*
T Okitikpi, *Mixed Race Children*
June Thoburn et al, *Permanent Family Placement for Children of Ethnic Minority Origin*
B Prevatt Goldstein, *Black Children with One White Parent*
Derek Kirkton, *'Race', Identity and the Politics of Adoption*
Marie Macey, *Transracial Adoption: What's the Problem?*
O Gill and B Jackson, *Adoption and Race: Black, Asian and Mixed-Race Children in White Families*
Frances Wardle, *Tomorrow's Children*
Adele Jones and Jabeer Butt, *Taking the Initiative*
Ivor Gabor and Jane Aldridge (eds), *In the Best Interests of the Children*
B Needell, *Preliminary Data Analysis on Biracial Children in California*
C Camper, *Miscegenation Blues: The Voices of Mixed-Race Women*

Alice Sawyer, *Identity Project on 'Myself'*
I also referred to a vast number of newspaper articles from the *Independent*, the *Guardian*, *The Times*, the *Daily Mail* and others. Television programmes on the BBC and Channel 4 provided some material and I have acknowledged these in the text.

The following institutions were also essential sources for my research:

The Institute for Public Policy Research, the Foreign Policy Centre, the British Agencies for Adoption and Fostering, the National Foster Care Association, Newpin Family Support, the Association of Black Social Workers and Allied Professionals, the National Institute for Social Work Race Equality Unit, the Commission for Racial Equality, the Post Adoption Centre. I am indebted to the local authorities that facilitated interviews with looked-after children.

Most of all I would like to thank all the people who agreed to be interviewed for this publication and previously for *The Colour of Love*. Authors of such books are only conduits, that is all.

Grateful acknowledgement is made to the following:

Allen & Unwin for *Mixed Race Children: A Study of Identity* by Anne Wilson.

BAAF for *Acting On Principle* by Ravinder Barn, Ruth Sinclair and Dionne Ferdinand.

Bloomsbury for *From Caucasia with Love* by Danzy Senna.

Cambridge University Press for *Ambiguous Ethnicity: Interracial Families in London* by Susan Benson and *Race and Empire in British Politics* by Paul B Rich.

Center for the Study of Biracial Children for *Tomorrow's Children* by Francis Wardle.

Dutton for *Children of Conflict: A Study of Interracial Sex and Marriage* by Fernando Henriques.

Free Association Books for *In the Best Interests of the Child* by Ivor Gaber and Jane Aldridge.

Hansib Publications and Ethos Publishing for *Remember Me* by Asher and Martin Hoyles.

HarperCollins for *Sexual Life Between Blacks and Whites* by Beth Day and *Imperial Fictions: Europe's Myth of Orient* by Rana Kabbani.

The Harvill Press for *On Identity* by Amin Maalouf, English Translation by Barbara Bray.

Jessica Kingsley for *The Construction of Racial Identity in Children of Mixed Parentage; Mixed Metaphors* by Ilan Katz.

Macmillan for *Voices from the Great War* by David Omissi.

Penguin for *Bulletproof Diva* by Lisa Jones and *Admiring Silence* by Abdulrazak Gurnah.

Routledge for *Scattered Belongings* by Jayne Ifekwunigwe and *Black, White or Mixed Race* by Barbara Tizzard and Ann Phoenix.

Sage Publications for *Racially Mixed People in America* edited by Maria Root.

Sister Vision for *Miscegenation Blues: The Voices of Mixed Race Women* edited by C Camper.

Contents

Terminology

The terms used, misused and battled over for so long in this area of human relations continue to be a problem. I do not use the word 'black' to mean mixed-race in this book unless this is how my interviewee describes herself or himself. Most other writers use the term 'black' to mean mixed-race, and when I quote them I do so too. I prefer the terms 'mixed-race' or 'mixed-parentage'. At times I use 'black' as a political term and apply it to all British people of colour. But when it comes to ethnicity, I use the word 'black' to mean of African and African Caribbean origin. The context makes this clear I hope.

Introduction

'I consider you are not fit to bring up your daughter with your ideas of mating her to a Negro. I sincerely hope that God will cut short your life and that you will *die soon* so that dear little white girl may be saved from the hideous fate you plan for her. A black blubber-lipped Negro on top of her.'

'Interbreeding is evil and nobody could be proud of half-caste children. The idea of everyone being a wretched khaki colour with thick lips and flat noses in the future is abhorrent to all right-thinking Englishmen.'
Letters received by the Reverend Clifford Hill after a broadcast in 1961 during which he said that he would not object to his daughter marrying a black man.'

'He looked at my fourteen-month-old child in his pushchair and said, "Another fucking nigger, another fucking coon."'

'I know how hard it's been and I sometimes wish I had done things differently. It is such a shock when one day you are suddenly seen as black, because your children are when you think of yourself as white. But my children? I would never change them, not for anything.'
Two white mothers of mixed-race children on *Woman's Hour*, 1986.

'My mum is pink like candy floss and my dad is dark brown like plain chocolate. I am light brown like toffee but I wish I was like my mum. It's better.'
Mary, the seven-year-old child of an Indian father and Scottish mother speaking in 1990.

'I sometimes wish my parents had just aborted me. What is the point of me? I am not white and not African. I look like nobody else that I know or have ever met. My hair is gold and then frizzy. My skin is both brown and freckled. I have blue eyes and an African nose and big mama lips. My father, he was shocked when I was born because I didn't look like him. But I did. Only he just saw my strange colour. So that is why maybe he went away and has never been in touch. My

mum, well, I think she tried to love me and then she pushed
me off to social workers. Why don't these grown-ups think
what they are doing? I want to be sterilised!

*Kora, a seventeen-year-old girl interviewed for this book in 1999. She was in
council care for five years and which she was to leave at the time of the
interview. She has no contact with either parents and no foster arrangements
have ever worked for her. She was excluded from school during the last year of
her education and has no GCSEs.*

This is a book about mixed-race Britons, a community which is
moving out from the shadows and heading purposefully into the
light, challenging existing ideologies of ethnic and national purity
and staking its claims on this nation. Research produced for a
Channel 4 series on slavery shows that one in ten Britons today
could have mixed racial origins[2] and progress in DNA technology
will lead to further evidence showing that far from being 'pure'
blooded, the indigenous people of this island are, in the words of the
culture critic Philip Dodd, a 'mongrel'[3] race. Over three hundred
years ago, Daniel Defoe recognised this in his poem *The True-Born
Englishman*, in which he pointed out that the blood of this nation,
even then, was 'Roman-Saxon-Danish-Norman English'.[4]

With such a heritage, perhaps it is not surprising that Britain now
has one of the highest rates of mixed-race relationships anywhere in
the occidental world and that the trend is upwards and accelerating
among ordinary people as well as the famous and powerful. Just
think of Trevor McDonald, Zeinab Badawi, Trevor Phillips,
Baroness Shreela Flather, Baroness Patricia Scotland, Lord Taylor,
Lord Hollick, Lord Dholakia, Frank Bruno, Hanif Kureishi, Oona
King MP, Sade, Michael Caine, Bernie Grant MP, Dawn French,
Madhur Jaffrey, Sayeed Jaffrey, Jung Chang (author of *Wild Swans*),
Jennifer Kendall, chef Ainsley Harriott, Salman Rushdie, Lisa Aziz,
Cleo Laine, Cathy Tyson, Shirley Bassey, Diana Princess of Wales,
and scores of other famous people. They have all been or are in
mixed-race relationships. In the case of Oona King, Sade, Kureishi
and others, they themselves are also of mixed parentage. We are
beginning to see the first wave of writing and art describing this
brave new world, for example, the acclaimed first novel *White
Teeth*, by Zadie Smith (herself mixed-race), which describes the
irreversible rise of hybrid London.

All these high fliers and, more importantly, thousands of ordinary
people have challenged one of the most persistent and universal of
social taboos in human history. For centuries communities have
protected themselves from the threatening 'other' by creating
barriers to desire. In this country, says the novelist Caryl Phillips,
'The "mongrel" nation that is Britain is still struggling to find a way
to stare into the mirror and accept the ebb and flow of history that

has produced this fortuitously diverse condition and its concomitant pain.'[5] But race, caste, religious, class or colour boundaries have never wholly succeeded in keeping any fenced off compound 'pure' and homogeneous. Neither apartheid nor the lynch mobs in the southern states of America could deter the truly committed. The murders carried out by furious Asian families when their daughters step out of community, the kind of national hysteria which greeted Jemima Goldsmith's marriage to Imran Khan, poisonous social disapproval, nothing but nothing can, it seems, stop love and/or physical attraction.

You cannot take three steps in any of our large metropolitan areas without seeing a mixed-race couple, often with exquisitely beautiful children. One mother from Kilburn in London, interviewed for this book, told me that these children are the majority in her son's class and that they compete with each other over who has the most labels:

It is lovely to see the pride with which they name their heritage. The winner at the moment is Gloria, who is a quarter each, Ghanaian, Irish, Pakistani and Cornish. The other children envy her and invent family trees to match hers. It is so different from when I was growing up. We had a mixed-race American girl in our class at secondary school and she used to be called 'mutt' and I remember her getting more and more withdrawn.

So does this mean that this is now – albeit reluctantly – a rainbow country? Or that the optimism of *Guess Who's Coming To Dinner!* has become a reality for most of us who have dared not to conform? No. The fact that *more* people are leaping across racial and other barriers does not necessarily mean that attitudes have radically improved. The journalist Gary Younge is right to advise caution:

By far the most common misconception, particularly among liberals is that a rise in mixed-race relationships signals, a priori, an increase in racial tolerance. People who would otherwise argue that politics should be taken out of the bedroom cannot help trying to slip sociology under the sheets. One wonders if this is the case why the group most likely to be involved in mixed-race relationships – young black men – is also the group most likely to be stopped. Searched, jailed and excluded. If 'every mixed-race marriage is building a better Britain' as one commentator claimed, then logic suggests that the break-up of any mixed-race Britain makes Britain worse.[6]

In some cases, like the example above, progress is clear for all to see and people have of course embraced these crossovers. But old prejudices die hard and in many cases they might even be strengthening because there is a panic that too many people are rebelling against social categories. Unimaginable acceptance has been achieved and yet intolerable (and intolerant) opposition still fights on. Both exist, neither cancels the other out. And where once it was usually mainly the white side which objected to interracial unions, nowadays such prejudice can be found in all the other communities too. As Donna, a mixed-race entrepreneur married to a Welshman, describes it:

> When my parents married, the white family sent my parents an abusive letter, a wreath and did not come to the wedding. When we married, my father, who is black, was so upset he could not even look at me. He thought I would marry a black man and bring black back in some way into the family. Instead I brought in more white. Now my son has blue eyes and Dad never stops commenting on this. You know, I don't think he can relate to him because of this, I see the distance in his eyes when my son is sitting on his lap.

The word 'miscegenation', used to describe the products of relationships across racial barriers, is infused with opprobrium and the implication of something not quite the norm, something deviant. Behavioural changes can occur without attitudes necessarily changing at the same pace and this is certainly the case with mixed-race relationships. When exploring this issue therefore it is vital to include both what is happening in this area of human relations and what people think and to include the positive as well as the negative experiences. It is essential too to assess how institutions and experts have (or more often have not) responded to the phenomenon which, many believe, is set to transform the ethnic composition of our major cities.

The 'problem' framework

A number of experts in the field now believe it is time to question the way in which the issue is discussed and framed in this country. Academics and others who pontificate on human behaviour, for example, have been locked into the pathological matrix. Interracial relationships, it seems, are a problem (the racist view), have unspeakable difficulties (the pessimistic liberal view) or provide a pretty coffee-coloured solution for all the world's problems (the view of hopeful liberals). If you remember the Blue Mink song about the whole world becoming a great big melting pot or Paul McCartney's 'Ebony and Ivory', you can see both the naïveté and appeal of these fond hopes and dreams. The media coverage over the decades from the forties to the seventies neatly illustrates these positions. In the forties and fifties, such families were seen as contaminators of a racially 'pure' country. In the sixties and seventies, this changed to people worrying about how many problems such families were creating for themselves by having mixed-race relationships and children. A few people also thought that this trend would help solve the endemic racism so obviously present in British society. The last two decades have brought in a militant pro-black position where mixed-race children have been labelled black regardless of whether they wanted to be.

These simplistic approaches are now increasingly rejected by mixed-race people and families although most accept that being who they are will demand great self-consciousness, whether spoken or silent, and an unavoidable backdrop of racism. As Zadie Smith says of her own life: 'When you come from a mixed-race family, it makes you think a bit harder about inheritance and what is passed from generation to generation...As for racial tensions, I am sure my parents had the usual trouble getting hotel rooms and so on but I don't talk to them much about that part of their lives.'[7]

However, it is vital to stress that there is now a critical mass of young adults who are of mixed origins and who do not see themselves as carrying either burdens or solutions for the entire society. Many people from these families are impressively articulate about their emotions and they provide role models of how prejudices can be confronted to create future possibilities, but they do at the same time resist being seen as symbols. When you talk to a wide range of people you discover that without necessarily being conscious of it, this community is changing and challenging settled ideologies, notions and labels. As social researcher Anne Phoenix writes: 'Given that there are an increasing number of people who are of mixed parentage or who are themselves in mixed-race relationships, it is not surprising that this is an area where terminology has been contested.'[8] She also believes it is wrong to presume anything any more. For example, from her research she has concluded that people of mixed race do not all suffer from racialised identity problems and that most identify themselves as 'mixed'.

These developments do need to be taken seriously especially as even now (when we should know better) rich and prolific human experience continues to be reduced to snapshots by those with predetermined views about this subject. They creep along with their cameras, catching people they define as living in the hinterlands of ordinary life. Popular culture has served to reinforce these views. Anne Wilson, in her excellent study of mixed-race children, argued some years ago that sociological work in this area has been influenced by and has influenced the 'problem' perspective put forth by the media, and that in the United States academics have gone even further, seeing these children as 'marginal': 'Apart from the occasional attempt to treat the subject sensitively and seriously, plays, magazine articles, novels and television programmes all tend to return to the same theme: that interracial marriages are fraught with problems and that mixed-race children are crazy mixed-up kids who are rejected both by black *and* white communities.[9]

Growing confidence and persistent barriers

Wilson wrote her book in 1987. Nowadays, we have more and better research in this area though still not nearly enough. There is a greater sense of 'normality' felt by a large proportion of people in mixed-race families and at long last ethnic monitoring forms are beginning to provide a 'mixed-race' category. Mixed heritage people themselves are asserting their own identities much more effectively. For some people, for example, changing attitudes – at least among thinking people – and the chance to live in mixed areas have provided a richness of life confirming what Wilson wrote over a decade back in *Mixed Race Children*: 'Contrary to the popular stereotype of mixed-race people as torn between black and white, many children seemed to have found a happy and secure identity for themselves ... This was particularly true of children in multiracial areas who were able to draw support from the existence of other mixed-race and "brown" children in the area.'[10]

Madeleine Ashtiani, an Italian-Persian, wrote a passionately felt piece about this in the newsletter produced by People In Harmony, a support group for mixed-race families: 'I want to speak for those who silently have been observed and quietly have been excluded from the raging debates on "race" both in academia and in the media, where sociologists and journalists alike have, at best, come to misunderstand conclusions on our behalf, or at worst ignored us ... we embody interraciality, we embody reconciliation.'[11]

But there is a danger in overstating the good news. A too-high dose of positive thinking creates easy illusions and discourages an engagement with the very real difficulties faced by people such as young and disenchanted Kora above, who since our conversation has attempted suicide and is now on high dosage antidepressants.

Unexpectedly, the good can turn sour and the impact appears to be greater in mixed-race situations. When I co-wrote *The Colour of Love*,[12] a book about mixed-race relationships, I met a young girl who was the very symbol of all that is so special about these families. She was beautiful, highly articulate and very bright. She excelled at sports and loved school. She knew all about black history and her English background too. And she was proud. Today the same girl, now a teenager, is finding it heartbreakingly hard to find her way in the world. She has dropped out of school and her parents have split up. All of this happens in same race families too, of course. But race adds heat to the mix.

Methodology and ongoing controversies

In this book I have tried to resist coarse postulations and simple assumptions, though I daresay that many who have lived experiences will not feel the entire depth and breadth of their individual lives adequately reflected in a book of this kind which is, by definition, limited. I detect some progress since *The Colour of Love*, but this is only one of the threads which emerged. Old prejudices and new doubts are equally present in Britain today. I have asked individuals with immediate personal experience to talk about their lives and thoughts. These are people who, through their relationships with partners, parents and children, have insights that no contained journalistic analysis or ponderous research tome can hope to capture. It has been an illuminating exercise. The conversations were not formal but unstructured and shaped by my interviewees. Their views were taken on board, they had access to me and I did my best to avoid imposing any pre-packaged notions on them.

Nevertheless, even a venture like this, which attempts to break out of sociological bondage, had to confront certain challenges. Some people saw the book itself as an affront. They argued that a relationship is just that and that such explorations are a meaningless and voyeuristic exercise. 'Would you do a book on blonde people having relationships with red-haired people? So why black-and white-skinned people?' I was asked. Of course it could be argued that all journalism and non-fiction is voyeuristic, but I hope that the sheer diversity of experiences I have included and the uniquely collaborative approach used have reduced the power I have as a writer to manipulate or make a spectacle of people. Yet the danger always exists and I acknowledge it.

Another more serious objection that can be levelled is that the book itself is based on racist premises. If we accept that there is only one human race (which is indisputable) and that hierarchical racial divisions were invented for ignoble purposes, the very notion of mixed race becomes a racist concept and by doing what I am doing, I am endorsing that racist construct. It is an important point but one which rests on wishful thinking.

Of course, scientifically speaking, biological differences in inherited characteristics do not denote the superiority or inferiority of any group of human beings. These are false edifices that have been erected, primarily by the white world, to prop up the brutal exploitation of non-whites around the world over several centuries. But racial stratification has a powerful *social* and *political* existence. Cultural, caste and religious hierarchies have, through history, been set up to advantage the privileged. Demarcation between groups on the basis of colour, culture and religious hierarchies persists with remarkable tenacity around the world.

Wishing passionately that these pernicious divisions did not exist did not seem to me a good reason to assume that they do not. These partitions and the attitudes they engender have permeated the lives of many of the individuals I talked to, although for others they have had less direct effect on their daily existence. But not one interviewee denied that these powerful social forces do prevail around their lives and those of their children.

Questions addressed in the book

A book like this is of value for two opposing reasons. The breadth of experience revealed across a wide spectrum of class, gender, age and history shows up the absurdity of any generalisation in the field of human relationships. On the other hand, this is not simply a collection of disparate ramblings. I was interested in testing certain assumptions and exploring connections. For example, is it really possible to overcome indefatigable historical prejudices through a defiant and/or romantic personal act? Or is this simply dismissed as an 'exception' by those bonded to their ideas of racial separation? And is the increase in mixed-race relationships in fact deepening prejudice as people see their imagined 'pollution' of the pure races becoming a reality? Do age-old fears, taboos and fantasies still weave themselves around the private lives of those in interracial relationships? And how through this forest of experiences can better social policies be devised which can take account of difference as well as commonality?

What became clear as I talked to people was the force with which the external world bears down on those in mixed-race families or relationships. In a society where our reluctance to become 'involved' leaves tortured children at risk in their own homes and raped women lying in gutters, perfect strangers think they have the right to abuse you, or your partner or your child, because you have different skin colours. Or at least to comment, express surprise and talk about you and yours as if they have an absolute right to do so.

For as long as racism and other forms of injustices against groups continue to create a divided and racially unequal society, people who cross the barriers will be forced to live in the glare of the public eye. Their lives will always be located within that bleak landscape, whether they succeed in their relationship or not. Susan Benson, who studied multiracial families in Brixton in the late 1970s, puts it aptly: 'To study the everyday lives of interracial families, then, is to study the nature of British race relations as it impinges on the lives of individuals.'[13] Many other factors come into play too, including class and economic status; the rise of black politics; increasing cultural and religious conservatism; the ever elusive dreams of integration; radical changes in education and childhood development; politics and demographic changes in inner-city areas and now the perils and possibilities of globalisation.

Add to this the changing male/female roles, sexual expectations, myths, psychological dynamics, evolving cultural identities, fame, economic success – and the picture becomes even more complicated. When everything is in a state of flux, old certainties become irresistible for many. But – and this is worth repeating – in the end whatever the outcome, however society has chosen to label these relationships, whatever impediments it has put in their way, including laws like those in South Africa and the Southern States of America, people from different racial groups across history have, for better or for worse, continued to have sexual relationships.

Changes in the past fifteen years

There appeared to be a new determination and confidence among many of my interviewees who now sense that they are growing into a critical mass. This is a significant development since 1989/1990 when *The Colour of Love* was researched and written, although it is interesting (and sad) that a number of happy couples in that book have since split up, often with much pain. But even among those who could not in the end stay together, most have few regrets. They feel their lives have been enriched and transformed by what they chose to do and a number console themselves that they are pioneers – who therefore have to suffer – leading society towards a better future with people much more at ease with each other.

Some spoke movingly about how, these days, it is just as likely for a black or Asian person to disapprove as it is for a white person and how much this hurts. As Susanah, a twenty-year-old mixed-race student said:

> I am at university in Liverpool. You can't get more mixed and hotch-potch than this city. But because I look more black than white, I get such hassle. Black students say I am a tart because my boyfriend is white – Irish, mind you, but that doesn't matter. And whites too will comment, nicely, about how difficult it must be. I can't believe that I am going through the same shit my parents did, only twice as bad because then at least the black community was more welcoming of stray whites who came into their families.

Many people have reached a new understanding about the direction of their relationships. It can no longer be assumed, as it once was, that white values would dominate and that the black or Asian partner would turn 'white', give or take an occasional ethnic headscarf or sari at the office Christmas party. You can see this change quite clearly if you look at the names of mixed-race children then and now. Thirty years ago, mixed-race children were often given the most common English names such as 'James' or 'Jenny' as if that way they would merge more easily and disappear into the crowd, not draw attention to themselves. Today many children are given names which reflect the non-white side of the family. Nothing is taken for granted, and this, said one woman, exercised the heart and mind constantly ('It's like your thoughts are going to the gym to get fit'), making you more conscious and a better parent.

Sexual fantasies and racial violence

On the other hand, there are many liberal whites whose assumptions about sexual relationships between white and black still seem to be based on historical stereotypes. Forbidden fruit takes a long time to lose its magic. Too often these days, white men, repelled, they say, by feminist white women, turn to Asian women as 'submissive' and black women as 'whores' and some are not afraid to let their fantasies hang out. In an article in the men's magazine *Arena*, journalist Tony Parsons asked this extraordinary question:

Why is the blonde all washed up? Why are more men turning to Pretty Ethnics? Why do most men prefer – either in their lives or in their fantasies – the comfort of brown-eyed girls rather than the big broad mares with dyed hair and sagging tits? *Why?* Are you *kidding?* ... would you rather share your toothpaste with some complaining, big-boned, post-fem ballsy chick or a creature of infinite beauty and grace?

Parsons goes on breathlessly to anoint such desires: 'Rather than sexual imperialism, I believe that a liking for Pretty Ethnics means that in your heart you are embracing the whole of humanity.'[14]

Steve, a successful journalist I met in London is unashamed of his not dissimilar fantasies:

I go for black girls because they have gorgeous bodies and smooth skin which never wrinkles. White girls have skin which sags and bags and wrinkles even by thirty. Black girls also know what to do for a man. There is nothing they won't do. It is as if their history of slavery has taught them a thing or two about what a man wants. They never say no.

Such attitudes are often openly discussed by people who see themselves as unafraid and hard new Metropolitans.

Other historical sexual and power fantasies still appear to infiltrate mixed relationships and are even more emotionally charged. These, like most other issues, are not new. Beth Day began to explore them in her heartfelt polemic in the 1970s:

The desire for the black man to prove himself sexually with a white partner has provoked a bitter conflict between black males and black females, just at a time when they most need to consolidate their ranks ... the competition for the black men has also succeeded in building a wall of distrust and anger between black women and white women, when co-operation would be valuable in breaking down the barriers of discriminatory employment practices and in pressing for more female political power. The myth of black super-sexuality also puts the white woman who is genuinely attracted to a black man in the potential position of being sexually exploited – a pawn in the revenge that the black male seeks to wreak on the white male for his history of oppression.[15]

This is also one of the most powerful messages in *Soul on Ice* by the black writer Eldridge Cleaver who, in the days of the civil rights struggles, wrote about the inner damage caused to so many older black men by inhumane racist treatment.

These writers are describing non-British experiences and many black Britons now argue that these have nothing in common with the British experience. I think this is an understandable, but flawed argument. Take the US and Britain. Of course the reality of actual slavery and violent reactions against black men in the US – there were no lynchings in the UK – means that emotions were more intense and raw and the physical perils altogether more present and pressing. But look at our newspapers and you soon find that some of the most violent racist attacks in British society, and in Southern Ireland too, are perpetrated against mixed-race couples and families. The sexist and racist assumptions of ownership, purity and pollution, of the barbaric black male, underpin British society to this day. Thirty years on, in the United States and Britain, these assumptions are still invading lives, as is confirmed by several men and women in this book. The histories are radically different but the effects of racism are similar. You only have to look at the employment, imprisonment and school exclusion rates of black men in both countries to see this clearly.

White and black women have had to think through where they place themselves in this often racist and sexist society, especially as these two powerful social forces are so often in opposition. Some of the women I interviewed had resolved this dilemma, others were still negotiating it and others, although obviously aware of it, saw their lives in entirely personal terms.

Inter-religious relationships

British racism has changed its face, mutated, extended its brief, and couples and individuals spoke of new challenges they had been forced to confront. Certain things have improved so dramatically that it is almost impossible to recall some of the realities just three decades back. Enoch Powell died without seeing blood foaming in the

Thames. But some religious groups are now under vicious attack; this is why I have included couples who have crossed religious boundaries, although miscegenation strictly refers only to race. In recent years, the new enemy resurrected out of old Islam is also being tested in terms of personal lives and relationships. White men and women married to Muslims have had a whole area of resentment to negotiate, and this has given them both courage and pain. During the Gulf crisis, these were the comments of the award-winning *Sun* columnist Richard Littlejohn: 'What I can live without are British women married to Iraqis, arriving back at Heathrow and Gatwick... in full Arab garb... They have chosen to turn their back on Britain, our values and beliefs. They should be left to rot in their adopted country with their hideous husbands and their unattractive children.'[16]

In response to such views, which are widespread, young Muslims are reasserting their distinct identity and regrouping as Muslims across the racial and ethnic divides. Mixed marriages within this new Muslim assertiveness are given space, safety and a 'home' which obviously helps many. The problem is that the deal demands of the 'outsider' that they should convert and give over their identity and future to be absorbed into the Islamic world. This is no different from the days when black and Asian partners had to go 'white' in order to be accepted. For many non-Muslim individuals the bargain is more than acceptable. They find it comforting to be included in a community with shared values, in particular if they were previously disenchanted with the secular, individualistic world. But others find these conditions of acceptance demeaning, difficult and intrusive. These are explored in Chapters 4 and 5.

The Jewish community is changing too. Many young Jews are now refusing to bury their heads in the sand or to become invisible in order to make themselves less offensive to the Anglo-Saxon eye. And when identities begin to reassert themselves, the issue of intermarriage is never far away. Old prejudices against the Jews are less obvious but can resurface, creating new fears of survival and longings for purity and integrity. Hannah, mother of David who has a black wife, feels things have been sliding dangerously in her own family:

I like my daughter-in-law, Shellie. She is straight, honest and loving. But I am seventy. My Jewishness is important to me. Shellie will not bring the children up as Jews. She says her blackness is more important. Love is making a monkey of my son. He doesn't understand that our survival depends on continuity. He is giving away our history without any care. She is due to have her baby any time and they want to call it Maya or Courtney. You see. It is all going. I said Jacob and they both said it was too Jewish. How can you be too Jewish?

The more orthodox sections of the Jewish community have long vocalised these fears and do so with greater urgency as the rise in mixed marriages, now up to 30 per cent of community marriages, seems unstoppable. And even people like Jonathan Romain, a Reform Rabbi who counsels mixed couples and is no purist firebrand, have expressed worries about where it might all end: 'At the end of the day I firmly believe that intermarriage is a bad thing. Intermarriage detracts from the religious continuity of Judaism...It also endangers the survival of Anglo-Jewry. This community is decreasing frighteningly rapidly.'[17]

Minority group prejudices

It is significant that many black and Asian people too are arguing in the same terms as Hannah above. But is a plea for racial purity to be condoned when it is uttered by oppressed minorities and condemned when it is put forth by a powerful majority? I believe not. These attitudes are dangerous and morally unsound wherever they arise and to those who choose to defy these ideas of purity, such justifications appear even more flimsy. One can understand why communities who think of themselves as minorities (a concept which seems only to apply to non-indigenous people and not, say, to the Welsh) imagine that in a few hundred years they will disappear from this soil. But culture can be passed on in mixed-race families by both partners and it is surely unacceptable to tolerate the vehemence with which purists from 'minority' communities argue for the right to prevent people – by whatever means – from making personal choices about who they wish to love.

Nasreen, a young woman in a refuge, tells her story of this simply:

> I fell in love with my colleague, another trainee teacher. He is a Syrian Christian. I am Muslim. But our roots are in the Middle East so our values are the same. But my brothers, they have threatened to kill him if he speaks to me. They say they are protecting our family and community against this poison. I still see him secretly but it is all ruined now. We are unhappy all the time instead of being happy the way we were. Guilt and fear dominate our lives. For what? I will never marry anyone else but I don't know if I have the courage to marry Mike now. I could ruin his life. Or maybe end up a widow.

Other complexities and confusions also came to light. Many interviewees thought these needed to be approached more honestly and not shrouded in secrecy. The nature of relationships between blacks and Asians and the kinds of prejudices involved was one such issue; another was the increasing tendency of many 'successful' black and Asian men to choose white partners almost as the finishing touch to their impressive CVs. These discussions were full of fire and fury as impossible questions surfaced. Do these men make these choices because of the myth of the emasculating black matriarch and the obsessively devoted (to the son) Asian mother? Why is it acceptable for a black or Asian man to cross the colour divide, but not a woman? Why is it right for black people to condemn these relationships when they would themselves cry racism if white people registered their disapproval in those terms? Why do so many Asian parents find it easier to accept white partners than black partners for their children? And why do many black people either reject mixed-race people as not properly black or accept them only on condition that they disavow their white side? These questions are dealt with in Chapter 5 on family life and relationships.

The culture wars

Another issue that emerged was the facile way in which culture is perceived by those who oppose mixed relationships. People rightly argued that cultures develop and change, and must do so if they are not to become fossilised. Dynamism is a positive life force and history shows that those who wish to preserve outdated notions in some mental attic full of cultural bric-a-brac eventually make themselves and their values obsolete. If this is so, it becomes meaningless to talk in dichotomous terms about choosing one 'culture' or another, because we are all composite creatures now. Immigration changes those who emigrate, as well as the places they leave and the places they move to. Things or people can never return to what they were. As Shahid, an artist in Bradford, put it:

> My father, who is a mullah in Bolton, is completely different from a mullah in Lahore. He is living within a context of difference. There people are living mostly within sameness. So to say that we have a culture which never changes is rubbish. Fathers are having to change towards their children. He has had to accept my wife, who is Turkish. He says, change is Allah's way of stopping us becoming lazy and like lizards.

One overwhelming conclusion I reached while researching this book was that however mixed-race couples and mixed-race children choose to live their lives, they cannot shake off historical baggage or isolate themselves from the assumptions and bigotries of the outside world. These attitudes infiltrate their lives. And for many it is the transition to parenthood that brings this realisation most profoundly. Some of the parents quoted at the beginning of this chapter are examples. My research revealed unbearable unforgiveness. I found that when children married out sometimes the parents died without making up or seeing their grandchildren.

But even when there is blessing all round, for those entering these relationships love is almost always never going to be enough. Outside pressures do dent and sometimes damage resolve and affect love. You have two choices: either you become stronger and fitter as a couple or you surrender. There is no shame in such a surrender.

I have learnt much during my own ten-year marriage to a white Englishman. I have seen how people like us develop an unreal and unhelpful sense that we are warriors for a cause. You can only do your best. Things *are* harder across the barriers and it would be foolish to deny that just because you do not want your racist granddad to gloat.

Mixed-race individuals

The children in these families are not black, Asian or white. Theirs is a complex identity which needs to be understood by mono-cultural parents and others. They are often rejected by all sides and have to develop their self-esteem in ways that are unique. From the age of three, my daughter Leila was told that she is half English and half Asian. She has found it confusing at times but she will grow up knowing she is different and that she should be proud of this fact. She is, like those other thousands of mixed-race Britons, a person of the future, but that future cannot be designed or planned by those on the outside of the experience. As Madeleine says: '...multiracial people are becoming more politicised...the time has come for us to demonstrate how racial inclusivity can celebrate ethnic difference and blur boundaries simultaneously...by nature we are ethnically fluid, our conceptualisation of "race" is complex, a process'.[18]

The need for further research and better policies

These are just some of the many strands which emerged during the course of my research. I am conscious of gaps in the book. There are no Irish Catholic and Protestant couples, or many other interesting combinations – German and Jewish, for example. These omissions do not indicate neglect or judgement on my part. I had to draw the line somewhere, even though it was tempting to go on with this project for another two years.

This book cannot provide all the stories or truths. There is more research available than a decade ago but not nearly enough. The complex lives of this growing and increasingly visible population within these islands need to receive sustained and broad attention from policy makers, demographic specialists and those engaged in race and ethnic studies. In his annotated bibliography published in 1996, Alex Hall of the Centre for Research in Ethnic Relations, University of Warwick, wrote: 'There is a dearth of information on mixed-race relationships in the UK. This is curious since it is often the area of "race relations" which excites the most public condemnation and personal hostility.'[19]

This paradox continues to manifest itself. In the absence of ongoing and sensible research, the subject has too often become trivialised and sensationalised by the media, especially by television and the popular press. The media understands all too well how the combination of sex, race and sometimes class makes for appetising copy which helps to sell its products. But it must be acknowledged that the media is also responding to a growing public desire to know more about mixed-race families. Maybe it is because of this spotlight that there are a substantial number of people who do not wish to be thought of as mixed-race. Some are violently offended by the attention. This reluctance of many Britons to describe either themselves or others as 'mixed-race' has another understandable explanation. Throughout history, as Chapters 1 and 2 show, people of mixed ancestry have been misrepresented, vilified, excluded and even punished by various societies. In the United States, as late as 1960, laws like the Virginia Code made intermarriage an act of felony punishable by five years in prison. Many of the earliest race riots in this country came out of the hatred white men felt for black men who had sexual relations with or married white women.[20] It is only in the last two decades that we have seen the emergence of real pride among mixed-race British families. But, as has already been described, this period has also seen new conflicts around this issue which have not helped the necessary process of liberation and reclamation.

Inexplicably, a number of these battles seem to have arisen out of the best of intentions and have been triggered off by many of those who have spent their lives challenging old prejudices and who have been passionately committed to anti-racism. Chapters 3 and 6 deal with this in detail. Since the seventies, many of these people have promoted a dogmatic position, which has taken root, insisting that mixed-race children should be defined by the racial background of the non-white parent. This strongly held belief permeated many local authorities, black community groups and relevant agencies. It is still remarkably difficult to persuade policy makers in key positions that mixed-race children are different from mono-racial children and that theirs is an identity which needs to be recognised.

There is an irony here. In the United States during the worst days of slavery and segregation and institutionalised racism, white supremacists used the 'one blood' rule to categorise mixed-race people as black and therefore deny them any rights. A single drop of black blood made a person uncompromisingly black. The rule ensured that the mixed-race children of white slave owners would remain slaves and never inherit privilege. In 1781, a British soldier who had fallen in love with a free black woman swallowed drops of her blood to become 'black' and thereby avoid draconian anti-miscegenation laws.[21] Similar rules destroyed the lives of people in South Africa. There were unspeakably tragic stories in both countries of mixed-race people trying to pass for white (because they could and knew that by doing so they could avoid the cruelty and injustice meted out to black people) and others who believed they were white because the family history had been kept hidden and were then denounced black. With such a history it is indeed curious that so many black, Asian and white professionals decided – without any credible consultation with those affected, like those who had direct experience of being in mixed-race relationships and their children – that one drop of black blood made you black.

The interviews and issues covered

I have tried to address these fascinating issues through the people who know best – those with actual experience of crossing over. A minority of interviewees did not mind being identified but for those who wanted to remain anonymous I have changed some details in order to protect identities. For the relevant chapters I deliberately sought out the views of young Britons (17 to 23-year-olds) in colleges, clubs and other informal settings. I wanted to see what they thought of interracial relationships. The results were not encouraging, both because I realised how little has changed and also because, with a few exceptions, the polarisation between the groups seemed so much greater than in earlier post-war decades or even ten years ago when *The Colour of Love* was written.

The people I talked to gave me endless amounts of time and coffee and allowed me intimate access to their lives, even when it was incredibly painful or when they could so easily have held back. Some people found the conversations cathartic after years of burying feelings about the issue. Others talked to each other as I talked to them, often for the first time, about their worries and realisations. Some claimed to have found renewed joy and vigour through being forced to excavate the past and remember what they gave up in order to be with one another. Many, many others needed to share the pain and doubt that they had kept hidden for years. There are three interviewees in this book who told me things they said they could never tell their partners. I feel privileged to have met all the people who talked to me and their exceptional insights. They made the book. Those many hidden voices and seeing eyes show that one can talk about common threads but in the end these are individuals, separate and unique.

I have included couples who began their relationships in the 1940s and 1950s, as well as those who have done so more recently.

I talked to the parents of children who have gone into mixed relationships and to mixed-race children, many of them now embarking on love affairs of their own. They told me about their lives within and outside their relationship, about the joys and traumas of parenthood and about their hopes and fears for the future. They discussed how their family reacted to them, how their friends and the wider community responded and what they felt their place to be in multiracial Britain. A few of my interviewees felt that the country was 'good at' certain kinds of diversity, namely food and sex, but that this should not be taken as an indication that racism is coming to an end. This point was made by Zadie Smith when some people described her book as a 'post-race' novel. In fact people make that assumption so that they can block out their own awareness of the serious problems which continue to destroy the lives of people of colour.

The chapters are divided thematically, but there is obviously some overlap. Chapter 1 and Chapter 2 concentrate on the long and fascinating history of mixed-race relationships in order to provide a context for our modern times. Chapter 3 assesses the trends today and uses statistics and qualitative research carried out for this book and by other researchers to describe contemporary experiences. It looks at the way terminology continues to grow and evolve when it comes to mixed-race Britons. Chapter 4 also deals with the central issue of identity. Personal identity, the identity of children and the challenges these create are the main issues. This is followed by a chapter on the intimately related subject of family life. Included are relationships between partners themselves, their children and the wider family group. In Chapter 6, I assess social policies which bear directly on the lives of mixed-race families. From relationship counselling to help with racist assault, people in mixed-race situations are not receiving adequate recognition.

At the end of my long, exhilarating journey I felt a strong sense that there was new energy among the people in mixed-race families, even when things fell apart and caused tremendous despair. This feeling is well encapsulated by Gary Younge who wrote in the *Guardian* in 1997: ' Beige Britain... a new race is growing up. It's not black and it's not white and it's not yet officially recognised. Welcome to the new mixed-race future.'[22]

Chapter 1
History up to 1900

'I have had three partners – all blonde – and have six children. Why? I ask myself. I have nothing in common with these women, but in my mind's eye beauty is white and blue eyed. I cannot fancy a black woman though I have tried. It is centuries of brain-washing, the deep memories of slavery and imperialism, of hearing your parents and grandparents going on about how lovely so and so is because she has straight hair and pale skin.'
Bernard, whose parents came to the UK from Jamaica in 1956 and who is convinced history is still playing out.

'If we could bleach her by any means we would, and thus make her acceptable in any company, as she deserves to be.'
An American who greatly admired Mary Seacole, the mixed-race nurse who went to the Crimea to tend soldiers and work with Florence Nightingale.

'If [my complexion] had been as dark as any nigger's, I should have been just as happy and just as useful and as much respected by those whose respect I value; as to his offer of bleaching me, I should, even if it were practicable, decline it without any thanks. As to the society which the process might gain me admission into, all I can say is that judging from the specimens I have met here and elsewhere, I don't think I shall lose much from being excluded from it.'
Mary Seacole's retort to the enthusiastic admirer above.

'We would do almost anything to avoid a collision with degraded natives; but in case of an invasion – our blood boils at the very thought of our wives, sisters or daughters being touched – we as men with human feelings would unhesitatingly fight to the death, with all the fury in our power.'
David Livingstone, explorer.'

Mixed Feelings is primarily concerned with the lives of people in this country and not in other parts of the world and the book concentrates mostly on contemporary experiences. But in any account of mixed-race relationships it is important to understand how the attitudes of white, black and Asian Britons towards miscegenation have evolved and are inextricably bound up with the history of this nation and the central role, as Bernard above points out, of slavery and colonialism around the world. Dr Fernando Henriques concluded this in *Children of Conflict*, his seminal study of interracial relationships: 'Contemporary manifestations of racial mixing have been very largely determined by the historical matrix of colonisation. The latter, particularly when associated with slavery, gave opportunity to the coloniser to abuse sexually the indigenous inhabitants of the colony. It is very rarely that this opportunity was not realised.'[2]

It is vital too to remember that during some of the worst episodes in human history, mixed-race people were ruthlessly victimised and this is part of the rich texture of memory of mixed-race people in Britain. When you talk to mixed-race families as I have done for this book, you realise that for many, these stories form a central part of their sense of themselves. Much of the material for this chapter and the next was suggested by these families who feel strongly that too many people are ignorant about the history and politics of miscegenation.

Before colonisation and slavery there was little evidence of any deep feelings of distaste and prejudice towards certain physical characteristics although it has been argued by a number of non-white historians that all early European civilisations were built on assumptions of superiority. Zia Sardar, Ashish Nandy and Merryl Wyn Davies assert in their pamphlet *Barbaric Others: A Manifesto on Western Racism* that:

> The two pillars of Western civilization, classicism and Christianity, shared a triumphalist self image. Each invented Otherness to define itself and the process of maintaining boundaries required the perennial reinvention of real peoples... Real people became object lessons for 'normality' by their shocking ability to live differently. Dwelling on the differences and similarities, extracting pen-portraits of the characteristics of the Others, was a process of distortion, one that became more garbled as distance increased, or as contact with Other cultures became more tenuous or non-existent.[3]

I agree with this analysis but only partially, because I feel that it is based on careful selectivity which fits in with the central arguments in the pamphlet. Indians, Chinese, Mongols, Egyptians, were all capable of showing superiority as were the Romans and Greeks and if one looks closely at the various classical texts, there can be little doubt that there was more respect for the Other among the Greeks and Romans than was seen in later centuries. Nevertheless, it is important to remember that the collective arrogance about the west did in part grow out of the self-image of Greeks, Romans and early Christians and the subsequent histories which perpetrated these ideas. And because the west has for centuries wielded an inordinate amount of power, these myths have acquired a mighty presence across the world.

As the colonial ambitions of Europeans grew, a demonology of black inferiority began to emerge and was used to justify the enterprise. Sexual contact between whites on the one hand, and Africans and Asians on the other, was thereafter largely confined to casual encounters and concubinage. After all, marriage between the races was a mark of equality, which could not be encouraged by people increasingly wedded to the ideology of white superiority. Miscegenation, particularly if it produced children, inevitably challenged that ideology.

Kenneth Ballhatchet, himself an army officer, wrote *Race, Sex and Class Under the Raj*, an excellently researched book which explored imperial attitudes towards mixed-race relationships between 1793 and 1905. Ballhatchet says in the introduction: 'The preservation of social distance seemed essential to the maintenance of structures of power and authority. Marriages that threatened to bridge this social distance were sternly discouraged.'

He goes on to say that it is vital to understand the way the British rulers attempted to control sexual behaviour in India in the interests of imperial power.[4] Much of the justification of British rule was built on manufactured beliefs about subject people. Africans, Middle Eastern people and folk east of Suez were deemed primitive, physical, irrational and naturally lascivious which is why God had enabled the people of the land of hope and glory to go forth and 'civilise' them by setting an example of firmness and physical self-control. So deeply ingrained were these prejudices that they still linger in the mental recesses of many white Britons.

But the connections between race and sex are more complicated than this. Ballhatchet believes, as do a number of scholars, that one factor which led to the massive colonial adventure was sexual desire for the wild and forbidden. It is likely, he says, that sexual frustration 'urged many into imperial pursuits'. An earlier writer, Ronald Hyam, argued this too in *Britain's Imperial Century*. In his view there were a number of pugnacious officials whose fantasies could not easily be satisfied in the repressed UK and who did find these more than accommodated in the Orient and elsewhere.[5] Both these responses can be detected in Tennyson's *Locksley Hall* where the hero fantasises about the possible delights of an oriental bride, but then decides that this would be inappropriate for a highly learned Englishman whose nation was destined to rule the world.

The views of subject people abroad created attitudes towards miscegenation in this country. There were links too, as Henriques points out, between attitudes in the United States and in the United Kingdom and there still are when it comes to race matters. Essentially it is impossible to understand anything about mixed-race relationships without studying how the European came to view and still views the non-European.

The early civilisations

Colour prejudice as we know it now did not appear to exist in classical times. The Greeks – including Homer – felt enormous admiration for the medical skills and organisational abilities of the early Egyptians while the Romans looked down on everyone (except the Greeks) and found Germans and Britons, in particular, savage and crude. What is unquestionable though is that both these civilisations believed devoutly in the idea of their own perfection. Barbarians were often depicted as gross, dog-headed, one-eyed, hybrids, satyrs or minotaurs. Skin colour was observed and recorded but this was never the sole cause of prejudice. Moreover those who were prepared to accept Roman or Greek were permitted to join the 'civilised'. What you did rather than what you were gave you value. Academics who have studied the history of miscegenation – in the West, in the ancient world and during early Christianity – have found that although there was an awareness of colour and physical difference, dark skin was seen as sensuous and attractive. Ovid described his love for a black slave girl in *Amores*[6] and begged 'dusky Cypassis' for some sweet caresses. Other poets wrote of their craving for women with skin darker than the night. Asclepiades, for example, wrote:

> She waved her branch, fair Didyme,
> And waving stole my heart away
> And now like wax in fire, see,
> I melt in sweet decay.
>
> If she is black, what's that to me?
> This charcoal too is black, but yet
> No rose more red can ever be
> When once alight 'tis set.[7]

In the Greek legend of Perseus and Andromeda, the devastatingly beautiful Andromeda is the daughter of the Ethiopian king. Ethiopians are present in a number of Greek myths and fables. Memnon, one of the defenders of Troy, was one of them. Herodotus thought that the Ethiopians were 'the tallest and handsomest men in the world'. Some evidence exists that stereotypes were already forming and an associated curiosity laced with derision was also emerging. Dr Henriques mentions as one example some overtly sexual frescoes from Pompeii showing black men copulating with white women and says that throughout the Mediterranean area there were superstitions built around the sexual prowess and physical attributes of black men. Satirists wrote sarcastically about adulterous women who might end up producing babies with unexpectedly dark skins. The Roman satirist Decimus Junius Juvenal who hated the excesses of the Roman Empire wrote:

... Things might be worse – just suppose
She chose to stay pregnant, to swell her belly with frolicsome
Infants: you might become some piccaninny's Papa
And find yourself making your will on behalf of a son and heir
Whose off-black face was better not seen by daylight.[8]

The early Judaic tradition is similarly ambiguous. It is said that Tharbis, also an Ethiopian princess, saw Moses as he fought with great courage against her own people. They soon fell in love.[9] The earthly paradise so central to the stories of Christianity was thought to be in Ethiopia. As Henriques says: 'In the reality of the early Christian Church no distinctions appeared to have been made in terms of skin colour or ethnic origins. In the history of Egyptian monasticism it is quite clear that Ethiopians and Europeans lived and worked for God side by side.'[10]

The Moorish invasion and conquest of much of Europe was extremely important in both the making and breaking of stereotypes about non-Europeans. Moors were themselves an inter-mixture of Arabs, Berbers and black Africans. This mixing was common in the pre-Islamic period. There was no 'pure' blood to be found in the Arab peninsula. How could there be with constant contact between the various racial groups? Islam too was self-consciously non-racist. As long as a person was Muslim, he or she was part of the brotherhood. There was a cultural openness too which must, in part, have come from the demographic hybridity which was common in the Muslim world. The Moors crossed over to Spain and Portugal in 711 AD. Within fifty years they established control over Andalucia. Granada, Cordoba and Seville became great cities of cross-cultural exchange, the arts and architecture. These Moors of Europe were admired for their literacy, aesthetics and culture even as they were loathed for their power. They were uniquely committed to the idea that cultures gained most when they respected others and when there was an easy exchange between them. Intellectualism, art, philosophy all needed this cross-fertilisation. For a period in history, the destructive notions of national and cultural purity were superseded by more enlightened ideas. Spanish Moors lived these principles too. They intermarried, did not demand conversion,[11] and promoted an Islam which was not self-denying. More puritanical Muslim groups from North Africa came to despise them for this and in 1086 they displaced the worldly and cultivated Spanish Moors and gained power. By that time, Christian Spain was also striking back and the sacking of Granada in 1492 by King Ferdinand and Queen Isabella ended the long battle for control and supremacy over Moorish Spain. Many Muslims today who fear the rise of intolerance in Muslim communities point to this golden period when it was possible for Muslim people to live together and marry across race and religion. The city of Seville is a child of this cultural miscegenation.

Europeans and abroad

There has long been another set of myths which determined the attitudes of Europeans towards non-Europeans. Travellers and adventurers were bringing back real and/or exaggerated stories about the strange places and people they had met abroad. They could be said to be continuing the traditions of the Greeks and Romans who found 'abroad' both rich and fascinating but full of strangely beastly human beings. Most of these men – including Marco Polo who first went forth in 1275 – felt a combination of awe and unease at what they saw, although there was no sign as yet of the whole belief system of superiority over people of colour which was to dominate Europe and America in later centuries.

The Crusades began in 1096 and ended in 1291. Western Christianity, led by France, England and Germany, embarked on these military missions in order to capture Palestine, Constantinople and other areas which were part of the Ottoman Empire. In order to justify the often ruthless exploits of the crusaders, myths were created of Islam as a barbaric religion, a conspiracy against Christianity. By the middle of the twelfth century, this was the image most westerners had of Islam and Muslims. And these persisted in the occidental imagination. In Dante's *Inferno*,[12] written in 1307, 'Mahomet' finds himself cleft in half 'from chin to that part that breaks wind', and in hell because he is a heretic. Italian traveller Ricoldo de Montecroce went to Baghdad in 1291 and came back with stories not about the intellectual life which flourished there but of irrational and dangerous Muslims. An Irish priest, Simon Simeonis, who travelled to Palestine in 1323, was only ever offensive about Islam and the Prophet.[13] Edward Said writes in his seminal work, *Orientalism*: 'For Europe, Islam was a lasting trauma.'[14]

These attitudes and the Crusades produced hatred on the other side too and the idea of dirty, pig-eating 'haram' Christians proliferated among many Muslims during this period. Meanwhile 'savages' in the New World were being subdued, massacred by those who claimed to have discovered these countries.

Renaissance England inherited these stereotypes even though relations with the Ottoman rulers for trade purposes made this period an ambiguous one. There are paintings in Florence and Venice which contain images of Muslim men who are not caricatured but shown as astute, elegant and dignified. But in the great flowering of drama and writing during this period, the Saracen, the Turk, the Blackamoor, the Jew and the Moor were often portrayed as villains, albeit with more complex characters than in previous centuries.

Some European travellers were drawn to and not repulsed by those outside their own world. Others took a strictly pragmatic approach. Fifteenth and sixteenth-century explorers like the Portuguese were more interested in trade and wealth than genetic purity. In Guinea, west Africa, they had informal relationships with native women or took them as long-term concubines. These Africanised Portuguese were known as 'tangosmoas' or 'lancados'. They fathered mulatto children and were largely assimilated into the way of life. Uninhibited by conventions of imperial authority, it was easily possible for them to take on the local dress, customs, languages and forms of worship. This kind of real blood integration made good economic sense as it offered an advantage over other European traders. As late as the seventeenth century, there were many contemporary accounts of this crossover such as the following:

> The Europeans have wives and children. Some of the children born here are as white as ours. It sometimes happens that when the wife of a merchant dies, he takes a Negress and this is accepted practice as the Negro population is both intelligent and rich, bringing up their daughters in our way of life, both as regards custom and dress. Children born of these unions are of dark complexion and called Mulattos and they are mischievous and difficult to manage.[15]

The Portuguese seemed to be able to respond with a sensuality that was held more in check by Anglo-Saxons although not in Goa in India where the British displayed similar behaviour to the Portuguese, giving in to their desires more readily than in many other regions. The more fastidious among people in both groups were starting to object to this behaviour. As early as 1550, a Jesuit priest, Nicolas Lancilotto, wrote a desperate letter to St Ignatius Loyola: '...the Portuguese have adopted the vices and customs of the land without reserve...There are innumerable Portuguese who buy droves of girls and sleep with all of them...There are innumerable married settlers who have four, eight or ten female slaves and sleep with all of them.[16]

Whatever prejudices were growing in their white hearts, it seems that Portuguese men could not resist brown-skinned women sexually. The hypocritical Catholic Church was keen to convert the darker races but had little real respect for them. In 1585, Alexandre Valignano, a head of Jesuit missions wrote: '... all these dusky races are very stupid and vicious, and of the basest of spirits... as for the mesticos[17] and casticos,[18] we should receive either very few or none at all; especially with regard to the mesticos, since the more native blood they have, the more they resemble the Indians and the less they are esteemed by the Portuguese.'[19]

There was a contradiction in the Portuguese view of these relationships. On the one hand, 'nativisation' brought certain trading advantages. But fear of contamination, especially with very dark-skinned people from the Southern states, was becoming a major perceived threat even though conversions to Christianity were seen as an essential part of the Imperial project. The British were later caught up in a similar web of values.

I interviewed Danny Desouza, a Goan immigrant to London, who recalls stories about his great-grandmother Esther Cohelo and her affair with a white clerk during the Raj. She became pregnant and was rejected by her family, the Church, and soon abandoned by her lover too. 'She ended up on the streets I was told and her child either died or was taken away by someone. When I wanted to marry my Swedish wife, the whole family recoiled because Esther's story had burned into our family history. White people betray you I was told.'

There is little scope in this book to go into detail about the attitudes to mixed-race relationships of the subjected non-white communities, but it is important to remember that these, with significant exceptions, were not usually any more supportive. Hindus had their own reasons to fear and despise these relationships. With their strictly defined class system, crossovers were and remain a threat to the stable order of things. Marrying across caste in India is as impossibly hard as marrying across the races in many parts of the world and can lead to the most unbelievable brutality towards the couples who try to break down the barriers. In a searing article in the summer of 2000, the Indian journalist, Samia Nakhoul, wrote about the case of two young lovers from a village who were hanged and then burnt beyond recognition by their two families for crossing the caste barriers. Kallu, 21, and Rekha, 18, grew up as neighbours and had learnt to love one another. Both belonged to the so-called 'backward' castes and were poor. But Kallu was of a slightly higher caste than Rekha. This was completely unacceptable said one of those arrested for the murders: 'We can only marry from our own caste. It is not possible for one to marry outside the caste. This does not happen in our society. It is not possible.'[20]

The Muslim Moguls, who ruled India from 1526 to 1857, were less rigid and some of their emperors married out to make the point that India was one country with many faiths. Akbar was one of the most open-minded and internationalist of these and it was he who welcomed the early English traders into his country. Many Muslims and Sikhs were as rigid about marriage partners as the British and Hindus, however there are important distinctions. Muslims and Sikhs were intolerant of out marriages for reasons of self-preservation and fears of contamination, but unlike Europeans and Hindus, they did not have carefully constructed ideologies to justify these fears.

In time, Europe developed shared beliefs about non-ethnic Europeans which grew harder and harsher over the centuries. Dark-skinned people were thought to be savage and born villains; the white man ever noble and favoured by the gods. Edward Said goes into painstaking detail about how these views solidified into prejudices. Their potency was still visible in the nineteenth century.

The purity of the British nation versus the power of attraction

Pre-eighteenth century

As black seamen and ever more servants and slaves arrived in Britain, fears of pollution began to grow in Britain. Inevitably perhaps, there were more frequent liaisons with white women – mainly poor or 'fallen' women, although it was not unknown for upper-class women to unleash their sexual appetites on their black servants. Children were born from these liaisons, as one George Best recorded in 1578: 'I myselfe have seene an Ethiopian as blacke as a cole broughte into Englande, who taking a fair Englishe woman to wife, begatte a sonne in all respectes as blacke as the father was...'[21]

The beginnings of a black presence included slaves, performers, musicians and others. Street pageants often had black people dressed up in extravagant costumes and they were seen at local fairs too. In 1604, Elizabeth I called for the deportation of blacks because there were already too many of them in her kingdom.[22] By 1650, numbers had grown substantially because it became fashionable to have slaves in rich households. Writers in the sixteenth and seventeenth centuries were attracted to the theme of interracial sex. In *Lust's Domain*, thought to be by Christopher Marlowe, the Queen Mother of Spain has an affair with Eleazer, a power crazy and brutal black Moor. He boasts about this to his Spanish father-in-law:

> The Queen with me, a Moore, a Devill,
> A slave of Barbery, a dog; for so
> Your silken Courtiers christen me.[23]

In John Webster's *The White Devil*, Zanche, the black servant, is the very embodiment of evil temptation. She is openly sensuous, seductive and exerts terrible power over white men. Sexual relationships between different races were explored in a number of Shakespeare's plays. Caliban in *The Tempest* evokes the horror of the 'uncivilised' male who threatens the vulnerable white woman. But in *Titus Andronicus*, when the mixed-race child of the Queen is described by the nurse as 'A joyless, dismal, black and sorrowful issue', he is defended by the black father, who says:

> Coal-black is better than another hue,
> In that it scorns to bear another hue...[24]

Othello is still arguably one of the finest dramatic explorations of race and sex but the character of Othello is ambiguous, you feel, in order to create an imperative for the tragic end after which 'normal' values can once more prevail. He is brave and noble, a servant of the Venetian state, fighting against the Turks, one of those rare outsiders who is taken in (in both senses) by a social group which determinedly excludes others of his kind. But we see that he is highly emotional, gullible and prone to irrational bouts of temper, still a barbarian. The play in the end is a clear warning against mixed-race relationships for, as Rana Kabbani observes 'Such intercourse can only lead to tragedy, upsetting as it does the fixedness of the status quo. The black man cannot simply be allowed to "tup" the "white ewe" uncurbed; both must be punished for such transgressions, even when their mutual affection draws a cautious amount of sympathy for them.'[25] Four centuries on these attitudes and contradictions can still be observed, even among young Britons. To date however, no other writer, in my view, has been able to produce such a compelling exploration of the passions evoked by mixed-race relationships and the presence of blackness in a white world.[26]

I once sat in a London secondary school when A level pupils were studying this play. It was a racially mixed group and I spent time talking to the pupils about their own personal feelings – as white, Asian and black girls and boys. A number of white boys told me that Desdemona was 'stupid for trusting a black man'. Andy went further: 'You see it everywhere. Our girls they think the boys are sexy and that and then they beat them, make them pregnant, kick them around you know? They are animals these boys, just like Othello.' Young white girls were more understanding but still talked about staying with your own. Only one said that she would have a black boyfriend. Another girl later told me she had had a black boyfriend and had got pregnant: 'He wouldn't use nothing you know? I had to have an abortion. He went off. But that could have happened with any boy. My parents said it was because he was black. I said they was wrong.'

One could argue that *Anthony and Cleopatra* is a similar cautionary tale; Cleopatra is the seductress who destroys the great Mark Anthony, once in command of his emotions, and the world. His captain's heart becomes 'the bellows and fan to cool a gypsy's lust'. As he himself says:

> These strong Egyptian fetters I must break,
> or lose myself in dotage.

Like Cleopatra, the North African is pleasure, sensuality and intransigence; Octavia, the Roman European, is duty, self-control, and civilisation.[27] We are bewitched by Cleopatra even though her excesses are destructive. Two strong leaders are trapped by her power over them and although the final scenes mourn the suicide of Cleopatra and praise her exceptional qualities, it is Anthony who is the greater loss. Like Zanche she is the lethal non-white female, one of the recurrent stereotypes through history.

Eighteenth century

Substantially more black people were seen in Britain during this century. On 5 April 1723, the *Daily Journal* expressed fears that London was being overrun by these arrivals: ''Tis said that a great number of blacks come daily into this city, so that 'tis thought in a short Time, if they be not supress'd, the city will swarm with them.'

In 1764, *The Gentleman's Magazine* had estimated that there were 20,000 black people in London alone.

In 1772, Lord Mansfield, the Lord Chief Justice, ruled that slaves on British soil could not be forced out of the country against their will and he estimated that there were 15,000 black people in the country, an estimate which is probably too low.[28] Black ex-slaves were welcomed by lower class women and there were many liaisons between them. The men panicked. In 1772, the white Jamaican writer and slave-owner Edward Long came to Britain and exploded with disgust at what he saw:

A venomous and dangerous ulcer that threatens to disperse its malignancy far and wide until every family catches infection from it ... The lower class of women in England are remarkably fond of the blacks, for reasons too brutal to mention ... By these ladies they generally have a numerous brood. Thus in the course of a few generations more, the English blood will be so contaminated by the mixture and . . . this alloy may spread so extensively as even to reach the middle, and then the higher orders of the people, till the whole nation resembles the Portuguese and Moriscos in complexion of skin and baseness of mind.[29]

Philip Thickness, who had spent time in the Caribbean, wrote in 1778 about the 'monkey cunning' of black men and the 'unnatural alliances' they formed with white women. 'Over a few centuries they will overrun this country with a race of men of the very worst sort under heaven . . . a race of Mulattos mischievous as monkeys but infinitely more dangerous.'[30]

But not everyone reacted with this kind of venom. When Anna Maria, the four-year-old daughter of the great abolitionist Olaudah Equiano and his English wife Suzanna Cullen, died in 1797, the church of St Andrews in Cambridge mourned her death and to this day, according to Professor David Dabydeen, there is a memorial service held to remember this little mixed-race child. Throughout the eighteenth and early nineteenth centuries, the presence of black men and white women was recorded in contemporary paintings and drawings, including some by Hogarth. Dabydeen has been excavating this hidden history for years and he wonders, provocatively, in one essay: 'Why were white women, from the evidence of portrait painting, and from social records, so fond of possessing little black boys – what psychological and sexual politics and neuroses were at play in the English boudoir or bedroom?'[31] Ignatius Sancho, the first black writer to be published in this country, was born a slave. He was a member of literary circles, was painted by Gainsborough and was a friend of Garrick. There were a number of stories and scandals about mixed-race relationships. The Duchess of Queensbury had a passionate affair with her black servant Soubise and turned him into someone who was accepted by high society. There are many other examples of this natural acceptance of lovers of colour during this period.[32]

Born in 1779, George Bridgetower is one of these. The son of a black Barbadian and a white Austrian woman, George was a musical prodigy. When he was ten, the *Bath Journal* described 'the astonishing abilities of this wonderful child [and his] exquisite performances . . . his taste and execution of the violin is equal, perhaps superior, to the best professor of the present or any former day.'[33] In 1791, the Prince of Wales took him under his wing and engaged tutors for him. By the time he was twelve, he had performed in all the major venues and, in 1803, he became friends with Beethoven who said Bridgetower was 'an absolute master of his instrument'. The composer originally dedicated one of his sonatas to the violinist.

It is very important to recognise the role of mixed-race people in the long fights for justice that have taken place in Britain, the colonies and the USA. One such campaigner was William Davidson, born in Jamaica in 1786, the son of the white attorney-general and a black mother. His father sent him to Edinburgh for his education when he was a teenager. He became a revolutionary and joined with others fighting for rights for the poor in this class-ridden society. He fell in love with a white woman who was not allowed to marry him and this led to an attempted suicide. Later he married a widow, also white and already a mother of four. They had two more children. They lived in abject poverty as did many others in this country. Davidson joined the Cato Street conspirators who were amassing weapons and, it was said, planning an insurrection. They were discovered by the authorities. During his trial, Davidson denied that he was guilty of high treason and instead argued he was fighting against tyranny and for the rights guaranteed by the Magna Carta. He was hanged and beheaded outside Newgate Prison in 1820 for revolutionary activities.

Dido Lindsay worked as a secretary to Lord Mansfield of Kenwood House, the Chief Justice from 1756 to 1788, who had ruled that no master could compel a slave to leave this country because all men and women on this soil were free. Dido was the daughter of a slave woman and Sir John Lindsay, a captain in the Royal Navy. He left her money when he died. Mansfield and his wife had no children of their own so they adopted Dido and brought her up as one of the family. She was accomplished, very popular and, judging from a painting of her by Johann Zoffany, a very beautiful woman too.

One remarkable fact which is mysteriously ignored by writers and academics on this subject is that these early black migrants disappeared in time through assimilation into the wider society. As the novelist Mike Phillips pointed out to me: 'If anyone bothered to carry out DNA tests we might find that a substantial number of white Britons have elements of African blood.' But as ever, in this century too, attitudes were unpredictable and contradictory. When Sierra Leone, the so-called 'colony for free slaves', was created in 1786 as a dumping ground for poor blacks and their 'fallen' white consorts from Britain, there is no doubt that behind the evangelical fervour lay attitudes not unlike those expressed by Long a few years previously. On one ship bound for Sierra Leone there was a record of 290 black men, 41 black women, 11 black children, 70 white women and 6 white children. The white women had had sexual relationships with black men. The territory became a haven for mixed-race marriages and relationships. Prejudice was never as rife there as in most other parts of the world and one of the governors,

Sir Arthur Kennedy,[34] sent home dispatches worrying about how easily people accepted such behaviour and how these relationships were 'infecting' the powerful and rich as well as those at the bottom of the social ladder.

Others were drawn to the very thing that created so much worry. Captain Cook's responses to Polynesian people in 1775 were genuinely admiring, even erotic: 'Their skin complexion is a fine clear olive, or what we call brunette; their skin is delicately smooth and agreeably soft...their motions are easy and graceful, but not vigorous; their deportment is generous and open, and their behaviour affable and courteous.'[35] Through the eighteenth and then the nineteenth centuries, a number of French and British painters and writers paid artistic homage to these island people, Robert Louis Stephenson, Baudelaire, Gauguin, Byron and Tennyson among them. Their fascination arose in part from chimerical ideas of an erotic paradise where lovely, passive, 'native' women did their best to please because they were innocent and unspoilt. This view fitted in well with the great myths of the Romantic Movement and Rousseau's beliefs about the 'noble savage' which questioned the domination of post-Enlightenment rationalism. Dark-skinned people were seen as closer to nature, sensual, even magical. Miscegenation (whether real or imagined) for these believers was a transformative and poetic experience.

Nineteenth century

As the century progressed, there emerged other European artists who were inspired by their fear of sexual relations with the Other. Terrifying images of bloodthirsty Muslims beheading men and enslaving women were commonplace. Delacroix's *La Morte de Sardanapoles* (1827) shows beautiful white women naked and helpless in the arms of dark-skinned men with cold, cruel faces. Rape is in the air. In Jean'Leon Gerome's painting *Le Marché d'Esclaves*, a naked, young, white woman is surrounded by Arab men, one of whom has stuck his finger in her mouth which she is still trying to clench shut. Ingres was obsessed with harems and Turkish bath houses. The effect of these paintings – all of which hang in prestigious galleries – is subliminal terror, a confirmation that white women need protection from violently lusty Orientals.

Romances were built around the brave Christian hero who kills and defeats vile Saracens. Usually Saracen princesses throw their hot bodies at these heroes, either to be rejected or embraced if the lady converts to wholesome Christianity. In *The King of Tars*,[36] a Christian princess agrees to marry a nefarious Saracen king in order to save her people. They have a deformed child who is miraculously cured when the mother has him baptised. The king follows suit and becomes handsome and white.[37] Sir Walter Scott and many others were infected by these fantasies. His heroine Zarah in *Peveril*[38] was a 'fierce torrent of passion' because her mother was from the East.

Dark-skinned people were now regarded as barbaric and sexually rampant. They had to be ruled, controlled, brought into civilisation. And the underbelly of this attitude was a sordid and growing fascination with the sexuality that whites claimed was so repulsive. This is what fuelled the obsessions of British Orientalists and sensualists who found much in the East to titillate them – Richard Burton, for example, who translated the *Kamasutra* and seems to have made it his business to sleep with women, men, goats and sheep in every country east of Suez and then describe his adventures in grotesque detail. Rana Kabbani believes these myths were essential to expansionist ambitions, whether territorial or cultural:

> In the European narration of the Orient, there was a deliberate stress on those qualities that made the East different from the West, exiled it into an irretrievable state of 'otherness'. Among the many themes that emerge from the European narration of the Other, two appear most strikingly. The first is the insistent claim that the East was a place of lascivious sensuality, and the second that it was characterised by inherent violence.[39]

Nineteenth-century idealists were not immune from anti-black prejudices and records reveal that these were openly declared. William Cobbett may have been a radical but when it came to this issue he was plainly enraged by the black presence in his country. In 1804, he wrote:

> Who, that has any sense or decency, can help being shocked at the familiar intercourse, which has gradually been gaining ground, and which has, at last, got complete footing between the Negros and the women of England? No black swain need, in this loving country, hang himself in despair. No inquiry is made whether he be a pagan or a Christian; if he be not a downright cripple, he will, if he is so disposed, always find a woman, not merely to yield to his filthy embraces, ... but to accompany him to the altar, to become his wife, to breed English mulattoes, to stamp the mark of Cain on her family and her country! Among white women, this disregard of decency, this defiance of the dictates of nature, this foul and beastly propensity, is, and I say it with sorrow and shame, peculiar to the English.'[40]

In this century, a whole new body of theories about racial hierarchies began to take hold. Count Arthur de Gobineau, a French aristocrat, was the most influential of these and he still exerts a powerful influence on modern-day racial theorists. Gobineau's essay, *The Inequality of Human Races*, written in 1853, divides humanity into three categories: whites, blacks and yellows of whom whites are genetically superior. He too believes that mixed-race people could be beautiful but that for the white parent, miscegenation always leads to the degeneration of the superior white genes.[41] Many other intellectuals were involved in the development and perpetuation of this 'scientific' racism.[42] In 1852, Robert Knox, once a professor at Edinburgh, believed totally in the inferiority of the darker races. In his book *The Races of Man*, Knox states that miscegenation is a danger to white people as it diminishes them biologically.[43] In 1859 came Darwin's *The Origin of Species*, which was used by race theorists as further 'evidence', more confirmation that human beings could be classified into the most advanced and the least evolved. This social Darwinism has always been regarded as suspect, but the appeal of the ideas remains strong among many.

During the early part of the nineteenth century, a number of mixed-race West Indians settled in Britain. Some were wealthy – the products of rich white plantation owners and black women who had been elevated in status. The children were sent to 'finishing school' and were cultivated and accepted in high- and middle-class society. Some examples appear in the prolific fiction of the period. Miss Swartz, in Thackeray's *Vanity Fair*, was the daughter of a German slave trader and a slave. She was presented at court and considered a good catch for merchant families. The character of Heathcliffe has fascinated black scholars for some time. He was a foundling, brought from Liverpool, a slave port which then had a large number of mixed-race liaisons. The boy is, says Mr Earnshaw, 'as dark almost as if it came from the devil'. His wife refers to him as a 'gipsy brat' but it is quite likely that he was a mixed-race child who looked like a gypsy. If so, this 'unfortunate' heritage underpins his flawed and volatile character. Leigh Hunt, that most English of essayists and a poet, was in fact mixed-race. His mother was descended from slaves in the Caribbean and his father was an English chaplain.[44]

As colonial rule intensified and solidified through the eighteenth and nineteenth centuries into the belief of manifest destiny, so did the animosity towards black and Asian people. Racial superiority and purity were the pillars on which to build conquest and rule. It is a little known fact that Indian slaves were bought and sold in the coffee houses of London in the eighteenth century. But as the century went on, a number of Indians started appearing to study, visit, trade or campaign against the Empire. Like black men before them, some ended up with white partners, English and Irish. Many of these Asian men (few Asian women were seen at the time) were what we would call today 'economic migrants' using their skills to try and eke out a living. Henry Mayhew has a record of these in his tome on London's poor in 1861. He notes that they had white partners and mixed-race children.[45] In her excellent book, *Ayahs, Lascars and Princes*,[46] the historian Rozina Visram describes in detail several of these individuals who not only had the wit to make a living on the streets of British cities (and survive constant hostility) but had the gall to take up white partners. These were frowned upon by white Britons of all classes and the papers were always full of scandalised comments. 'It would surprise many people,' thundered the London City Mission magazine in August 1857, 'to see how extensively these dark races are tincturing the colour of the rising race of children in the lowest haunts of this locality; and many of the young fallen females have a visible infusion of Asiatic and African blood in their veins. They form a peculiar class, but mingle freely with the others. It is an instance of depraved taste that many of our fallen ones prefer devoting themselves entirely to the dark races of men.'

But it was not only the lower orders of whites and Asians who entertained these preferences. There were teachers, professors, healers and others too who found favour among middle-class white women. Monshee Mahomet Saeed, Professor of Hindustani at University College, London, had a white wife, as did the famous Sake Deen Mahomed. (Then, as now, class made a huge difference to their status.) Sake Deen Mohamed, a poor Indian who became 'Shampoo Surgeon' to King George IV, curing him and many members of European aristocracy of chronic illnesses and problems through his special oil massage, was married to a solid and dependable white woman called Jane.

During the worst periods of Victorian bigotry and hubris, that most imperial of monarchs, Queen Victoria, developed such a deep (and some believe more than platonic) fondness for her Muslim Indian servant Abdul Kareem that she had his portrait painted and made him her Indian Secretary and Companion of the Order of the Indian Empire. All the letters and written records of this relationship were later carefully destroyed by courtiers, on the order of key politicians.

The famous case of George Edalji showed up the hypocritical attitudes prevailing at the time and particularly the way educated Indians were regarded as upstarts who needed to be shown their place, just like in India. George was the son of Charlotte Stoneham, an Englishwoman, and Shapurji Edalji, a Parsi man who had converted to Christianity and who became the vicar of Great Wyrley in Staffordshire in the 1870s. George was a brilliant lawyer but in 1903 he was accused of maiming horses for ritualistic purposes – a false charge. He spent three years in prison before Arthur Conan Doyle and others took up his cause and proved that he had been the victim of malice, probably racist.

Shapurji Saklatvala, one of Britain's first non-white MPs elected as a communist, was not only married to a white woman but had a huge following among working-class women. A reporter from the *Daily Graphic* wrote in 1924: 'He wields a magnetic influence over his audience that verges on hypnotism...I saw excited women waving his handbills and actually kissing his portrait pinned on them.'[47]

Samuel Coleridge Taylor was a world famous composer. His mother was English and his father was a doctor from Gambia who, although qualified in England, found it so hard to get patients that he returned to West Africa in order to practise. Elgar described him as 'far and away the cleverest fellow among the young men'. He composed the hugely successful 'Hiawatha's Wedding Feast' and became a professor of music but this did not stop many critics saying that there was something misguided about such high praise for someone with 'negro' blood. He himself married a white woman and before his early death at the age of 37 was working on an operetta about a mixed-race relationship.

Mary Seacole, quoted above, was another extraordinary example. The daughter of a Scotsman and a free black woman, she came to England and went to the Crimea during the war to work with Florence Nightingale and administer to the wounded. Using traditional medicines from the Caribbean and modern medication, she was so good at her work that military bands in Britain played for her and *The Times* wrote glowing tributes to this great healer saying the nation was indebted to her and that her role should never be forgotten. It was. The book *Remember Me*,[48] quoted from above, gives a wonderful account of these and other heroes and heroines of mixed-race origins.

There is no doubt that in Britain many white women responded at a human level to the black and Asian arrivals, but most white men and some white women reacted with fear and distaste, attitudes not uncommon today. Indians, whether in India or in Britain, were deliberately treated as inferior by those in power in order to halt any claims to equality or a great culture. The hatred directed at black people was less ambiguous because it arose from the simple notion that Africa knew no civilisation and that 'niggers' were barbarians. In spite of all the prejudices however, people carried on their relationships and produced children, a number of whom were exceptional human beings who made a mark.

Particular geographies

There follows a detailed exploration of three areas which profoundly affected attitudes on miscegenation in Britain, some of which have briefly been touched on above.

East Indian territories

Dramatic displays of bigotry against mixed-race relationships were found in undivided India, Burma and other eastern countries, especially after colonial rule was established and the ambitions of the mother country moved from trade to ownership. In the seventeenth century, the East India Company had positively encouraged the growth of a Eurasian population. White men who married Indian women and had children were given financial gifts, and official papers confirm that this was done 'to give encouragement to increase such marriages'.[49] The main reason for this was commercial; men who had partners would be more likely to remain in the areas for long periods and trust was easier to obtain. Journeys home and back took too long and it was expensive to transport families all the way from Britain. A wonderful painting in India House, of William Palmer and his Indian wife, Bibi Faiz Baksh, painted by Francesco Rinaldi in 1786, shows how relaxed relationships could be at the time. The wife, her head covered, is wearing huge Indian earrings and cradling a baby. Palmer gazes at her and his infant adoringly while two other young children and a group of Indian women look on, all obviously rejoicing in the new arrival.

There are several other examples of mixed-race relationships and ancestry, including Job Charnock, the founder of Calcutta who married the widow he saved from suttee. A large number of senior officials in the East India Company loved Indian art, architecture and artefacts and although a great deal of illicit looting of these objects took place at the time, at least there was an acknowledgement of a great civilisation. However, by 1784, when the ambitions of the East India Company began to grow beyond trade, all this began to change and in 1791 Eurasians started to face prejudice.

The eighteenth century deepened the divide between the so-called civilised European and the untamed non-European as the age of reason arrived and colonialism became entrenched. In *The Lords of Mankind*, VG Kiernan shows just how the case was built up for white superiority by colonialists. In India, for example, the white taboo on intermarriage had the effect of '...worsening the tinge of racialism always present in the British make up. When the Englishman turned his back on the invisible Indian beauty, as on a poisonous orchid or a sour grape, he turned his back on India altogether.'[50]

Officially, it was after the Indian uprising in 1857 that the British took over the subcontinent and Queen Victoria proclaimed it part of her grand Empire. But for several decades previously the British in India had been treating the natives with disdain and had grown to believe that their power depended upon keeping a vast social distance between themselves and their 'uncivilised' subjects.

Sexual attraction across the races was now seen as something wholly destabilising to the natural order of things. In Goa, for example, the Church Missionary Society started to denounce any cross-racial liaisons and campaigned for missionaries to bring across their white wives.

As more white memsahibs began to arrive in India – an inevitable consequence of the disapproval of mixed relationships – the gulf between the two races widened. The Indian mistress soon disappeared, at least among the higher classes of the imperialists. Ballhatchet writes: 'Of all the areas of sexual behaviour which embarrassed the authorities, relations between British soldiers and Indian women proved the most troubling.' Ordinary soldiers, it was assumed, did not have the high moral capacity of the officer classes and were prone to 'mercenary love' which in turn made them vulnerable to VD. 'Lock up' hospitals were created for Indian prostitutes where they were confined until they were cured.

The British view of Indians was that they were by nature more promiscuous than white people. Interestingly this was reflected in a set of identical notions on the part of the Indians, who were shocked at the way white women bared their shoulders and touched men in public. This is why Indian men never brought their wives when they were invited to receptions organised by the rulers. At least three works of fiction have been written exploring this tension between physical and emotional attraction between the races (often imagined) and social disapprobation. In E M Forster's *A Passage to India*, the greatest of these because of the dense and detailed way it creates the atmosphere of the Raj, the climax of the book is an alleged attack in some caves. The victim is the unmarried Englishwoman Adela Quested and the accused attacker is Aziz, a Muslim doctor who presumes to come closer than he should to white individuals who, on their side, seem not to display the usual arrogance of rulers. This intimacy proves more destructive than anybody imagines. We never do find out if the attack took place. That is not the point. White society believes it did and blames Miss Quested for not knowing her position and befriending Dr Aziz, a widower and never-to-be-trusted native. Among its many other themes, the novel captures the central anxieties of race and sex in an unequal political system.

Four decades later, Paul Scott, who went to India in the early 1940s when the Quit India movement was becoming stronger, found a society where there was no bridge possible between the ruled and the rulers. In the *Jewel in the Crown*, the first novel in his brilliant Raj Quartet published in 1966, the pivotal relationship is between an intelligent and proud Indian man, Hari Kumar, and a naïve white woman, Daphne Manners, who is engaged to be married to the racist English policeman Ronald Merrick. Like Adela

Quested, she fails to understand the importance of keeping her distance from colonial subjects but in her case she goes all the way and ends up pregnant with Kumar's child. Both are made to suffer for this act of effrontery, the man paying more severely than the woman. Ruth Jhabvallah's *Heat and Dust* is about the love affair between an attractive Nawab and the sexually frustrated wife of a British official who breaks all the rules and leaves her husband for the oriental aristocrat for whom the affair provides excitement and an excellent opportunity for revenge against the British. The point is that neither side is comfortable with this relationship and it does not last.

This is literature reflecting something that has for too long disappeared under the weight of stereotypes. The cold, superior memsahib was certainly the norm, but there were many white women who were less formal and racist than the men and who themselves were victims of the sterile world of Anglo-Saxon masculinity and sexual repression. They did not go unpunished. Several well-publicised cases show how hard it was for white women to free themselves of the official racist attitudes of those around them. A Christian missionary, Mary Pigott, refused to treat Indians as second-class citizens. This so incensed her fellow Christian brothers that they tried to destroy her reputation by claiming that her behaviour with Indian men was immodest and even sexual. She went to court three times in order to clear her name.[51]

Anxieties were only increased as maharajahs (especially those who were educated at British public schools) started to behave as if they were equal to white people. In 1893, consternation rippled across the two nations when it was announced that a white woman, Miss Florry Bryan, was to marry the Maharajah of Patiala. He received an official letter from a representative of the Viceroy:

> An alliance of this kind, contracted with a European far below you in rank, is bound to lead to the most unfortunate results. It will render your position both with the Europeans and Indians most embarrassing. Europeans will certainly object to treating this lady as a suitable consort for a ruler in your position. They will also resent the idea of a European lady being married to a Native Chief as one of a number of other wives.[52]

The marriage went ahead. Maharajahs were kept away from Britain because it was feared that white women would fall for them. Indian soldiers were also considered dangerous. Viceroy Curzon wrote to the conservative Secretary of State, Lord George Hamilton, in 1901: 'The "woman" aspect of the question is rather a difficulty, since strange as it may seem, Englishwomen of the housemaid class, and even higher, do offer themselves to these Indian soldiers, attracted by their uniform, enamoured of their physique and with the sort of idea that the warrior is also an oriental prince.'[53]

There were extraordinary scandals too of white women who had joined brothels of their own accord but who were believed to be held as white sex slaves. One of the most famous of these cases involved Fanny Epstein, a young but wilful prostitute who escaped to Bombay in order to get away from her father. The National Vigilance Society in England was convinced that Fanny was a victim of the 'white slave trade' and insisted that an international search was required to find and return her to her father. Fanny eventually went to the police in Bombay and confidently told the Inspector that she was of sound mind and knew what she was doing. The police were convinced that the young woman was not acting under any kind of duress and that she, in fact, ran her brothel. In the end she was 'captured' and forced to go back to her father.[54]

The saddest stories, however, are of true cross-racial love which the imperialists made it their business to destroy. In Burma, particularly when the policy changed from encouragement to the virtual banning of interracial marriages, a number of couples were either forced to separate or give up their positions. An order was passed announcing that nobody with a Burmese wife would be promoted. Active encouragement was also given to the men who already had such families to abandon them and move on.

The Caribbean

Black slavery was introduced into the Caribbean in the early sixteenth century after the original inhabitants of the islands had been wiped out. Almost from the start, miscegenation became a feature of the slave and master relationship. By the seventeenth century this was so common that the colonial government of Antigua passed an edict forbidding 'Carnall Coppulation between Christian and Heathen'.[55] If it was found that the law had been broken, the white person was fined. The black person had his indenture extended or was flogged and branded even if there were proof of pressure or rape. This island was the only one to follow the example of the southern American States. Elsewhere in the Caribbean mixing seems to have been accepted as a norm even when interracial sex was often the result of exploitation and cruelty. A whole new vocabulary emerged to label mixed-race people and a new hierarchy to match. The status of light-skinned people was higher than those with dark skin, African features and hair. Pure white people did not consider any of them equals even though many of the men officially kept 'coloured' mistresses. This group included governors who permitted these concubines to act as hostesses at functions. Henriques writes: 'To consort with black and coloured people in terms of a sexual relationship was acceptable. What was not was the notion that such women could ever aspire to marriage with a white man...Lightness of colour and a great deal of money might, however, overcome the barrier.'[56]

As recently as the 1960s academics provided questionable explanations for these relationships in the Caribbean. One of these, R G Ragatz, wrote:

> The white man in tropical America was out of his habitat. Constant association with an inferior subject race blunted his moral fibre and he suffered marked demoralisation. His transitory residence and the continued importation of Africans debased life. Miscegenation, so contrary to Anglo-Saxon nature, resulted in a rise of human hybrids. Planter society was based upon whites and blacks, removed to unfamiliar scenes and their unhappy offspring. The saddest pages of imperial history relate the heartrending attempts to effect adjustment between these discordant elements.[57]

There was some pity forthcoming from a few writers for the mixed-race women who could never hope for real status and many observers began writing accounts of the degradation, abuse and sexual violation of slaves by the master class. Bryan Edwards, who wrote the hugely popular *History of the West Indies* in 1801, recorded unhappy mulatto women who had no hopes of ever acquiring a respectable married life because their status was too high for the black population and too low for the whites.[58] Overseers frequently kept written accounts of their treatment of female slaves, including entries such as 'Sally was ravished, whipped and locked in chains...She has the clap very badly.'[59] They also advised visiting men about the costs and 'value' of various female slaves they might wish to have in their beds; light-skinned ones were always more expensive than darker-skinned ones. White women were as bad, if not worse than the white men, when it came to the treatment of female slaves, and sexual jealousy played its part in motivating the attacks. By the time white women arrived in the Caribbean, sex between their men and non-whites was flourishing and white women extorted their revenge for this on the black women whom they blamed for drawing their men away from their noble natures. Captain Cook wrote about this cruelty in great detail. Two young white 'ladies', angry that a slave girl had got pregnant through intercourse with the surgeon's son, tied her up with their own garters and then nearly beat her to death with their shoes. He records seeing another such beating where the head of the slave was beaten 'almost to a jelly' and stuffed into a commode. Masters too inflicted horrible torture on slave women who resisted their advances. Stories appear repeatedly of slave women being hung from trees, having their genitals burnt or limbs mutilated. One such woman was flogged with thorn bushes so badly that the skin from her front and back was totally taken off. Less well known than these stories are those of forced prostitution. White mistresses trained slaves from childhood to service men and in fact one of the beatings above was doled out to a young girl who had not brought enough money from the ship where her mistress had sent her to carry out whoring activities.[60] Where money exchanged hands, dark girls came the cheapest with the price increasing for lighter women. Accounts by nineteenth-century observers were, at times, more appalled by the 'normality' of crossovers than by the violence they surely must have observed, although most understood that the system of slavery was responsible for all that they saw. One observer noted:

> ...the most gross and licentiousness continues to prevail among all ranks of the Whites...Every unmarried White man, and of every class has his Black or Brown mistress, with whom he lives openly and of so little consequence is this thought that his White female friends and relations think it is no breach of decorum to visit his house, partake of his hospitality, fondle his children and converse with his housekeeper...the most striking proof of the low estimate of moral and religious obligation here, is the fact that the man who lives in open adultery – that is, who keeps his Black and Brown mistress in the very face of his wife and family and of the community – has generally as much outward respect shown him...as if he had been guilty of no breach of decency, or dereliction of moral duty.[61]

It was the lack of proper hypocrisy which was condemned by such writers, not the way plantation whites dehumanised, used and abused those they considered lesser beings than themselves.

But not all white people could behave with indifference once their sexual desires were inflamed. Sometimes these women and the children of the relationship would gain their freedom and even inherit some money from the master. The poet Robert Browning's grandmother, for example, was a mulatto who had inherited a plantation. This trend became such a cause of anxiety that in Jamaica a law was passed as early as 1748 limiting such inheritances to £1200. Understandably, a number of slave women thought that sex was the only way out of the desperation of their lives and they deliberately engineered these relationships but only a few ever found the freedom of their dreams.

However, in time some within the 'coloured' population became rich and more confident and developed their own social circles. These rich Creole beauties were considered highly desirable by some English gentlemen. The first Mrs Rochester in *Jane Eyre* was just such a woman. Her character – crazy and cruel and deserving of pitiless imprisonment – offered a moral lesson to men who allowed themselves to be seduced by alien beauty. In her novella *Wide Sargasso Sea*,[62] published in 1966, Jean Rhys makes this Mrs Rochester the heroine and mines her background. Born in Dominica, Rhys herself, half Welsh and half Creole, paints a poignant picture of what it meant to be a mixed-race woman in the early nineteenth century. Her heroine walks fast past a little girl who is screaming 'white cockroach' at her and realises: 'Real white people, they got gold money... old time white people, nothing but white nigger now and black niggers better than white niggers.' She is a misfit both in the Caribbean and in England. At one point in the book, her faithful Caribbean servant confronts her husband who is weary of his wife and her strange ways: 'She is a Creole girl and have the sun in her. Tell the truth now. She don't come to your house in this place England they tell me about, she don't come to your beautiful house to beg you to marry her. No, it's you come all the long way to her house – it's you beg her to marry you. And she love you and give you all she have. Now you say you don't love her and you break her up. What you do with her money eh?'[63] The tragedy moves on and she ends up mad and dangerous as her husband goes back to the safety of a good English woman.

From 1730 onwards, coloured folk, the term used for mixed-race people in the Caribbean, were systematically excluded from any important positions, even those within the church. They were considered a threat by white people because they had white blood and because many felt themselves to be closer to white than black in terms of status. In Antigua, coloureds and blacks could not even be buried in churchyards where white Christians were buried and for whom a larger bell was used to announce such a death. The meanness of spirit is staggering. Moreover the effects of such racism can also be to corrupt its victims. Many coloured people in the Caribbean took up white snobbery and values about light and dark skins. A traveller from England, Mrs Flannigan, who wrote pages describing all the shades of colour in Antigua noted this: 'The coloured women participated in the prejudice of their masters, and as they became mothers of female children, they reared them in the same spirit and inculcated into their heads that it was more honourable and praiseworthy to inhabit the harem of a white man than to be the lawful wife of a man of colour.'[64]

It is clear though that neither laws passed against miscegenation nor merciless social disapproval could shame sex and/or love into submission. In some areas the interracial mixing was much higher than in others. Trinidad, by the beginning of the nineteenth century, had a population of three times as many free coloured people as whites. Similar proportions were emerging at the same time in British Guyana. Free coloured people – symbolic living proof that racial theories were unjustified – were regarded with more intolerance than black people who knew their place. In 1859 Anthony Trollope wrote:

> Both the white men and the black dislike their coloured neighbours. It is useless to deny that as a rule, such is the case. The white men now...dislike them more in Jamaica than they do in other parts of the West Indies because they are constantly driven to meet them and are more afraid of them.
>
> ...they cannot be refused admission to state parties or even to large assemblies; they have forced themselves forward and must be recognized as being in the van. Individuals [white] decry them – will not have them within their doors – affect to despise them.[65]

But why did black people resent coloureds? Because they felt that people of colour believed themselves to be on the side of whites and superior to blacks. But whichever side was contemptuous of the coloured, the effects of the prejudice were pain, hurt, humiliation, rejection and defiance.

There are many people who believe that one reason so many black British men and women have relationships with white people today is because there was, for centuries, a white bias in Caribbean societies. People tried to marry lighter than themselves. There was a tendency up to the 1960s to worship Europe and European values and to look down on the African heritage. The Caribbean men who fought in the Second World War and those who were part of the post-war migration to Britain were also irresistibly drawn to white partners, partly for this reason and partly because there were few black women in this country at the time.

The rise of black power and the Civil Rights Movement in the US had a significant influence on this tendency but the effects of a long history cannot easily be erased with slogans and assertions of self-belief. A study carried out in Jamaica in 1969 to test the self-esteem of various groups revealed some startling truths. Respondents – all teenagers living through the black-is-beautiful era – were divided into physically differentiated groups. Seventy-three per cent of the total sample said that 'fair' was the best colour to be. In fact the most outspoken black power advocates often had white wives themselves. But of course the Caribbean is composed of more than a white-black mix. East Indians were brought in after abolition in 1836 as indentured labourers to work on the plantations. Chinese immigrants also arrived. Both these groups set down roots and although they did marry out, the tendency within both is towards in-group relationships. The major exception to this is Trinidad where there is a large mixed-race population descended from Indians, blacks and whites. Tensions between the groups however do still emerge and underneath the public image of the multi-coloured Caribbean, inter-communal prejudices are rife.

The United States of America

With the exception of South Africa under apartheid, the USA has enshrined more laws against mixed-race relationships than anywhere else in the world. Responses to these relationships have often been vile and violent. And yet the USA maintained a grand narrative about equality, personal freedom and individual choice. And to this day, there is still a national resistance to the recognition that, for better or worse, from Pocahontas to Malcolm X, the national story is one of interracial mixing.

The legend of Pocahontas is perhaps the best known early account of a mixed relationship in the United States. It symbolises the ever present central ambiguities of how white Anglo-Saxon Americans regard 'the Other'. Here was the daughter of an Indian chief who fell in love with a white man, John Smith, and saved him from being killed by her tribe. She converted, left behind her 'primitive' ways, became one of the chosen ones and then died young and far away from home in cold, cold England. In other words, she assimilated, gave up her heritage and confirmed the superiority of white Christian values. Little wonder she is so adored. But at the time Smith was accused of high treason. There were some pioneers who thought that these prejudices were not only wrong but unwise and immoral. An observer wrote at the time:

> ... we ought to have intermarried with them, which would have incorporated them with us effectively and made them staunch friends, but [our politicians at home] put an effectual stop to all intermarriage afterward. Our traders have indeed their squaws, alias whores, at the Indian towns where they trade but they leave their offspring like bulls or bears to be provided for at random by their mothers ... [66]

Soon after slaves first started landing in the US, hostility against mixed-race liaisons began to appear. In 1629, two white men found 'fornicating with Negresses' were whipped in public. Black people and native Indians were both treated as contaminators yet intercourse between whites and these two groups was rife. Just like in the Caribbean, attitudes were based on deep beliefs about the essential inferiority of the enslaved with the same manifestations of control, cruelty and debasement described above. Slavery and sex were an intimate pair. Many black women resisted their masters and there are innumerable stories of bloody punishments, torture and death. As early as 1661 in Maryland, interracial relationships were banned. A law was passed proclaiming that if an Englishman slept with a black woman the children of the union would automatically be slaves. The black radical activist WEB Du Bois wrote in 1900 that whilst he could forgive white people for slavery and many other injustices, he could not forgive white people: '...neither in this world nor the world to come: its wanton and continued and persistent insulting of the black womanhood which it sought and seeks to prostitute to its lust...'[67]

Attitudes towards the growing numbers of children of these black–white liaisons under slavery were complex and deeply problematic. It is only in the last few years, for example, that white Americans are beginning to accept the reality that Thomas Jefferson had a slave mistress who was mother to some of his children and that there are both black and white descendants who can lay claim to this lineage. In the early days of slavery, children of these mostly forced sexual relationships enjoyed certain privileges. Having some white blood and a lighter skin colour gave them status. Some white masters provided for them and a minority rose to become plantation managers but no higher, except in very exceptional cases where the fathers felt a genuine bond with the child and its mother and tried to give them legitimate rights. A few lucky children found themselves with real status, freedoms, rights and an income including a proper inheritance which in some courts were upheld even though the marital family disputed the will.

But ironically, as miscegenation became more commonplace, more vociferous views took hold. In certain states, one drop of black blood made you black – a law that ensured that mixed-race children of white slave owners would never inherit privilege.

White women – for all the passion which went into their protection by white men – were also more attracted to black men than has really ever been acknowledged. From 1800–1850, in Virginia, divorces were granted to men because children were born to their wives who were obviously mixed-race. Here is one example of a petition presented to court:

> [Elizabeth was] a woman descended from honest and industrious parents and of unspotted character... your petitioner lived with the said Elizabeth with all the affection and tenderness that could possibly exist between a man and a woman... when to the great astonishment and inexplicable mortification of your petitioner, the said Elizabeth was delivered of a mulatto child, and is now so bold as to say it was begotten by a Negro slave man in the neighbourhood.[68]

White men in the South could not accept that white women could give themselves freely to black men and so in many such instances the black man was accused of rape even when there was no evidence that force had been used. A census carried out in 1830 in one particular county in Virginia showed a number of black men with white wives and lovers.

Maybe it is easy to dismiss all this as long-gone history, simply part of the regrettable slave trade which did not, after all, go on in Britain. Certainly the British have never experienced the extreme racial violence of the US, yet the horror and hostility to black/white relationships did cross the ocean.

The above is a brief and necessarily incomplete account of the past, a story far longer and more complex which merits an entire book. The next chapter explores attitudes in the first sixty years of the twentieth century. Both are intended to create a context to help understand the situation today. As we will see in the ensuing chapters, history is still trapped in people and people are still trapped in history – to quote the words of the great James Baldwin who had many white lovers.

Chapter 2
History after 1900

'Black men were thought to be sexually very much more vigorous than white men. People felt that women fell for them for that reason, for sexual indulgence, that sort of thing.'
Margaret Simey, a local councillor in Liverpool in the thirties and friend of Muriel Fletcher who wrote a controversial report on mixed-race families.

'I was living in Europe and everywhere around me were the "monuments" of the plunder of my people – the European pirate-heroes, the slave-built castles and the continuation of the subjection of black and coloured peoples. Tony wanted us to get married from the moment he realised how we felt about each other. He said he didn't want anyone to be confused that this was a slave-plantation type situation all over again.'
Elean Thomas, the Jamaican novelist speaking in 1990 about her relationship with her white British husband Lord Tony Gifford, a QC and human rights lawyer.

'In the early sixties when I first started the Rio in Notting Hill, people were still coming over from the West Indies, and the only women who were available were white. Some were prostitutes, but not all of them although prostitution was very common at the time.
That included Christine Keeler. You know Christine Keeler used to call me 'dad'. She used to come to the Rio. You must recognise the guts that these woman needed to come out on the streets with their black men. Nobody talks about it but they paved the way, they were brave women.'
Frank Crichlow, one of the people who started the Notting Hill Carnival, talking in 1992.

'No separate history of people of mixed black and white parentage has been written. In this sense, as a group, they have no past and no heroes or heroines with whom to identify.'
Barbara Tizzard and Anne Phoenix, 1993.

William Du Bois said the key issue in the twentieth century was the 'problem of the colour line'.[1] In the twenty-first century it is culture which is causing the great fissures around the world. But the two are deeply connected. Those who believe in the genetic purity of the species have much in common with the people who have an essentialist idea of culture. Both detest mixed-race couples and their children. Too few people recall that in Nazi Germany, mixed-race people were sterilised or killed in concentration camps. In 1925, Hitler said:

> Any crossings of two beings not exactly at the same level produces a medium between the level of the two parents. This means: the offspring will probably stand higher than the racially lower parent but not as high as the racially higher one. Consequently it will struggle against the higher level. Such mating is against the will of Nature for a higher breeding of all life ... the stronger must dominate and not blend with the weaker thus sacrificing his greatness.[2]

These ideas had long been argued and circulated by those in the Eugenics movement which sought to replace 'inferior' races with those who were born better. In 1937, one writer said that mixed-race people were: '... the work of the devil, that they inherit the vices of both parents and the virtues of neither, that they are without exception, infertile, unbalanced, indolent, immoral and degenerate.'[3]

In 1944, another believer in Eugenics, JA Rogers, wrote: 'I have never found an inter-mixed or inter-married white-negro couple where the stamp of social inferiority was not plainly traceable as a result.' He goes on to say that such impulses are 'antisocial' and 'opposed to the teachings of sound Eugenics in the light of the best knowledge available to both races at the present time'.[4]

Those who were not biological determinists of this dubious kind came up with their own theories about what was wrong with mixed-race people. In 1928, Robert Park, a Harvard sociologist, introduced the theory of the 'marginal man' who was 'condemned by fate to live in two cultures and worlds' and was always therefore a divided rather than whole self. But Park conceded that this lack of commitment to one world made the person capable of greater tolerance, rationality and cosmopolitanism. In his view this made mixed-race people more capable and not less than black people.[5] Other sociologists – more influential than Park – believed that there was net loss and not gain with the marginal status. Everett Stonquist was the best known of these pessimistic theorists. He believed that as a mixed-race child grew to adulthood and awareness, there was always a crisis of confrontation with rejection. After this pain and confusion there came a period of 'adjustment' where the mixed-race person either opted to pass for white (if this were physically possible) or to join in with 'blackness'.[6]

These theories had a profound impact on the lives of thousands of mixed-race families around the world. Australia has yet to come to terms with the fact that from the time white settlement began to the 1970s mixed-race children were treated in shamefully inhumane ways. Children, especially those whose fathers were white, were forcibly removed from their Aboriginal mothers to be brought up in special children's homes. This was an active policy to erase the Aboriginal culture from their lives. Bob Randell, one of these children, wrote this song later when he was an adult:

> Yowie, yowie, my brown skin baby
> They take him away from me
> Between her sobs I heard her say
> Police 'bin take my baby away
> From white man boss baby I had
> Why he let them take baby away?
> To a children's home the baby came
> With new clothes on and a new name
> But night and day he would always say
> Mummy, oh mummy why why they take me away?
> Yowie, yowie, my brown skin baby
> They take him away.[7]

In Britain, as late as the 1960s, mothers of mixed-race children were also pressured into giving up their children who were then classified as 'hard to place' children. This category is still used by some children's agencies. Mixed-race children are grouped with children with learning difficulties, special needs and physical disabilities.

Many of us who grew up under the Imperial sun, which did not set until the late sixties, remember hostility towards mixed-race families. I recall a striking example of this as a child in Uganda. In the block of flats where we lived there was a rare mixed-race family. Thomas was Goan and Anglo-Indian himself. His wife Mary was white South African. Thomas's parents had been ostracised because they decided to marry and have a family. Thomas still could not understand how two English-speaking Christians were seen as criminals by whites and other Indians. He was tormented by the way his parents had been humiliated. But then why marry a white woman from South Africa? Perhaps, he said, because he was still so angry and wanted to carry on fighting the world on this issue. The couple lived in constant terror as Mary's father kept sending death threats and referring to their children as 'mongrel dogs'.

During the days of colonialism in Africa, it was more or less impossible for white women to step into a relationship with a black man, whereas white men could and did succumb to the charms of black women. Other communities in Africa displayed the same attitudes towards black men who were always presumed to have huge sexual appetites from which Arab, Asian and other women had to be protected. Asian and Arab men had black mistresses and children (cruelly named 'chotara' which meant half-caste) but their women had to be preserved. This created a terrible ferment among many African men. In 1964, following a military coup in Zanzibar, several young Arab and Asian girls were taken by the African military leadership to be raped and enslaved. Idi Amin's act of revenge against Asians was triggered when an Indian woman, the widow of a rich industrialist, rejected his advances and offers of marriage.

Double standards for men and women created silent havoc. A white American school friend of mine in Kampala came from an evangelical Christian family. Her father was an American missionary who would not allow his wife to leave the house without him. One day, he suddenly ran away with a young African woman and was never heard of again, leaving his family more confused than distraught. The image of Africa as the dark continent – a metaphor which persists – created some of the strongest barriers to white–black relationships. Attitudes in the twentieth century did not appear to have changed much from previous centuries. The view of the Other, both overseas and within the British Isles, was based on a deep sense of white British superiority mingled with irrational desire for the objects of their contempt.

In a fascinating Radio 4 programme, *Eros and the Empire*,[8] Professor David Dabydeen explored these ambiguities in fine detail. For Conrad, he points out, the continent of Africa contains not only the heart of darkness but is a place of overwhelming sexuality, bestiality and 'unspeakable copulation', drawing to its 'pitiless breast' those who have civilised themselves to live down to their forgotten instincts and go beyond the permissible.[9] How different is this from the fantasies of earlier centuries, asks Dabydeen? Very little, he rightly answers, quoting earlier travellers to Africa such as Thomas Herbert who said that Africans were close to apes and fornicated with beasts which is why they could never be truly human.

In South Africa this belief became the basis of Apartheid after 1948. The forced separation between the races created untold misery for those who dared to break the taboos and the children who were born of the unions. The 1927 Immorality Act was to 'prohibit illicit intercourse between Europeans and non-Europeans'. Other laws separating the different populations and restricting their movements were all passed in the name of racial purity and white power.

We are only now beginning to hear some of these stories. Mixed-race people in South Africa could not live with the white parent and were rejected by the 'pure' blacks too. In other parts of Africa, strong social disapprobation was enough to keep the numbers of liaisons pitifully low. In East Africa, for example, there is no large 'coloured' or mixed-race population and this is also true of West Africa. When such relationships did happen, there was usually rejection on all sides. One of the most poignant cases which only really came to light in the eighties was the marriage of Sir Seretse Khama, a chief and political activist from Botswana, to his English wife, Ruth. They met and fell in love in London in 1947. Both were Christians and had met at the London Missionary Society. Yet when they arrived for their wedding at a church in Kensington, they discovered that Seretse's uncle had arranged for the marriage to be cancelled. Ruth's father then disowned her and although the couple were married anyway, that was just the beginning of their long struggle for acceptance. Soon after their wedding, Apartheid was established in South Africa. Britain needed the uranium deposits in that country and the British government colluded with the South Africa regime to declare that Sir Seretse was an unfit chief. The couple was forced to live in exile until independence when he became the president and was awarded a knighthood. His wife said in 1980: 'All their efforts to keep us apart were useless. Trying to split up Seretse and me was like trying to split the atom. We knew that nothing could drive us apart.'[10]

Fleshing the historical stereotypes

In western countries and particularly in the United States, persistent images of dangerous black sexuality resulted in similar pain and inhumanity. In 1941, James Weldon Johnson wrote the most succinct and precise description of this:

> ...in the core of the heart of America's race problem, the sex factor is rooted; rooted so deeply that it is not always recognised when it shows at the surface...Taken alone, it furnishes a sufficient mainspring for the rationalisation of all the complexes of white superiority. It may be innate; I do not know. But I do know that it is strong, and bitter; and that its strength and bitterness are magnified and intensified by the white man's perceptions of the Negro complex of sexual superiority.[11]

Paranoia over the corruption of fair maidens by the untrammelled sexuality of black men was visible in the Southern States well into the 1960s, when black men were publicly castrated for the 'crime' of looking at a white woman. This is mapped out in Beth Day's work, quoted below. Today the knives may have been put away, but in many of these places the venom felt by white men remains. This was and is 'chivalry' unasked for by either party, says Day, in her angry book, *Sexual Life Between Blacks and Whites*: 'One of the sad features...is that the white women never did ask to be protected from those black men. It was their fathers', husbands' and brothers' idea...white women were as much victims of the system as black men. They were allowed no sexual freedom of choice.'[12]

In 1958, Mildred Jeter, a mixed-race woman married to Perry Loving, a white man, went to live in Virginia. They were both imprisoned for a year. Similar cases were seen in courts in most Southern States even though the judgments contravened the Fourteenth Amendment which protects the individual rights of citizens. In one judgment the Court of Virginia stated categorically that it was the responsibility of the state 'to preserve the racial integrity of its citizens...to prevent the corruption of blood and the creation of a mongrel breed of citizens'.[13]

There is still a terrible lack of honest discourse on the deeper motives which drive a large number of mixed-race relationships. Earlier, two brave writers, Frantz Fanon and Eldridge Cleaver, exposed all too well how politics, economics and power could and often did provide explanations for passion. In 1952, Fanon saw these relationships as crops growing on the soil of inequality:

> Out of the blackest part of my soul, across the zebra striping of my mind, surges this desire to be suddenly white. I wish to be acknowledged not as black but white...who but a white woman can do this for me? By loving she proves I am worthy of white love. And loved like a white man...When my restless hands caress those white breasts they grasp white civilization and dignity and make them mine.[14]

Three decades on, in his searing book *Soul on Ice*, Cleaver created a fictional character, Lazarus, who muses thus:

> There is no love left between a black man and a black woman. Take me, for instance. I love white women and hate black women...I'd jump over ten nigger bitches just to get to one white woman. Ain't no such thing as an ugly white woman. A white woman is beautiful even if she is bald-headed and has only one tooth...it's not just the fact that she's a woman I love; I love her skin, her soft, smooth, white skin...there's a softness about a white woman, something delicate and soft inside her. But a nigger bitch seems full of steel, granite hard and resisting, not soft and submissive like a white woman.[15]

This is the context in which the film *Guess Who's Coming to Dinner* exploded on to the screen in the mid-sixties revealing that it was not only the ignorant rednecks in ex-slave territories who had problems with miscegenation, but also highly educated white liberals. Nor was this a simple issue for black people either. WEB Du Bois, much admired leader and himself mixed-race, said:

The history of the American Negro is the history of [a] longing to attain self-conscious manhood, to merge his double self into a better truer self. In this merging he wishes neither of the older selves to be lost. He would not Africanise America, for America has too much to teach the world and Africa. He would not bleach his Negro soul in a flood of white Americanism, for he knows that Negro blood has a message for the world. He simply wishes to make it possible for a man to be both a negro and an American.[16]

The ramifications of sexual relationships with white people still rage in the United States today, raising questions of identity and integrity and fundamental questions about the rights and wrongs of sleeping with the enemy. The struggle for recognition as equals and Americans is the context in which interracial relationships have to try and succeed.

Mixed-race relationships in the UK in the early twentieth century

By the beginning of this century there were core black and Asian communities in the port cities of Cardiff, Bristol and Liverpool, and significant numbers of mixed-race families. But white Britons in these areas did not approve and 1919 saw the first large-scale riots against blacks in Liverpool, Cardiff, London and elsewhere. One of the main reasons was the eruption of emotion on the part of some white men who could not bear the liaisons between black men and white women: 'Flung out into the slumland culture of the port towns, the black seamen focused upon themselves considerable racial hostility as they became linked in the public mind with growing crime rates and prostitution when they cohabited with white women and produced "half caste" children.'[17]

On the streets of Liverpool, gangs of white men up to 2000 in number roamed the streets beating up black men. 24-year-old Charles Wotten , a discharged sailor from Trinidad, was murdered by one of these roaming gangs. The Liverpool Echo described how 'the howl of the mob dies away on a delighted note when word goes about that "another bloomin nigger has been laid out"'. But then in an editorial, the Echo goes on to pronounce:

One of the chief reasons of the anger behind the present disturbances lies in the fact that the negro is nearer to the animal than is the average white man and that there are women in

Liverpool who have no self-respect...many of the blacks in Liverpool are of a low type, and they threaten respectable women in the street.[18]

The *Manchester Guardian* blamed black men for defending themselves.[19] Sir Ralph Williams, a former British colonial administrator, wrote to *The Times*: 'To almost every white man and woman who has lived a life among coloured races, intimate association between black or coloured men and women is a thing of horror...[how can we blame] those white men, who seeing these conditions and loathing them, resort to violence?'[20]

Susan Benson, in her book *Ambiguous Ethnicity: Interracial Families in London*, argues that there were other underlying reasons for this riot:

> Economic tensions, and especially competition for employment in the unfavourable conditions of 1919 were clearly responsible for much of the hostility directed towards the visible, and therefore vulnerable, black dockland communities. The selection of interracial sexual relationships as a significant issue reflects not simply local tensions, but also the focusing of concern upon one aspect of race relations in the English context: the dangers and problems of miscegenation.[21]

A decade later, Cardiff's chief constable, James A Wilson, made a public plea for South African-type legislation to keep the races apart sexually.[22] There were official government inquiries into the health and hygiene of 'hopeless' hybrid children. Contamination fears were giving way to the syndrome of the hapless passive victim, the hybrid child who did not ask to be born.

A joint report by the British Social Hygiene Council and the British Council for the Welfare of the Mercantile Marine, both keen anti-venereal-disease campaigners, declared in the 1930s: 'Morality and cleanliness are as much matters of geography as they are dependent on circumstances. The coloured men who have come to dwell in our cities are being made to adopt a standard of civilisation they cannot be expected to understand. They are not imbued with moral codes similar to our own.'[23]

Margaret Simey from Liverpool remembers the horror and fascination, the rumours which swept through Liverpool as mixed-race families began to become more visible: 'People could not accept that any decent Englishwoman would live in those dockside communities. It was beyond their imagination. They thought only prostitutes could do this.'[24] Her friend Muriel Fletcher then became embroiled in one of the major furores of that period after writing a controversial research report which concluded that white women who were in mixed-race families were deluded and uneducated, often trapped in loveless marriages: 'They almost invariably regret their alliance with a coloured man, and realising that they have chosen a life which is repugnant, become extraordinarily sensitive about their position.'[25]

The report, *An Investigation into the Colour Problem in Liverpool and Other Ports*, published in 1930, was commissioned by the Liverpool Association for the Welfare of Half-Caste Children. The whole report needs to be read to see just what the attitudes were in this country at the time, but here is a taste of the tone and substance:

> The bad moral surroundings of these girls makes it impossible in most cases to recommend them [for domestic service]... the girls were slow workers, lacking in initiative, needed constant supervision... From her mother the half-caste girl is liable to inherit a certain slackness, from her father a happy-go-lucky attitude towards life... from an early age she knows that she will have no difficulty in finding someone to keep her.[26]

One of the most shameful episodes in the thirties, and one which illustrated that all classes of white people were capable of overt racism, was the reaction to the performance, in 1930, of *Othello* at the Savoy Theatre with Paul Robeson playing Othello and Peggy Ashcroft as Desdemona. People hissed and there was an audible intake of breath when the two touched. *The Times* would not review the play; critics walked out because there were black people in the audience. According to Ashcroft, Robeson could play at the Savoy Theatre but was not allowed into the Savoy Hotel. She herself received racist mail and was shocked that the play had unleashed such overt prejudice.[27] Some of the reviewers who did stay concentrated on the physical qualities of Robeson and his movements, concluding that these showed him to have an inferiority complex. Several biographers since have struggled to make sense of the electricity between the two protagonists and some concluded that Peggy Ashcroft had fallen under Robeson's spell, both in the play and outside it. The ironies are obvious.

With such social attitudes in place, perhaps it is not that surprising that the Fletcher report should have been written at this time. But what is astonishing is that this pre-dates large-scale immigration and that there was such a massive furore by people who objected to the report that Miss Fletcher had to flee Liverpool. In 1940 and 1952 further reports were produced on this 'coloured' population but they were more sensitively written and concentrated on economic deprivation and the very difficult social position of white women married to black men. An unpublished thesis by Sydney Collins of Edinburgh (1952) describes how white women had to protect the men and took up the role of finding homes, interacting with schools and other functions. The women often had jobs of higher status than the men and the relationships were observed to be equal although it was true that many of the women were from less 'respected' classes and some may have settled for loveless relationships. The pressure to regain so-called 'lost' respectability – something which you see in a number of mixed-race families even today – meant that both parents tried to ensure that the daughters in the family often had a very strict upbringing because of worries that they would be seen as 'low class' and impure. In an earlier study (1949–51) in docklands areas, Collins had found that 90 per cent of West Indian men were either married to white women or mixed-race women. He also found that the white families rarely accepted these relationships.[28]

The war lovers

In the First and Second World Wars, millions of black and Indian soldiers joined up, but despite fighting and dying for the Motherland, these 'coloured people' could not achieve the same status as their white counterparts and their contribution was largely forgotten. Even now, few people realise just how much was done by these troops and how deeply they cared about this country. The responses of Europeans to the Indian soldiers have only recently started to come to light and it does seem to be the case that on the whole the women responded with greater enthusiasm than the men. Letters by soldiers to their families back home contain many such descriptions: 'The women of this place are very pleased to see us. They are like opening flowers. They shake hands with our men when they disembark and attempt to feed them from their own pockets.'[29]

In *Indian Voices of the Great War*, a collection of these letters, it is clear that the admiration was mutual and that there was a great deal of fantasising about sex with white women. One soldier sent home a cigarette card with a picture of the Duchess of Gordon painted by Sir Joshua Reynolds and wrote: 'This is the woman we get. We have recourse to her. I have sent you this and if you like it, let me know and I will send her. We get everything we want.' Another soldier writes: 'The Ladies are very nice and bestow their favours on us freely. But contrary to the custom in our country, they do not put their legs over the shoulders when they go with a man.' In another delighted letter a wounded soldier writes: 'The Indians are very much liked here. The girls in this place are notorious and very fond of accosting Indians and fooling with them. They are ever ready for any purpose and in truth are no better than the girls of Adda Bazar of Indore.'[30]

All these letters were censored, as were the ones which described how Indian soldiers were being used as cannon fodder. But there was awesome gratitude too for those genuinely caring white women who looked after the wounded at the Brighton Pavilion, which had been converted into a hospital specifically catering for the Indian soldiers, who had different religions and customs. In one moving letter an Indian soldier writes:

> ... the ladies tend us, who have been wounded, as a mother tends her child. They pour milk into our mouths, and our own brothers and sisters, were we well, would only give us water in a pot. There you see the brotherhood of religion. Here you see the brotherhood of the English who are kind to us without any further motive. The ladies even carry away our excreta so kind are they; and whatsoever we have a liking for, they put it into our mouths. They wash our clothes every week and massage our backs when they ache from lying in bed.[31]

The authorities soon grew uneasy about this easy flow of affection between the Indian men and white women, concerned that Indians were getting the wrong idea of an Englishwoman's reputation which would 'be most detrimental to the prestige and spirit of European rule in India'.[32] Rules were subsequently put in place to keep white women out of the hospitals devoted to the Indian war wounded.

The Second World War produced similar tensions between desires and prohibition. A number of white women were attracted by the uniformed black and Asian men and paid a high price for it. In the early nineties, I interviewed Ethal, a frail old woman in an old people's home who has since died. I am including her story in full because it is such a powerful account of those times. Born in the North of England, the youngest of five children, she left home, came down to London and worked as a prostitute for several years.

> You will change my name, won't you, and you won't tell them where I live? You see I am seventy now and I live here in this home, but they don't know nothing about me. But I have had a life, I tell you, a real life. Back then, when the war started and all those handsome men went off. My mother cleaned and my father was sickly for quite a long time. Then he died.
> I had to leave home and come down to London, where there was no work. I did try. I remember feeling as if I was alone in the world. London was like that. I found a job with this gentleman, next to the lodgings; he was very kind, he introduced me to other nice gentlemen. I didn't walk the streets then, you know. But then he died and I had to leave. But one of my customers was this black gentleman – the first one I had ever had. He wore these polished shoes and looked after himself really well, and those hats! Harry was his name, I think. I think I fell in love with him

a bit, but one didn't, you see, not with a black, not even a girl like me. He used to visit me well into the night after he had been in one of their clubs, and he would tell me stories about the gambling and the drinking. He sang and the neighbour didn't like that. Not one bit. He didn't come back one day and that was that. Then things were rough and I had a few black sailors and even an Indian sailor who didn't speak any language and didn't know much about anything else either, you know? He was so skinny and had these dark hairy legs. I know I couldn't tell my English customers about it, they wouldn't have liked it very much.

Then I met Frank. He was in the RAF, a good-looking man, a pilot, from Jamaica, I think. He spoke so posh and he would bring me flowers and treated me like a lady all the time. He had a lot of money to throw away and he hated it in the service. But I knew he was getting attached. Anyway, a few months later I knew I was...you know...in the family way. I didn't know for a long time and then when I did I couldn't get rid of it. I was a Catholic, you see, my mother was. I didn't know whose it was. But when it was born it was as black as soot. They were shocked, all of them. I was too. I couldn't even hold him. I told Frank and he was a gentleman. Others would have run away. I was going to put the little one up for adoption, but Frank would have none of it. He called his mother over and we all lived together in this small place, there was no shutting of doors. She was a good woman. I couldn't understand what she was saying at first and then I fitted in. They were all marvellous to me – the aunts, the girls. The men would tease, but never flirt. I was Frank's girl. Nobody made me feel low.

The white neighbours took it rather badly. They would turn away when we came down pulling the pram. The children used to call me a 'nigger' and I saw such hate in the eyes of the women. I sometimes wish I could have told them how these people had helped me to find a family again. And my black family was better dressed, though we could not get a decent place to stay then. They had those white gloves, those long nails, hats. And on Sunday they dressed in their best as they went out to church. I still couldn't get close to the boy, though. I didn't feel he had come from me. Mothers want their children to look at least a bit like them. He was just Frank's mother's boy, I think. He thought I was his aunt or something. Frank was good to him. But he was a good man. He suffered when the war was over. Couldn't get the work he wanted – he was an engineer and so proud. But all he could get were these low jobs. But he never thought he was too good for them. He worked and kept us all going. Me, the boy, his mother and sister. Then the uncle would come over sometimes. On Saturday the small place would be full of them and they would play cards and talk about back home.

At first I felt strange, a white woman living with black folk. I think it was like changing colour. And I found the food and the noise terrible at first. But at the end I thought they were my people. And they were. I had no white friends. One friend, Martha, who used to be very nice, did come a couple of times but she soon stopped. I remember once going to a market with a group of West Indian women, and this man asked me why I was so white and did I have any white blood in the family! And I must have started talking a bit like them – you do, don't you?

Frank kept them from what I did before. Them being so religious, he didn't think it would go down very well. He used to say to me, 'Ethal, I see human beings. Others see what your job is and the colour of your skin.' He was marvellous. So wise, so educated. I often wondered what he was doing stuck with someone like me. I had never read a book. He would read all the time. But it was an honourable thing to do, to marry me. Not love, not the way it happened. But we did love each other after. I thought it was very funny. My white friends could accept me when I was a woman of the streets, you know, but not when I was married to a nice educated black man. I hated the way the family was treated. At first I would say things in shops and cafés. But the insults would get worse, so I just gave up. I mean, we are supposed to be civilised and they were not – to me in my life it didn't look that way.

And I suppose people were shocked to see us all out together on a Sunday morning, dressed in our Sunday best, going to church. At first I found all that moving and singing in the church a bit funny, and I never really joined in, even at the end. I was the only white person there. But those people believed so much, they would cry, it was marvellous, simple real faith. I think all this made me more religious. They were good for me.

I am sure the family was disappointed that Frank didn't marry one of his own. I remember his mother showing me this old picture of a young West Indian girl standing outside on a balcony, with this swinging skirt on, she said it was one of his girlfriends a long time ago. I didn't feel jealous or angry.

I enjoyed my life in those days. We used to go to black clubs and dance, I felt really quite proud on his arm there, when they called me his girl. Once when we were coming out of the club, a policeman, a big man, stopped us and asked what I was doing with 'the nigger'. He would not believe we were married and thought I was picking him up – it was funny when you think about it. And then he came to the house. I could tell he was really more shocked that I was married to him. Frank was so strong when this kind of thing happened. He would say nothing, but I could see how he was controlling himself. 'Yes, sir', 'No, sir', but his eyes were like red fire. Even when we got married in the registry office, they were all so shocked, you could see, nobody was smiling and when the registrar had to shake our hands it was like he was touching dirt.

Did I feel sad at the way white people treated me? Yes, sometimes. I remember when one woman had been very rude to me when I had the boy with me. She pulled her child away when she came to play with him, she said I was dirty and I really felt that.

I think a lot about those days now and about how life has been. I have always been outside, you know, not a part of anything. Not because I wanted to, it just happened like that. When I saw the gentlemen, I had to keep it from my family. People would reject you if they knew, so I used to say I was an office worker. All those lies. Then living with Frank's family I was more of an outsider and even within the family I was not quite one of them. They were always so kind to me, not like the whites, but I was outside. Now here I can't even show these ladies my pictures, I have them locked up and if they could see – my, my, they would be so shocked! So here too there is all this hiding. I think they are curious why nobody comes to see me. I read a lot of books now, Frank would have been proud. But then I was so full of dresses and music and fun. I missed him so much when he died, just like that, suddenly, twenty years ago. I stayed on, they were my family, but it wasn't the same. The boy, Randolph, had gone away to America, and he still sends postcards. But I haven't seen him. I wasn't that close to him. It was his grandmother and aunt he felt were his family. I think I was ashamed of him.

I left the family and went up north and started cleaning for offices and lost touch really. It was another life. I do miss Frank though, he was such a gentleman. He gave me this brooch once, the only present he gave me, we were quite poor. But this was special and I still wear it. It is a rose, you see, and he always used to tease me about my white skin and being an English rose.[33]

A large number of white American GIs in Britain during the war were overtly prejudiced and they objected to racially integrated forces. The Civil War had ended slavery, but racism against black Americans was still rife and remained so until the United States was forced to address the issue as a result of the struggle for civil rights which gathered force after the end of the Second World War. Soon there were calls from high and low for segregating the barracks. In 1940, President Franklin Roosevelt issued a directive which said: 'The policy of the US War Department is not to intermingle coloured and enlisted personnel in the same regimental organisations. This policy has proved satisfactory over a long period of years, and to make changes would produce situations destructive to morale and detrimental to the preparations for national defence.'[34] An impression was given that this was a requirement, a condition of the US coming in to support the Allies. In July 1942, Colonel Eisenhower, who two years later assumed command of the entire allied military operation in Europe, spoke to journalists outlining his strongly held view that in the army it was essential for whites and blacks to be absolutely equal but separate.

For far too long there has been a massive pretence that racism in the army was brought over by the Americans. In reality, US attitudes were used by the British authorities to validate the bigotry which had long prevailed in these islands. Limits were imposed on the numbers of black GIs although (this being discreet Great Britain) no official colour bar policy was announced. Private correspondence between the colonial and war office shows that the main reason for this antipathy towards black GIs was the fear that white women would liaise with them. The Cabinet concluded that 'It was desirable that the people of this country should avoid becoming too friendly with coloured American troops.'[35] As the war went on, the Cabinet carried on fretting over this issue and the risk of cross-racial sex. At RAF camps, special lectures were delivered to women officers and other staff about the dangers of sexual intercourse with black men.

Andy Shepherd, one of the Caribbeans in the RAF, remembers this all too well:

A vast number of Caribbeans were in the Royal Air Force and working as engineers and munitions workers. So there we were, in 1945 in Sussex, with all the WAAFs. We all used to have medical examinations, what was known as 'Free From Infection' parade – we would wait with our underpants and overcoats on while the doctors examined us.

I remember very well the hostility towards us then. Both Tories and Labour used to say that blacks would corrupt white women and live off their immoral earnings, that that was their stock in trade. High Tories took it further and said that we would take their women and hide them; they said this even when we were fighting with them in the war.

The WAAFs were told not to sleep with black men because they would have mulatto children and would harm themselves. One girl, who was quite precocious and pretty experienced, demanded to know how sleeping with a black man would harm her. She was told that West Indian men were unusually large and that our lovemaking had no sophistication about it, we were animal-like in our behaviour. That was the kind of nonsense that was pushed down these girls. The irony was that I was twenty-one years old and a virgin – I had never had sexual intercourse in my life. So when I did have sex, it was an experienced WAAF who introduced me to it. But the politicians and bosses in the army, they did not like these women being so friendly and familiar.[36]

There are records of fights between white American soldiers and black men out with white women. Mary Watson, who married a black airman, remembers this herself: 'There were a lot of white and black Americans at the time and there was animosity between these two, almost like segregation. So the white Americans didn't like it when the white girls seemed to prefer the black Americans.'

Black GIs carried on having relationships with white British women but it is only now that we discover that unmarried mothers giving birth to mixed-race babies were shunned and forced to give up their children who were often sent by the various philanthropic agencies to specially selected orphanages where large numbers of such children would grow up together. There was no support forthcoming from the British or US governments. Mary Hebditch, a former nursery nurse, said that she looked after many such children at a special farm in Dorset: 'They were lovely children. I had dozens of them.' Many mothers even now refuse to acknowledge their children, who are now in their fifties, and only in the summer of 2000 did it become known that a number of these 'removed' children were now actively seeking the families of their fathers in the US.[37]

Andy Shepherd witnessed these painful events when he was in the RAF.

This particular girl, a Scot, wasn't going to accept this nonsense about not going with black men. And many of the WAAFs knew that we weren't as primitive as we were made out to be – they saw how polite we were. I would never sit down until a lady had a seat. We all had pictures of home on the wall – I had all my graduation pictures, when I passed my senior Cambridge examination; pictures of my father and mother; and my home – and the girls loved seeing them, seeing what our lives were like before we came here, how lush and green everything was.

And by the time the girls got their instructions, relationships had already begun – maybe that is why the warnings had to be given. You mustn't forget that white men had gone off to fight the war so there was some frustration, although in those days there was a strong philosophy that you had to get married and hold off, but you were still kissing and cuddling.

Two of the girls became pregnant – one of them, a cook on the camp, was very much in love with the guy. When that happened they both had to leave the camp. She was told that if she put her child up for adoption, she could come back. But she refused to do so. I think in spite of all the racism, they were women first, and women on the whole are more human. In fact when so many black men were repatriated after the war some of these white women tried to protect them, to hide them and help them. Many of the relationships which started in the camps thrived. I know of many long and happy marriages between white women and black men.

It was no accident that many of the women who ventured into these relationships came from disadvantaged backgrounds, just as in previous centuries, and no accident either that the pressure on the couples often meant stress, and in some cases led to a lack of trust and a destructive cynicism. Many of these couples met in dance halls. Dashing, immaculately dressed Caribbean men were increasingly seen in public dating and courting white women and there were many popular clubs in London, Birmingham and Manchester full of such couples. What is instructive is that such clubs do not exist now, in spite of the rise in mixed-race relationships.

Trevor and Mary Watson, who were still happily married in 1992 when I met them, found each other on the dance floor. Trevor remembered the moment as if it had happened yesterday: 'I was in an RAF camp in Nottingham called Newton Aerodrome and we really met through our love of dancing. I used to go to the Greyfriars ballroom and that is where we met because my wife is also a good dancer and we used to meet to do a little jitterbugging.'

Mary added her own clear memories.

The girls went there for a good time and of course when the West Indians came it was a thrill to us, you know, to see other nationalities coming over. As a young girl I had always had a thing about black people. They always intrigued me. It was a thrill because the Jamaicans used to press their uniforms differently to the Englishmen. They had their own style. We used to say they were really lairy, you know. That means they looked fancy and smart. The passes would come from both sides. They were good dancers – oh, they could dance. I was a lot slimmer then and he used to throw me up and swirl me around. You have to understand that what was important in the past was the way the black man treated the white girl. He was a gentleman. He knew how to talk to a girl. I find – and I shouldn't say this, I know – but Englishmen, they haven't got that thing about them that makes a woman feel good.[38]

Hannah and Bob Murray, who is from the West Indies, met at a dance in 1946. Bob did not tell his family back home when he married Hannah. Eventually, under pressure from his father, he wrote and said he was married to a 'black Irish woman'. The couple are still married more than fifty years on. Their love is so solid it seems to prove that adversity, if it does not destroy, can create unbreakable bonds. Teresa Alleyne and her jazz musician husband Hanky, who met in the same period, are also still together. Yet when they wanted to get married the Catholic priest went to Teresa's home and said what she was planning was 'not a Catholic thing to do'.[39]

Andy Shepherd also recalled these social meeting places:

I spent most of my early life in Soho. I was introduced to Soho by a Trinidadian seaman called Happy Blake who ran clubs in the Harrow Road and the East End, and I too ran clubs. In those days there were some clubs that wouldn't allow black people in and there were also some public places that wouldn't allow us in. But I can't think of one club run by black people which didn't allow whites in. It would have been stupid because the majority of us were men so we either had to be poofs or befriend white girls, so mostly it was white girls who came with us. White artists and people like that used to think it was very classy coming to the black clubs. If you were a young black woman, you were a pearl. You couldn't get near a black woman, everyone would flock round her like bees to a honeypot – and most of those women married white boys.

Many Englishmen have asked me: 'How come you got all the girls?' Well, we were a meagre minority among a vast array of women whose husbands and lovers were killed during the war. Many of them were married and they used their superior skills in love to attract us, and I learned a lot. When two people decide to be close, the one who is more advanced helps the other on. Now in spite of all the sexual stories about black men, I was shown sex by a white woman from Nottingham. Everything was rationed – clothes, food and all that – and those women used all manner of encouragement to attract us. If someone uses their clothing coupon to buy you a kerchief or some socks, you understand what that person is giving up. I have never felt rejected in this place, never – maybe because I am fortunate and can look at a problem and be analytical about it, and I could do that even when I was pretty young. Of course I felt hostility, a lot of it, but it washed over me. If you allow these things to affect you...I had been to the United States and seen what can happen, I think I was more hurt in the USA. The Englishman's sophistication means he can carry off the hypocrisy in a very suave way. When we were with white girls, we never got any remarks – they were scared of us, I think – although the girls did; they were seen as fast and cheap. Of course there was racism. It increased when the Americans came, but it reached a crescendo when the men who had fought with the East African forces came back – they brought the worst forms of racism.[40]

After the 1939–45 war

The flow of large-scale immigration began after the Second World War and at this time the outflow countries were mainly in the Caribbean. The post-war reconstruction in this country created a need for skilled and unskilled labour. On 22 June 1948, the Empire Windrush started this movement of people bringing 492 Jamaicans who arrived with pride and the hope that they would be embraced in the motherland. But even as the boat landed eleven Labour MPs wrote to Clement Atlee expressing their concern that 'an influx of coloured people domiciled here is likely to impair the harmony, strength and cohesion of our public life and cause discord and unhappiness among all concerned'.[41] In these responses, says Kenan Malik, 'are contained the assumptions that have shaped both official and popular attitudes to post war immigration'.[42]

Academic research, official reports and media hysteria scaled new heights in the mid-1950s as immigration from the Indian subcontinent and the Caribbean increased and accelerated. Despite the war, anti-Semitic feelings were evident too especially on the issue of mixed relationships. A rash of 'human interest' stories asking 'Would you let your daughter marry a...?' pandered to the racism of the period.

One of the most disturbing interviews on the subject was with Wentworth Day, a parliamentary candidate in 1958. He had said no first-class nation could be made of mongrels and that if his daughter wanted to marry a black man, he would remind her that she would find a 'coffee-coloured imp' next to her on her bed. Mixed-race children, he said, were mentally deficient. Most suffered from an inferiority complex too. Mixed marriages, he said, came out of 'downright sex or sloppy sentimentality'.[43] A Gallup poll in the same year found that 71 per cent disapproved of mixed-race relationships and another study carried out in Brixton found high levels of disapproval and disgust expressed by white interviewees.[44]

It was in this year that the powerful novel *To Sir With Love* by ER Braithwaite appeared. The hero is a black teacher who goes to work in a school in a deprived area and, in spite of prejudice, he builds up an extraordinary rapport with his pupils. But the inner and outer struggles are never simplified and some of the most moving moments show him beginning to feel ashamed of his blackness just as he realises he is falling in love with a white woman to whom race does not matter. The impact of the book was felt across the country and even more so when it was filmed with Sidney Poitier playing the role of a decent black man. But the year 1958 will be most remembered for the Notting Hill riots, the worst race riots seen in this country. As with the earlier riots in Liverpool, Cardiff and London, one of the causes was the anger of white men who felt black men were corrupting their women. Joan was a white woman married to a black bus conductor:

> I was pregnant and had the older child in a pram, still only eleven months old. The gang of white men saw us and ran towards us. There was nothing I could do. They tore off my skirt and one tried to tear off my stockings. One of them started kicking the pram saying 'bastard or bitch?' I was screaming, my son was screaming. I then fainted as people started coming out of the flats. They took me into the house and called my husband. I lost the baby. And I never was myself again. But he was a strong Christian and said these things are sent to try us. I told my son this story for the first time the other day and he couldn't believe that I had kept it in all these years.

John her husband remembers all this and more:

> They were hard times. The Empire was striking back. I am not saying that there aren't these problems elsewhere. Wherever imperialism has been, these attitudes survive – white skin, light skin, is better than black in India, in Guyana – between Indians, between the descendants of the slaves in Guyana. But the attacks on us were orchestrated. The blacks who were here had got themselves rented property, thanks to Rachman. You know he wasn't a bad man. They hated him because he used to let rooms to us blacks. He got on fine with blacks – he drank with them, gambled with them and would give rooms, particularly to black women. In 1957–8 the National Front started holding meetings in this area, saying blacks had taken the jobs at a cheaper rate and were putting whites out of work. This was Mosley's message. Now many of us at that time were ex-servicemen. We were proud and had learnt to take no nonsense. The Southern Irish stood by us and there were some whites who supported us, physically and morally. The police – their attitudes were as they are now. I remember when all this was going on I was arrested and questioned so many times. But I believe in Jesus.

The 1960s brought marked changes in attitudes towards mixed-race relationships and children. Alongside the image of the poor mixed-race child who would belong nowhere, caught in the crossfire of culture, race and politics, developed a bizarre belief that intermarriage would be a good thing because it would lead to a useful assimilation of the alien wedge. Newspapers intermittently ran romantic stories of Love Winning Through as heroic individuals crossed into this minefield. But these were a small distraction from the obvious hardening of attitudes. This letter, not untypical, was published in the *English Churchman* by a 'nice' lady from Kingston-upon-Thames:

> With their extremely high birth rate it has been estimated that by the end of the century through intermarrying with us they will completely have mongrelised the British race... The irresponsibility of the negro and the fatalism of the Asian will have passed into our make up and we shall never be the same again. Do we really want to see our island peopled with either Mulattoes or Eurasians? The Marxists do, as a hybrid race – with its diminished patriotism – is much easier to manipulate than a thoroughbred with its roots in its country's age old traditions – the Devil would like to see us, the race which has done most to Christianise the world, disappear.[45]

Unsurprisingly, in 1963, from 1000 parishes questioned, only eighty-four had recorded marriage across the races.

In the early sixties, the country witnessed the arrival of large numbers of black women and children from the Caribbean and the subcontinent. Black society started restructuring into its own family groupings, but in a number of cases there was a past which had to be confronted. Loneliness, desire and love had led some black and Asian men into relationships with white women. When their wives from back home appeared, they found themselves in inextricably difficult situations. The women, both white and black, suffered great distress too.

Elsa (black) and Harriet (white) did not know that they were both partners of the same man, Harry, a bus conductor from Guyana who died in 1995. It was at this time that the two lives came to light. There are five children between them and slowly, through one particularly affectionate relationship between step-siblings, the families are coming a little closer. Elsa is not bitter any more: 'God has allowed me to forgive him. He must have been lonely when he came over and all the racism and that. She was just a comfort to him. I understand that now. But maybe when I was younger I would have thrown him out with my own strong arms. So he couldn't tell me.' Harriet is less forgiving: 'I thought why can't he live with us here in Birmingham? He said it was his job and his parents. But all those years and nothing to show for it. My mum and dad, they never wanted this. It was like *EastEnders*. Both of us cows at this funeral.'

Andy Shepherd does not think it is right to blame the black women for the anger many still feel:

> When black women began to arrive here in the sixties, some of them found that their husbands had not only white girlfriends but another family. I don't know if they knew before they came. I would not have sent for my wife from the West Indies without telling her

what had been going on – that wouldn't have been fair, and most women wouldn't have taken it. I know of one woman who actually thanked the white woman, an Irish girl, for looking after her man when she came here, and they are friendly up to today.

Fewer Asian women had to go through these experiences. Although there had been some casual alliances between their men and local women, they were over a shorter period and often had a temporary status. But Marion, now sixty, is still bitter about the way she was treated by her Asian partner of ten years.

I loved Sanjay. He was my life. I gave up my family, my friends, everything. He and I were happy. Then his parents arranged his marriage and he didn't tell them about me. So he got married and still came to see me. I got pregnant at the same time as his wife, but my son was abandoned. As soon as his real son was born, he was gone. I never married and my son was a manic depressive. I called him Sanjay. He killed himself when he was eighteen.

The effect of Powellism

Politicians, who had always been ambivalent about black immigration – workers were needed but not wanted – started overtly addressing the issue of black immigration. The National Health Service, British Rail, London Transport and heavy industry all competed to recruit overseas workers. Enoch Powell was in the Department of Health between 1960 and 1963 and he welcomed overseas workers to work in the NHS.[46] Advertisements were put into Caribbean newspapers inviting nurses and auxiliary staff to join the workforce in Britain. Yet racism was rife. Open racist notices were everywhere. Private homes, public places such as pubs and clubs were free to put up notices saying 'No Blacks'. Immigration laws, unfair policing, discrimination – all became a way of life for many black Britons and the swamping rhetoric which reached its climax in Enoch Powell's 1968 'rivers of blood' speech began to be heard. But increasingly, young blacks and Asians were not prepared to suffer the rejection and injustice that their parents had had to endure. The Black Pride movement in the United States was growing and this exerted a powerful influence on black and Asian people in Britain. Some mixed-race children began to see themselves as black. And within communities which might once have been more tolerant of mixed relationships there began to emerge the 'purity' rhetoric previously seen only among white racists, although this response came out of years of rage and powerlessness.

In 1968, the late Desmond Wilcox made a brave film for *Man Alive* about the racism faced by mixed-race families, showing the wedding of a white woman to a black man. The Radio Times would not feature the couple on the cover. Vox pops illustrated the hostility to such marriages. It was 'disgusting', said some, that people were crossing racial barriers all because of sex. Others said it was fine as long as no children were born. A number of contemporary feature films showed the emotional brutality suffered by people who dared to cross the colour line. In *A Taste of Honey* (1961), a young white woman is ostracised for becoming pregnant with a black man's child. In *Flame in the Street* (1963), the mother of a young woman with a black lover says she is disgusted, that the thought of the two of them in bed makes her feel physically sick. 'Go to your nigger,' she shouts as her daughter rushes out of the door. In 1962, the *Sunday People* ran a feature headlined: 'Is this Hope or Horror?' It started: 'A secret fear will gnaw at the hearts of thousands of British mothers in 1962...they dread the thought of their daughters marrying a coloured man.'[47] Other common stories in the papers spoke about white British women who claimed to have had lives of hell married to black or Pakistani men. And the same kind of angry debates about black women being betrayed by their men went on in the black newspapers too. This was the loving sixties.

In 1999, I interviewed two of the black movie actors who were stars at the time. Earl Cameron and Harry Baird explained how hard it was for audiences to take love scenes between a black man and a white woman. After watching *Sapphire* (1965), one of the first films to show this kind of scene, the two actors said that 'audiences left the cinema like they were leaving a funeral'.

Susan Benson's study around Brixton in the early seventies provides an important detailed picture of attitudes and behaviour in the following decade. It did not set out to prove any hypothesis or fondly held theory on the issue, but to provide a textured picture of what life was like for mixed-race families in urban Britain. It was a small qualitative study but an important one. She found that white women who had black sexual partners were no longer seen as respectable and had to move into the black milieu. She concluded:

I cannot see, in interracial unions, a 'solution' to the racism and hostility that characterises relations between black and white in Britain today. Rather they reflect in microcosm all the tensions of a racially antagonistic society. But in the resolution or, perhaps more germanely, the neutralisation of these tensions, these families offer, perhaps, some not insignificant insight through which these various forces may be more fully comprehended.[48]

As late as 1978, an article in *The Listener* showed just how negatively people reacted to the idea and reality of mixed-race individuals:

[Many half-castes] are the product of liaisons between black seamen and white prostitutes in Liverpool 8, the red-light district. Naturally they do not grow up with any kind of recognised home life. Worse still, after they have done the round of homes and institutions, they gradually realise that they are nothing. The Negroes will not accept them as Blacks and Whites just assume they are coloured.[49]

Finally, it is in the twentieth century that mixed-race people began to be represented in greater numbers among those who are regarded as heroic or as role models. These include WEB Dubois, Bob Marley, Malcolm X, Shirley Bassey, Cleo Laine and Walter Tull, who was not only an officer in the First World War, but a brilliant footballer playing for Tottenham Hotspurs at the beginning of the twentieth century.[50] It is vitally important for mixed-race children, who need to have a sense of their own, rich heritage, to be aware of such figures. As the population of mixed-race Britons grows – and it is growing fast as the next chapter shows – pressure will increase for recognition within the narratives of British society.

Chapter 3
The Current Landscape

'People tell me that things have got better and that families like mine are now thought of as normal. So you explain to me why my children are abused every day and why I sometimes wish I had never had them. White mothers like me have started to go out in a group so that we can help each other. We go to Iceland in a gang. Somehow it hurts less when you are with other women like you when they shout "Paki fucker" or "slag".'
Tracy, a lone mother of two mixed-race children living in Bristol.

'My friends and I don't even think about race and that. We are Londoners. My girlfriend is Chinese and others in the group are the same. If you fancy someone what difference does race make? My parents, who are Hindu, are trying to get me settled with one of our own. And I have said "No way." They brought me here to broaden my mind and now I choose who I am and who I love. Actually they are okay about it now they have met Lin.'
Suresh, a medical student in Bath.

These people are exactly the same age, twenty-three. Both live in British cities and have loved or had sexual relations across the racial and cultural barriers. Neither has a problem with difference but the outcomes could not be more different. Tracy, who is white, has no GCSEs and is unemployed. She was in care for a long time, as were the black fathers of both her children. They met as teenagers. She is a very committed mother, but it is hard for her now to feel positive about mixed-race relationships.

I just didn't know about young black men. That they have to have so many different women and children without caring for them. I know this is a horrible thing to say but I am hurting, you know? I trusted them and they treated me like a slut. A white slut, who they think is even worse than a black one. I know there is racism and all that but it's not my fault is it? I think it is best to stick with your own. And what about all those black men who use white women? Why does no one say they are racialist? My new boyfriend is white and I hope he won't leave me. He doesn't like my kids though.

Suresh's views have been moulded by the fact that he is middle class, very articulate and male. His family is culturally conservative but he does not find this oppressive. They are not delighted with the choices he is making but the fact that he is a man makes them more acceptable. The complicated realities of contemporary mixed-race relationships are represented by both these examples and it is vital to remember this when looking at emerging research data.

There is a whole emerging discourse too on this issue which itself is starting to invite a range of sophisticated responses. The American journalist Lisa Jones is one of those who has interrogated much that is happening in the USA in the name of biracial empowerment and what she writes resonates for British mixed-race people too. Jones, of mixed-race origins herself, thinks of herself as 'black':

> Are we *special*? ... interracial and biracial 'nationalists' as I refer to them playfully... claim biraciality as a mark of 'racial singularity'. Their insistence on biraciality's unique status borders on elitism. They marvel at the perks of biraciality: That biracials have several cultures at their disposal... Can you fight essentialism with essentialism? ... Is there to be a biracial party line to tow and a biracial lifestyle to upkeep?[1]

For Jones and others it is only now that they can ask themselves such questions and one reason for this is that people with these backgrounds are now assertive and visible and acutely aware of the complexity and diversity within their groups

Lives, lives and statistics

In the last decade long-overdue, reliable statistics on mixed-race relationships and children have started to appear, although as Alex Hall points out in the Introduction, there is still an acute lack of good, detailed and ongoing research in this area of human relations. When Anne Montague and I were researching *The Colour of Love* in 1990, the information was sparse and ad hoc. It was enormously helpful, however, to use data provided by the then Office of Population Censuses and Surveys (OPCS) and the Office for National Statistics (ONS) which publishes regular Labour Force Surveys (LFS) containing updated information on mixed-race families and relationships. There were some local studies before 1979, but nothing to give us a national picture. Direct questions on ethnicity were asked in the 1979, 1981, 1983 and 1984 LBS surveys. These are useful because they give the figures for inter-ethnic marriages and also socio-economic variables. Some of these are described in greater detail below to provide some kind of tracking.

The 1980s

An analysis of the 1981 LFS by David Coleman of Oxford University[2] found that Afro-Caribbeans were three times as likely to marry a white person as were members of other non-white groups. At that time 22 per cent of Afro-Caribbean men and 10 per cent of Afro-Caribbean women were married to white partners and 3 per cent to spouses in other ethnic groups. Coleman believed that there was 'considerable scope for under-estimating the number of existing marriages and other unions of young West Indians'. This is because there are fewer 'formal' marriages than in many other communities and a variety of arrangements which are not covered by the survey.

Among Indians 8 per cent of men and 4 per cent of women had white partners. Seven per cent of Pakistani men had white wives but only 2 per cent of women had white husbands. In the Chinese community, the figures for men were similar to those for Indians and Pakistanis, but Chinese women were twice as likely as Chinese men to marry out. Twenty-four per cent of these women had white husbands. Africans were found to be even more likely than Afro-Caribbeans to marry out. A quarter of African men had white partners and one in ten African women were married to white men. Some of these were East African Asians. Other key figures included the following:

- 6 per cent of the adult non-white population was of mixed-race origin.
- Among younger people, the dominant mix was West Indian/white.
- Married mixed-race individuals were more likely to have a white partner than a partner from any other ethnic group.
- One in five marriages with one South Asian/white partner were between husbands and wives both of whom were of South Asian/white ancestry.

Trends picked up then indicated that large numbers of spouses were coming from India and Pakistan to marry young South Asians and that younger West Indians were marrying out in increasing numbers.

Mixed-race people were over represented among the under 20 year olds. Seventy-one per cent were under this age compared with 29 per cent of whites, 44 per cent of West Indians and 45 per cent of South Asians. The black/white population was the most youthful. The total mixed-race population was 9 per cent of the total non-white population and 1 per cent of marriages were between people of different ethnic groups. You only have to compare some of these figures to the 1985 LBS survey to see how change was already becoming manifest.

The 1985 survey showed that 27 per cent of black British husbands had a white partner. The figure for black women was 14 per cent. In the Asian community, 10 per cent of men and 5 per cent of women were in mixed marriages. 1989 figures showed 24 per cent of black men and 18 per cent of black women had a white partner. Charlie Owen of the Thomas Coram Institute analysed the 1987–1989 surveys and found that among young people, the gender gap had narrowed substantially. Twenty-seven per cent of black men and 28 per cent of black women had a white partner.[3]

Outcomes of mixed-race relationships were barely studied. Dr Jawad Sheikh, a senior registrar in psychiatry, carried out research in 1989 which confirmed that ethnically mixed couples were more likely to divorce than couples from ethnically similar backgrounds.[4] This was a rare and important piece of work which need to be replicated and developed.

The 1990s

The 1993 LFS revealed that there were over 200,000 ethnically mixed couples in England and Wales. But other evidence, mostly media generated, showed that more complex developments were taking place besides the increase in mixed-race relationships and individuals. A Harris Poll conducted in 1990 for the BBC Asian programme *East* showed that only 10 per cent of British Asians had married out of their racial and religious communities and that among eighteen to twenty-four-year-olds, only 3 per cent had done so. Furthermore, unmarried young Asians were just as conservative and said they would not marry out of their race, religion or even caste. A survey carried out for the Asian magazine *Tan* found that 35 per cent of young white men interviewed would never even consider having an Asian partner. Three-quarters of the men interviewed and a third of white women interviewed said that they had been attracted to Asians but only 12 per cent had actually had a relationship with an Asian. Fourteen per cent of the white interviewees said that they would be upset if someone close to them decided to opt for an interracial marriage.[5]

In the nineties we have a good deal more quantitative information and it is possible to see trends, although it would still be true to say that we are lagging behind the United States where universities have long and established traditions of studying miscegenation, past and present. Scores of books have been written on the subject and more appear there every year. The dearth of such material in this country is surprising because as is apparent from Chapter 1 and Chapter 2, mixed relationships have been central issues in both countries for centuries.

However, one fact is now indisputable; in the year 2000, against all the odds and most expectations, Great Britain had among the highest rates of interracial marriage anywhere in the western world. If this were taken as one indicator of integration, British society (which is still blighted by massive racial inequality as well as unconscious and deliberate racism) is now conclusively more integrated than any of the countries in the European Union and the United States.

Census figures and other recent surveys

The 1991 national census was one of the first major sources to indicate this trend. Figures showed that black and mixed-race men were more likely than other non-white ethnic groups to have a white partner. Younger people were more likely to be in mixed-race relationships. Ten per cent of the 'ethnic minority' population was mixed-race. More recent evidence from the LFS,[6] the Policy Studies Institute[7] and other sources indicates not only that mixed-race Britons are increasingly conspicuous in our urban centres but also that the trend is upwards. Almost half of Caribbean men born here and a third of Caribbean women have or have had a white partner. This is, at present, the most common pattern. A fifth of Indian and African men also have a white partner. Half of all 'Caribbean' children have one white parent.

A recent LVS estimate puts the mixed-race population of Great Britain at about 350,000. This amounts to 11 per cent of Britain's 3.25 million ethnic minority population, or 0.6 per cent of the total population of 56 million.[8] A large proportion of mixed-race Britons were born in the UK – over 80 per cent, as compared with 49 per cent of all ethnic minority Britons.

This is vital data which adds immeasurably to our understanding of what is going on. Looking in detail at these and other sources of demographic information, the picture which emerges shows that this is an aspect of British society which must now be taken into account in any serious analysis of the state of the nation. It is also important that the complexity of this development is better understood and routed. At present too many people excitedly rush to conclusions when statistics are produced, a tendency which is reckless and ultimately unhelpful.

Charlie Owen, one of the few academics to emphasise the need to take a less simplistic view of figures, has carried out a closer analysis of the 1991 census[9] than most and has scrutinised the findings of this major information gathering exercise. This census was the first to include a question on ethnicity. It offered a range of racial and national categories but did not provide a distinct mixed-race category, which itself demonstrates how research continues to lag behind reality. The choices were as follows:

White
Black-Caribbean
Black-African
Black – other (please describe)
Indian, Pakistani, Bangladeshi, Chinese, any other ethnic group (please describe)

Without a specified category of 'mixed' given, the information which is available is based on how people described themselves. On that basis four groups emerged. 'Black-White', 'Asian Mixed', 'Other-White' and 'Mixed-White'. Surprisingly, the 'Asian-Mixed' group was bigger than the 'Black-White' group which may be due to the fact that many 'Black-White' people describe themselves as black or may have described themselves as 'Other-White'. Nevertheless, the 'Asian-White' group is too often disregarded in debates and policies because there is now an assumption that the biggest group is 'Black-White' and that issues which affect that group must set the agenda. Other facts highlighted by Owen include the following:

Children

- In the 'Black-White' group, 30 per cent are under five years old and more than half are under the age of ten. It is a group which is growing rapidly.
- Four out of five 'Caribbean' children have one white parent.
- The total number of mixed-race children grew by 40 per cent in the eighties and Owen predicts that such children will form an increasingly large percentage of the ethnic minority population.[10] Although mixed-race Britons are a small minority in the total population of this country – constituting one half of 1 per cent – their numbers are expected to grow rapidly.

Adult relationships

- The mixed-parentage group formed about 10 per cent of the total black and Asian population in 1991. The numbers are expected to be higher in the next census.
- Younger people are more likely to be in these relationships than older people.
- Similarly, although mixed-race relationships account for only about one and a half per cent of all marriage and co-habitation in this country, the numbers are expected to rise

disproportionately.
- The mixed-parentage group formed about 10 per cent of the total black and Asian population in 1991.

Altogether in the census, 228,000 mixed-race people were recorded. This is almost certainly a serious under-estimate as is the figure given by Haskey above, for the following reasons:

- Many mixed-race people refuse to fill in ethnic monitoring forms because they feel that to do so would endorse racial classification.
- Mixed-race people who marry someone from the black and Asian communities, or another mixed-race person, do not see this as a mixed relationship. Instead the tendency is to regard this as marrying in. The same values operate when people are describing relationships.
- As stated above, a large number of mixed-race people describe themselves as black.
- In some areas, like Cardiff and Liverpool where there has been a long history of racial mixing, people may either not be aware of or may choose to disregard this description of themselves.
- A minority of mixed-race people prefer to pass as white and would therefore describe themselves as such.
- Many local authorities do not use the term 'mixed-race' to describe children in care or in schools, preferring instead to use the term 'black'.
- Some mixed-race people find it offensive to be asked to fill in a 'biological confession' on forms. They think of themselves as part of the human race and say it is not anyone else's business to ask the intimate details of the family history for administrative reasons.

This reluctance of many Britons either to describe themselves or others as 'mixed-race' comes too from an unspoken anxiety. It is the same fear that is felt by many Jewish people who remember all too well how such counts then became programmes for destruction. Counting Jews has always preceded pogroms and institutionalised persecution against Jewish people. Numbers have a potency which political leaders keenly use, as the rhetoric and policies on 'floods' of asylum seekers demonstrate all too well. Throughout history people of mixed ancestry have been misrepresented, vilified, excluded and even punished by various societies. It is only in the last two decades that we have seen the emergence of real pride among mixed-race British families. Historical memories go deeper than either white people or people of colour like to imagine and this period has also seen new conflicts around this issue which have not helped the much-needed process of liberation and reclamation of mixed-race identities. William Tell, half Jamaican and half English, simply lies and laughs, he says:

> I'm William Tell who will not tell. I say I am white on one form and black on another. Last time I said I was Austro-Hungarian. It is just shit and I will not play their game. Form filling so they can say they take us seriously. Shit. This is all a plot. To get us, man. To put us into a concentration camp when the likes of Le Pen and Haider rule all over Europe. They hate mixed-race people even more than pure blacks.

Hidden fears and unspoken disagreements

While exploring this reluctance to 'admit' their identity on paper I came across other evidence that monitoring forms as tools of inquiry are somewhat blunt and simplistic when it comes to mixed-race families. For example, if members of the same mixed-race family use completely different labels, what conclusion can one reach? I came across a number of such groups where not even the parents had come to any agreement about what to call themselves and their children. Take Paula who is English and her husband Bipin who is an Indian. He says his children are Indian because India is a multicultural country which makes no distinctions between various citizens. His children are just another part of that great nation which has always absorbed diverse groups. Paula insists that her children are black British because as a social worker she has been taught that this is the right way to describe them. Little wonder the children refuse to answer questions about how they see themselves and resort to statements like: 'I don't know. I am just me.'

Many identities are in flux in the world today but with mixed-race families unsettled identities are more pronounced, more vulnerable to personal circumstances, the social environment and people's attitudes. Nothing can or should be predicted in these situations. I found many families where the adults who had crossed racial barriers now wished for their children not to do the same and were almost ashamed of what had happened. This was as true for harmonious families as disrupted ones. In some families white and black partners would say to me in private that they wanted the children to reclaim a 'pure' identity but when they were talking together these same people would extol the virtues and delights of a mixed heritage. Jennifer and Murumbi have been together for fifteen years. She is Irish and he is Tanzanian. They have two children and live in South London. They are both teachers. Murumbi said this when we were on our own:

I came here as a student and was seduced by this country and its ways. They all fell in love and so I fell in love with Jennifer. But I still don't understand what that means. This is not the African way. I like my wife and would kill for my children, but I feel like an alien in my own home. There is nothing here that reminds me of my family or the values back home. I want my children to marry Africans so that some balance can come back into their lives and mine too. Jenny tries but it cannot work. She is white. I need her so I stay.

There are many other people who think like Murumbi or Lawrence, from Guyana, who is married to Iris, an Englishwoman:

I know I married out and I love my family and my wife. But the children are neither here nor there. I have told them that they should try and marry black, so that the blood line lost can be replaced. I sometimes think I betrayed my people. Love can make you betray your people. I feel shame. After slavery and colonialism I go and marry white. I try not to tell anyone new about this and I know it hurt Iris who is a good woman. In the end, as I get older I want to be with my own people, but they see me as a stranger.

The children in this family do not describe themselves as mixed-race. One tries to pass for white and has been successful. The other two say that they are black.

This sense of pain and loss is the central theme of the film *East is East*, in which a Muslim man married to a white Yorkshire woman cruelly tries to coerce his children into becoming good Pakistani Muslims. What makes the film so powerful is the evocation of the almost irredeemable guilt and shame the father feels and how these then make him violent and authoritarian towards his whole family.

Full fulfilled lives too

So am I saying that all mixed-race families are living in dread and sorrow? Not at all. Some are thriving and do feel themselves to be blessed.

Sumira, a British Muslim, is married to Samad, a Moroccan Muslim:

We are both Muslims but I am a Shia and he is Sunni. We couldn't come from more different backgrounds. To me Arabs were all scary people who sat on camels and had harems. He had never met any South Indians so we had a hard time in the beginning. But now I think I am so lucky. Look at this house, the beauty Samad creates out of Moroccan colours and pots. Our children have that sophistication of two major old cultures. If I had married an Asian boy, my life would have been exactly the same as my parents and grandparents. Closed, interested in money making, weddings every weekend. I am so glad to have been shown other worlds.

Samad was equally and genuinely optimistic. He wants their children to learn four languages and to be self-consciously 'Eastern' because that is their unique heritage.

Asher and Martin Hoyles are similarly excited by the possibilities open to their mixed-race daughter, Rosa Aretha Hoyles, to whom they dedicate *Remember Me*, a book they co-wrote to highlight the accomplishments of mixed-race people through the centuries. In the introduction to the book they write: 'Why should mixed-race people have to wait until later life to see the benefits of belonging to more than one culture? ... This book challenges the view that being of mixed race is a problem. By looking at positive achievements of mixed-race people, it shows how belonging to more than one cultural tradition can be an advantage.'[11]

Ian and Babs are another mixed-race young couple obviously in love and with few doubts about the future. Ian is Scottish although he has lived all his life in England and Babs is black British. They met as students and married in 2000 with the blessings of both parents. His parents are both doctors. Babs's mother is a senior health visitor and her father is a businessman. This year they all went on holiday together to Spain. Ian says it was the best holiday of their lives:

> It felt like both our families opened up windows to let in fresh air. There was so much to discuss, so much to enjoy. They had shared a country but as if they lived in different ones. Suddenly they had to question their own stereotypes. Babs's mother was really surprised that my parents always take my gran on holiday with them. She thought we all stuck our old in institutions. My dad, I think, realised for the first time how racism affects black businessmen when it comes to bank loans and that. I really do think that mixed-race families are changing and that you get much less rejection and anger.

Public attitudes

There is little doubt that over the last decades of the twentieth century, attitudes towards mixed-race families have been more accepting and less antagonistic. At least social researchers are finding this. More tolerant views are being expressed although this could mean that great care is taken not to offend or say 'the wrong thing'. The recounted experiences of mixed-race families show that opposition to what they stand for is still very much in evidence but that there are marked improvements which cannot be denied. The statistical evidence on attitudes does go back many years, and although it is always important to be cautious, it provides useful and important information about the changes that have taken place in society.

The British Social Attitudes Surveys (BSAS) found little change between 1983 and 1996 when white people were questioned on the acceptability of other white people marrying out. But when it came to an assessment of intermarriage in their own families the acceptability rates had gone up significantly. In 1987, the BSAS found that only 27 per cent of white people polled said they would mind if a close relative were to marry a West Indian. A Runnymede Trust survey in 1991 came up with another positive figure. 58 per cent of those interviewed disagreed that people should only marry within their own ethnic group. Over the past years other research across Europe on this issue has shown that young people have more liberal attitudes than older people.[12]

Research commissioned by me for my book, *True Colours: Government Policies and Attitudes to Multiculturalism*, at the Institute for Public Policy Research, and more detailed research carried out by the Policy Studies Institute, provided important evidence on attitudes of the various communities towards racial mixing but, like other research findings, these have to be treated sensibly and with due care. Quantitative data on this emotive issue can be notoriously unreliable. Some people give answers they feel they should in order not to be seen as bigoted, a fact which emerges when you carry out more in-depth qualitative surveys with some of the same people. That said, figures can be important indicators and are especially revealing on how social attitudes change first through saying the 'right' thing, which is also progress. Such surveys help to map out the attitudes of various communities to different combinations of relationships. But surveys can contradict one another too and this adds confusion to complexity. The IPPR survey showed a mixed picture:

- 33 per cent of white, 38 per cent of Asians and 49 per cent of Jews thought that most people in Britain would mind if one of their close relatives were to marry an Afro-Caribbean.
- 74 per cent of whites said that they themselves would not mind, with the figure for young people rising to 88 per cent.
- Only 47 per cent of Asians and 46 per cent of Jews would not mind.
- A third of whites felt that most people in Britain would mind a lot if a close relative were to marry an Asian.
- Afro-Caribbeans and Jews in particular thought that most

white people would mind a close relative marrying an Asian.
- One in ten whites and Afro-Caribbeans said they personally would mind if a close relative were to marry an Asian.
- One in eight whites felt that most people in Britain would mind if a close relative were to marry a Jewish person. When asked if they themselves would mind, 5 per cent of whites said they would.
- 30 per cent of Asians said that they would mind if a close relative were to marry a Jew.[13]

In our survey white Britons, especially younger white Britons, appeared to be most accepting of marriage with Afro-Caribbeans, which is significant. Compared to this only 47 per cent of Asians and 46 per cent of Jews said they would accept marriage with Caribbeans. Prejudices have not disappeared but the picture is far from clear.

The PSI Fourth National Survey found that: '... while attitudes to "mixed marriage" were in a process of flux, in most groups, based partly on perceptions of white prejudice and partly on concerns to do with community identity, the issue was an important topic of debate.'

PSI attitudinal research on this issue produced the following findings:

- 75 per cent of Pakistanis felt that people in their communities would mind a close relative marrying a white person.
- The figure for Bangladeshis was 50 per cent.
- 33 per cent of Afro-Caribbeans said they would mind.
- 68 per cent of Indians said they would mind.
- 43 per cent of Chinese expressed similar reservations.

When broken down into religious groups, further important evidence of attitudes emerged from this study:

- Pakistani Muslims were the most disapproving at 75 per cent.
- Only 42 per cent of Bangladeshi Muslims objected.
- The figure was the same for Sikhs.
- Only 32 per cent of Hindus said they had reservations.

In both studies older people minded more than younger people although there were some exceptions. The PSI survey found that 35 to 49-year-old Afro-Caribbeans were the group which most minded relationships with white people. On the whole people without qualifications and in manual work minded more, though the reverse was true of Afro-Caribbeans. When it came to gender differences, Caribbean, Bangladeshi and Pakistani women minded more than the men but there was no gender difference among Indians.

When asked if they themselves would mind, the PSI study found the following:

- 84 per cent of Caribbeans and Chinese people said they would not mind a close relative marrying a white person.
- 52 per cent of Indians would not mind.
- 41 per cent of Pakistanis had no objections.
- 52 per cent of Bangladeshis were in the same category.

Of the white people questioned, 52 per cent said that they thought most white people would mind a close relative marrying a black or Asian Briton and only 11 per cent said that they themselves would mind. This may be understating the true picture with people becoming conscious that some views are no longer socially acceptable and need to be withheld.

Impact of social attitudes on individual lives

What is the impact of such attitudes on families and individuals? Perhaps the most damaging influence is subtle. Sarah, a twenty-year-old mixed-race drama student explained it like this:

> The thing is that we are always in a goldfish bowl. We have no personal lives, no private lives. Society feels they have the right to comment on us, to us, about us, as if by right. Or there is an expectation that we will confess our innermost fears for all to consume. This is why so many of us are defensive. We have never been allowed to feel normal. Even when we claim we are, we have to say it, which really means that we are not though we wish we were. My parents' marriage broke up, not because they did not love one another. I think they still do. Neither my black father nor my Irish mother have married again. But they found the spotlight terrifying. My father, who is black, had a breakdown and turned to drink. My mother could not handle this on top of everything else. So we ended up in care for part of our lives. I can't blame them. I find it hard now, in the nineties. They were coping with the seventies.

This is one side of a serious conundrum. When you talk to mixed-race families or individuals who are in mixed-race relationships, the complaint you get is that not enough attention has been paid to them by policy makers and the general population for far too long . A number of interviewees felt that this was because there is still shame attached to these choices and that this shame leads to a willed invisibility deep in the national psyche. Some say that this invisibility is worse now. Shyla, a mixed-race twenty-year-old dancer, puts it like this:

> At least before when my parents got married people were open with their ugly prejudices. Now they will say how lovely I am but then ask if I mind that I am not one or the other. They don't really want to hear what you have to say. They really wish you had not happened to upset their cosy world of black versus white.

But on the other hand, many mixed-race people feel that they have been, for too long, the objects of obsessive curiosity, examined in what Sarah above calls 'a goldfish bowl'.

Emerging trends and attitudes

New trends are beginning to appear, although these have yet to be confirmed by more wide-scale sociological research. One of these indicates that an increasing number of Asian women are marrying out because their own rising ambitions for greater personal autonomy and freedom are not accommodated by some Asian families, especially after marriage. Rightly or wrongly these women believe that they can have a career within a marriage and an equal partnership with a white man more easily than they can with an Asian man, even one who is of the same educational and economic background. For a set of completely different reasons, anecdotal evidence would also suggest that black women are getting together with white men because many of them are high earners whose lifestyles are making it harder for them to find black male partners who are at present some of the most excluded members of British society. As Di, one such woman, interviewed for this book, put it:

> I always wanted to have a black partner and beautiful black babies. But you show me where someone like me – a high-earning barrister – can find such a man these days. I have settled for a white guy because my biological clock is rushing. I have a child now and he has blue eyes. I have to be honest and say I regret that. But I have a wonderful house. I live in Surrey and we have three cars, security for life. Where would I find a black man who can give me that today?

Crucially, as has been stressed already, the fact that we have so much more interracial mixing does not mean that society is becoming more accepting of what is going on. Quite the contrary. Stan, a teacher at a comprehensive school, is appalled at the number of mixed-race liaisons he sees among his pupils.

> Don't get me wrong. I am not a racist, but this kind of thing will kill off all cultures, white and black. White girls can't keep their eyes off the black boys who are thought cool and dudes and hard.

These boys can't keep their hands off the girls. They are ending up pregnant with half-caste bastards. Neither has any qualifications and the kids end up in care. I know I am sounding harsh, but nobody wants to come out and say what they think. They all murmur in the staff room, but they don't come out with what is bothering them. At least with same race babies the families will rally.

Interviews carried out for this book show how these days prejudice against mixed-race relationships is as likely among non-white Britons as it is among white Britons. In some surveys substantially more black and Asian Britons were hostile to these relationships than white people.[14] In the *Voice* and the magazine *Pride*, black women are often heard deriding famous black men, like Trevor Macdonald, Lenny Henry, Frank Bruno and others, who have white partners. They are accused of wanting trophy wives and of assimilating into white society. Many people do not think that these are wholly unacceptable criticisms even though they do reveal levels of prejudice which the same people would not tolerate if it were expressed by white people. But it is a valid question to ask why so many well-known people – men and women – from the black and Asian communities do seem to have white partners. It shows a certain level of acceptance and entry perhaps which is not available to vast numbers of others from these visible groups. If this is perceived as a strategy (even though it clearly is not) it is an understandable perception. A very powerful white editor cornered me one day at a party in the spring of 2000 and said: 'I must say, you are doing very well now. You are everywhere. Of course you couldn't have done it as an Alibhai. Adding the Brown to your name was a stroke of genius.'

Black men too are unhappy about the way black women are now going with white men, arguing that this is going to lead to the end of the black community. Sexism and racism and racial prejudice underpin many of these discussions. This means that clashes over the recognition of the rights of mixed-race families can no longer be explained simply in terms of white racism.

In some communities, sections of the British Asian community for example, there is such concern that the young people are abandoning their roots by marrying out that families are choosing to use threats, violence and even criminal actions to thwart their younger members.

Surjeet is a nineteen-year-old British Sikh. She is in hiding because her family want to kill her. There has, she tells me, already been one such killing in the extended family. Her cousin, who fell in love with a Muslim, was tricked into going to the Punjab and then killed. Surjeet is in love with a black man.

This is the last taboo. A white man they would have hated but not as much as Martin. It doesn't matter that he is better educated than the whole lot of us. Or that he has a job with a top firm. But what they see is not even a human being. Only black skin. When I told them my uncle grabbed me and tried to strangle me. My mother just watched. I broke off because the door bell rang and I left. And they say that blacks are uncivilised.

Martin's parents are none too happy either. They feel that their Christian values are under threat from this relationship. His younger brother wants to know what he is doing with a 'Paki'. In recent decades, new tensions have started to appear between black and Asian Britons and again these remain hidden because few commentators have the courage to accept that white racism does not necessarily create unity between various victimised communities or deal with the fact that individuals from these communities too often end up venting their frustrations by blaming and attacking one another rather than those who create the systems which exclude and undermine all of them. Inter-ethnic strife has increased among the young of all backgrounds and any relationships which breach 'tribal' demarcations are not tolerated. During the Notting Hill Carnival in 2000, a young Asian man was beaten to death by black youths who appeared to have deliberately targeted Asians to rob and assault.[15] Around the same time, a black man was killed in Bradford by a gang of Asians. In January 2001, a gang of Asian and Afro-Caribbean men was convicted of the murder of a Somali college student.[16]

Economic inequality is one of the main underlying causes of the deteriorating relations between black and Asian Britons. Some Asians have been able to better their prospects through self-employment and small business enterprises. A few have joined the ranks of the top millionaires. Thousands of others among working-class Pakistani and Bangladeshis are unemployed and locked in poverty. Yet a new stereotype has taken hold among white and black Britons and among middle-class and affluent Asians too that Asians are the perfect, super successful immigrants who are all living the good life. Young black people resent them for this and this is why so many of them these days assault Asian shopkeepers and school children. I have seen evidence of this in my journalistic work. It works the other way round too. Some Asians have come to believe that they are superior to black people. Those who grew up in East Africa seem to be most prone to these prejudices.[17] Mohan Patel, who owns a chain of stores, is quite open about his distaste for black people: 'They have no ambition and culture. They live for now and are full of drugs and the bad habits like too much sex and like that. Sometimes I think they are more like animals. I have forbidden my children playing with them. White children are the same these days.' What Mohan does not know is that his daughter, Bindi, who is sixteen, has been dating a Caribbean musician for a year and that his son Harish, nineteen, has a white girlfriend who is pregnant with their child. Harish is worried sick about what he is going to say to his parents and tells me that although he hates the views expressed by his father, he has never had the courage to confront him. Harish himself though (who does not know about Bindi) believes that black people are 'untrustworthy and have no sense of responsibility'. He says that he would be very unhappy if his sisters ever married out. But isn't that hypocritical? 'Yes. You can say that. But you see I can make my wife into an Indian whoever she is. An Indian woman who marries outside cannot carry on her culture in the same way. So they must marry Indian. It is correct that they must.' So within one 'normal' family in Harrow-on-the-Hill, race, culture, prejudice and gender are all swilling about and will, in time, shake up the values and assumptions which have hitherto tied this close-knit group.

Shahnaz, a British Muslim who is a youth worker and mother of a son whose father is black, has suffered for years because of these attitudes. Her parents refused to accept the boy and are still pretending to the community that she is single and away working. Her partner has left and his family does not get in touch either. Shahnaz did not see her family for ten years but then she missed them so much that she has started to force herself on them. Her son is not welcome:

> My son has a right to an identity which is complete. Both sides have let him down, refusing to give him what is rightfully his. We have such rich cultures on both sides, but they are not available to my young man. Why not? I have a mammoth task to give him what he needs. I cry sometimes. Why did I bring him into this world to suffer?

Meanwhile, he keeps asking why he has no other family to go to and why he never gets presents at Christmas from grandparents and others. Her other battle is to stop people talking about him as a 'mix' as if he were a 'bag of sweets. He is a whole person, a wonderful boy, centred and himself. I am with him, behind him and I will do what it takes to protect him.'[18]

For those marrying into different religions a whole crop of other issues have to be settled before and during marriage. Some faiths demand conversion at any cost. I know of a Muslim woman who is fading away because her parents will not agree to her marrying an English actor unless he converts. Her lover cannot, for he loves his dope and drink too much. She cannot accept these demands even though, she says, she loves her parents very deeply and would never want them to be disappointed in her.

> This is sheer hypocrisy. How can God be fooled like this? You get people to convert because they fall in love with a Muslim, not because they respect Islam. I will never marry anyone else. I will

die single. But these people don't understand anything about personal happiness. To them my needs are as important as the needs of a cauliflower.

Marcus is a black songwriter. He is an ex-member of Nation of Islam and has uncompromising views:

I want to throw up when I see my black sisters on the arms of white trash. They will destroy us faster than slavery did. Once I actually pulled a sister away on the road and told her she was worse than a whore because a whore had no choice. My mum, she was white. I don't know her. She binned me. Threw me to the social workers. My father, he was off too. It never works this mixing. If Allah had wanted us to do this he would have made us all the same. But he didn't.

I would like to stress once more that is important not to underestimate or demonise those who resist mixed marriages. Many are genuinely worried that their entire history and ancestry is cut off as a result. The 'minority' status of Jews, Asians and black people is all too real as is the experience of being regarded as alien and a threat. There is a worry too that marriage in modern times is hard enough without adding all the extra pressures that difference, racism and ethnicity bring to the relationship. As one Asian mother put it to me:

For me my whole history disappeared. My language, values, everything was swallowed by England the day they stole my daughter. And I explained to her that her values will not fit with theirs and that spending your whole life with another person is hard. So why to make it harder? Her father and I came just from different villages and we still had so many problems in the first years. I came from an area where we had abundance of water and food. His village suffered from droughts. So we had so many quarrels about how I thought he was mean and he thought I was wasteful with the use of water in our house here in Wembley.

But trying to understand these worries is not to condone them. There cannot be one rule for white racists who attack mixed-race relationships and another one for non-white people who do the same.

Unexpected expectations

It is important to remember too that people are changing all the time. These changes accelerate in multiracial societies and as global communication becomes available to increasing numbers of people. The reactions of individuals, families and communities are now as capable of confounding as confirming expectations. Not everyone behaves in predictable ways. There are families which see these crossovers as something to celebrate and not mourn.

I remember my mother, a Muslim with deep faith, weeping when I told her that I was going to marry an Englishman who was not going to convert to Islam. These were tears of joy. He was the third white man to come into our small family (not counting the casual relationships which the family chooses to ignore) and for my mother who can speak only basic English, these men have been sent by God: to drive her to mosque, to mend her cupboards and take her to flash restaurants where she still cannot believe her luck and the prices. In her case and in the cases of many of my Asian friends who have married out, there is little family resistance. One man whose beautiful solicitor daughter married a white teacher is quite overwhelmed because: 'these boys don't demand these killing dowries. They marry our daughters for their qualities not other stupid things like wealth.'

Many white parents too have changed their attitudes profoundly. An old builder, now in a wheelchair, cannot forgive himself for standing at the airport in 1972 chanting racist abuse when expelled Ugandan Asians were arriving here penniless and frightened. His daughter-in-law Sita, then six, was one of them. Now Sita bathes and clothes John and although she has a taxing job as a business consultant, she feels this is her duty and something her deceased father always taught her she should do.

Old myths and national fantasies

I found much disturbing evidence, however, of old stereotypes and fears around racial mixing which rise to the fore whenever there is a crisis, whether nationwide, local or individual. This is true in European countries and in the United States too. In 1998, Channel 4 broadcast a programme about young gang rapists in certain parts of London. The majority were Afro-Caribbean and some of the victims were young white females. There was a massive furore over the programme, with the black community accusing Channel 4 of being racist (even though the presenter was Darcus Howe) and with right-wing white commentators playing to ancient prejudices about blonde sex slaves and over-sexualised, brutal black men. In New York, the rape of a young white investment banker by black and Hispanic teenagers in Central Park turned into a media circus and ended up being a symbolic fable about public space, belonging, the vulnerable white insider and the dark and devilish 'stranger' who can never be trusted. White rapists in the city that week and non-white rape victims never featured in this hysterical outpouring.[19] The rape of black women by black men or of black women by white men never raises the same sense of national violation or level of outrage. Writing on this subject of violations and stereotypes,

Theresa Wobbe believes that in Germany we see the most stark and dangerous examples of how this works and how dangerous it can be:

> There is a link between the violence of racism and everyday violence against women. In Germany, the stereotype of the 'Turkish man who rapes German women' signals this linkage. This stereotype represents one construction of foreigners as rapists. This in turn implies that 'foreigners' are exclusively men who threaten Germans who are exclusively women...[this narrative] implies that German/white women are the only victims of rape and that German/white men do not rape. Non-German/black men are constructed as rapists whereas non-German/black women are constructed as not being raped.[20]

In some ways it is not surprising that individual cases of rape across the races or ethnic difference are perceived as more than a criminal act. Rape has long been a manifestation of political powerlessness and power. Throughout history rape has been used as a weapon of war and oppression especially where ethnicity is the central feature of the conflict. From Partition on the sub-continent to the Serbs and Hutus today, interracial rape represents all that is most vile in human nature. The stereotypes which then arise out of these periods persist for centuries.

While there is no research that I know of on this controversial subject, I believe these cross-racial sexual fears and fantasies have a devastating effect in other areas. We know that over 60 per cent of young black men in London are unemployed. Young black boys are also over represented in prisons and are more likely to be excluded from schools. Can we be sure that white employers, teachers, police officers and judges are not passing judgements on these men on the basis of the 'black men as rapists' stereotype? And should we not establish through proper research whether having this label thrust on young black men generation after generation is causing them to behave in certain anti-social ways? Lennox is a young man who has been in and out of prison. He is now transformed, he says, because he has found Jesus.

> I was bad, bad, bad. And I liked that. People thought guys like me want to destroy white girls, so I did. I won't tell you more. But I did. I am not saying it was not my fault. But I wonder if I would have done the things I did if I was a white doctor's blue-eyed son and everyone expected different things? I remember when I was eight and I was big for my age. I was playing outside my house and a little blonde girl came to see what I was doing. They had just moved in opposite. In five minutes this angry white woman came and carried her off without even looking at me. She just shouted at the kid saying she was stupid and naughty.

There are other equally potent images. Details about these and the relationships which knowingly or unconsciously arise out of these will be dealt with more fully in Chapter 4.

These stereotypes may still persist, but life has found a way of thwarting them. We appear to have reached a stage in our history where one can talk about a major shift in attitudes which is not confined to a few cases. Like Ian and Babs above, I found examples of immense joy and love towards newly established mixed-race families. There was an awareness of need and empathy which is less obvious in same race families. Julie, a white woman in her thirties, is a violin player in an orchestra. For her and her family, Theo, an African percussionist, the man she is due to marry, is a gift from the gods:

> I have had several relationships in my life. Mostly with white, upper-middle-class men with no soul. Theo has a depth, a knowledge, that comes from centuries back. He treats my parents and grandparents with such sublime consideration, they adore him too. He has taught me my family obligations. He got me – in the gentlest of ways – to visit my grandmother's grave which I had not done since the funeral ten years ago. He wants children, but not until after we are married and properly mature, he says. We have been together for five years so I am not talking like an airy fairy here.

But few people seem to want to acknowledge that just because people decide to love across the boundaries does not make them any less susceptible to racial generalisations. Those within these relationships can surprise themselves about how they too can succumb to easy assumptions and stereotyping about racial characteristics. When I am mad at my husband, I am ashamed to say we can both stoop to this too. I call him an imperialist when he criticises me for my lack of organisation and he pays back in kind by suggesting that the empire might never have taken such a hold if my people hadn't been quite so shambolic. Of course neither of us means this but it is a good hard stick. Sometimes strange differences creep up on us. As an Asian I have no notion of private space. Rooms are left open. There is no privacy except for the bathroom. It drives him mad. Talking endlessly is the only cure for these tensions. Our daughter, Leila, and our love are worth every argument but I do worry that one day he will so tire of this hard work that he will slope off and find a nice girl in Shoreham-by-Sea where his mother lives and where both partners would understand exactly the meanings of things.

Hard choices

In *The Colour of Love*, my co-author, Anne Montague, and I were determined that the book would not focus only on the problems and negative aspects of life in mixed-race families. We worked hard to find new ways of presenting the issues and thereby avoid the dominant problem paradigm. An entire chapter was therefore devoted to people who felt that they had proved the cynics wrong, that their relationships and families were an illustration of how mixed-race relationships could work. Alas today many of the people in that section admit defeat and are trying to cope with very painful break-ups never knowing really if the differences which emerged between them came out of the fact that they had different skin colours or ethnic origins. In several of the cases, the individuals expressed feelings and fears built around the belief that mixed-race relationships don't work and that it is better to stick with your own. One wife, an Asian, whose husband left her and their small children for another woman feels, race did have more to do with it than she had ever thought possible:

> He left to go off with another white, middle-class woman. They have the same backgrounds, the same world view. They could be siblings I guess. My children are complex – they have a heritage which is incredibly mixed. I am British but I can never be English. So I look at what has happened and of course a part of me thinks it is because I did not fit in. Because I was hard work and because my children – who do feel terribly abandoned – are mixed-race.

What will help these children is the fact that there are an increasing number of other children like them. They will not easily be contained or restrained by others. This is why it is so important that our experts and institutions should be taking more than a passing interest in mixed-race families. They should be setting out to find out how these young people define their racial identities, their attitudes to the way society labels them, their experiences with white and non-white Britons including their own parents and families, and how they feel public institutions like schools help them as they grow up.

What is needed even more urgently is information about dysfunctional mixed-race families and research into why so many mixed-race children are ending up in care in this country.

Media obsessions and proper research

As I have already said, in the absence of sustained and sensible research, mixed-race relationships have too often become trivialised and sensationalised by the media, especially by television and the popular press. Over a twelve month period from 1998 to 1999, I was asked to appear on programmes about mixed-race relationships or comment on these relationships by 59 journalists. I declined all but three of the invitations because the rest seemed to be treating a complex subject in a dangerously frivolous way. Programmes such as *Kilroy* and *Esther* never tire of featuring individuals who have something shocking to say on the subject. As I write this in the spring of 2000, I have had a further 39 requests for help, advice, and interviews on the subject. I have declined all the requests although it does make me wonder why there is such a massive curiosity at a time of serious dumbing down on our television screens. Are television programmes reflecting a genuinely serious interest in this subject because they feel that there has been a shameful neglect of it in the past or is this simply part of the sex, sex, sex agenda where race adds additional and piquant spice?

I believe that both are happening. The media is in part creating the appetite for such stories, but it is also responding to a growing public desire to understand more about mixed-race families. In her work as a developmental psychologist Anne Phoenix has observed: 'Over the last ten years there has been a burgeoning interest in the subject partly because there has been an increase in the number of those in mixed relationships and those who are of mixed parentage.'[21]

As I end this chapter, I would like to highlight one key thread running through the whole of this book. It is essential to counteract the idea that mixed-race people are locked in an interminable cycle of misery or that their existence should be a permanent cause for concern in any society. Most of the interviewees in this book would, in part, welcome an approach which did not automatically assume this. None of them would argue though that there are no serious barriers and prejudices which complicate their lives. But there is a substantial number of young people who do not see themselves as constantly burdened and confused people. Their testimonies reveal how misguided it is to claim that an individual's culture and personality is almost wholly determined by one race or religion. Many of them are emotionally highly literate and need no lessons on identity. And indeed some of them are excellent role models on how prejudices can be broken down to create future possibilities. But although most can articulate clearly how they have dealt with ignorance and simple-minded categorisation, they universally resist being seen as symbols. What is beyond dispute is that this community is changing, getting more influential and vocal and is challenging settled notions, ideologies and labels. As Bob Purkiss, the National Secretary for Equalities of the Transport and General Workers Union and Commissioner of the Commission for Racial Equality, who is mixed-race himself, says:

It is important to debate mixed-race families because they are a growing group who are often made to feel invisible because their identity is not recognised. This is because they do not fit into the social categories used in ethnic monitoring...We must make sure that mixed-race families are made more visible so that the ever growing numbers of mixed-race children do not have to face a society which sweeps their experiences under the carpet.[22]

And these experiences are complex, diverse and ill-understood and have more to do with society than the individuals concerned. As Nick Banks of Birmingham University says: 'It is clear that mixed-race relationships and children are here to stay. The biggest difficulty facing such relationships is not one of inherent pathology or "maladjustment" of children. The difficulty is one of social stigma which exerts outside pressures on relationships.'[23]

The need to understand what is going on is only going to become more urgent in the coming years because of the anticipated demographic developments described above. The significance goes far beyond pragmatic policy considerations. When a nation begins to grow a population which is of mixed heritage, the national identity of the country is transformed. The myths of purity and bloodline begin to lose their grip and in many ways private acts by individuals redefine the country itself as hybrid. None of this is easily done, nor can it be easily undone. Audre Lorde has pointed out: 'It is out of chaos that new worlds are born.' Those new worlds are here and we should be better aware of them.

Chapter 4
Identity

I'm not black and I'm not white
I'm my own colour and that's all right
A colour is something that I cannot change
A colour is something with a very big range
But I'm not black and I'm not white
I'm my own colour, and that's all right.
Giselle Richelieu, aged 9, in a People in Harmony newsletter, August 1997.

'I was born in Winchester to a mixed-race American father and a white English mother and grew up in a little village in the New Forest all my life. My personal and employment experiences have contributed to my understandings of how the terminology of race and mixed race shifts over time and from place to place as well as that there are similarities and differences between the way people of mixed-race are treated and how black people are treated. In the 1950s I was called "nigger" and later, "half-caste" or "coloured". Later I became a person who was part of an "ethnic minority" and/or "visual minority" but always thought of myself as black. In the 1960s there were "half-caste gangs" in Liverpool. They were proud to be "half-caste", but were beaten up as black by the National Front! At fifteen-and-a-half years of age I joined the navy and went to South Africa. In South Africa I was called a "Cape Coloured" and given some privileges over black people, but not the privileges of white people. In the mid-1960s, I went to Charleston in South Carolina and became black again. In Jamaica, I was classified as "brown" because of my job.'
Bob Purkiss, National Secretary for Equalities at the Transport and General Workers Union and a Commissioner of the Commission for Racial Equality speaking a seminar in 1998.

'I say that I am "mixed-race" but if my dad heard me, he would box me round the head; he likes me to say I am black.'
A child interviewed by researcher Sian Peer for her report on identity.

'My mum is English, my dad is Jamaican. He took me away to Jamaica. I am glad he did. I am light and I could pass for white. My child says I am light. But black is what I feel on the inside. It is inside you. It makes you. I am black.'
An adult interviewed for a self-help video.

Africa
Sud America
Britain
North America
Many may claim me
But no one can really own me

Black
Light Skinned
Coloured
Red
Nigger
Half Caste
White
I will colour myself

Extract from a poem, 'Towards the Eradication of Social Chameleons Or It Was Your Assumption Not Mine', by Jayne Ifekwunigwe, March 1991.

Tribal identification has been both a feature of human history and an influence on it. The chapters on history in this book demonstrated how miscegenation was an affront to this manner of shaping thought and actions which is why it has been treated with such cruel disapprobation by those in power whether in the home or in society in general.

The politics of identity is a much more recent phenomenon. Liberation struggles in India, Africa and the Middle East led to the development of pride among subject people and writers such as Leopold Senghor, Gandhi and others were instrumental in beginning that process of self-love, an essential development after centuries of subjugation. The Black Power movement in the United States in the sixties is regarded by many as another key turning point. Being proudly black was seen as one way of fighting racism. The idea was imported here too. In America, the term black was inclusive of mixed-race people and in Britain it went further, embracing Asians and other groups which were united through their experiences of racial prejudice and discrimination. But this unity soon began to crumble although the reasons for it were different in the United States and the UK. Through the eighties and nineties the assumptions of integrationists in the USA were challenged mercilessly and we saw the growth of quotas, the deepening of ethnic differentiations and depressing new antagonisms between Hispanics, African Americans, Asians and so on. In the UK the black label began to be applied only to Afro-Caribbeans and others of African heritage. Asians, Muslims, Sikhs and Hindus took on more specific and inherited name tags. Other major forces contributed to this explosion of identity politics. Feminism grasped the idea of gender identity and developed it into a full political critique. As communism fell, old ethnic conflicts resumed leading to savage physical battles over identity.

Once individuals and groups start consciously to attach themselves to particular identities, it is but a small step to engineered national identities and demands for isolation from 'the other'. Citizens of hybrid nations have questioned, sometimes overthrown, diversity in favour of more simple 'original' labels. Serbia shows one grotesque side of this attempt at purification and return to ancestral rights. In other countries such as India, Pakistan and Rwanda brutal struggles have resulted from groups claiming to represent the true soul of a nation. The result is that the twenty-first century sees both fast and unstoppable globalisation and hybridisation, and alongside it the opposite, a retreat from hybridity and cosmopolitanism. As the French Algerian writer Amin Maalouf says in his brilliant new book on identity: 'I am challenging the notion that reduces identity to one single affiliation and encourages people to adopt an attitude that is partial, sectarian, intolerant, domineering...their view of the world is biased and distorted.' But Maalouf accepts that 'Unfortunately the "tribal" notion of identity is still one of the most accepted everywhere and not only among fanatics.'[1]

There are still so many struggles when it comes to the identity of mixed-race families of which respect and self-determination are the two most crucial. Several programmes on BBC television between 1994 and 1996 offered heartbreaking first person accounts of how mixed-race people are denied these two rights. One family spoke of having bricks and excreta thrown into their home. The white mother, a working class woman said: 'We don't smell. We're a clean family I'm proud of.' Her words show how much crass stereotyping she has internalised. This is what people think of them and so she is trying to prove them wrong instead of asking why such judgements are made by bigots. Her teenage son started weeping.

The politics of separation, racism and inter-ethnic hatred have a direct bearing on individuals and how they see themselves. Identity in that sense cannot be 'internal' alone. It changes; it is influenced by what happens in the world out there. In Yugoslavia as it was under Tito, mixing across the various ethnic and religious groups was not considered a betrayal. But when the ethnic cleansing programmes began, suddenly people had to describe themselves as one or the other. Among mixed-heritage families, there were forced separations and a number of divorces in order to protect lives. Leila is a refugee from Bosnia:

> I was married to a Serb and I was pregnant. Then the trouble started and suddenly our family was a target. My brother-in-law, who was only thirteen when I married his brother and like a son to me, joined the Serb army and stopped talking to me. My own family asked me to abort the child. The pressure got too much so I left and actually lost the baby. Thank God. What kind of life would it have had as a mixed nobody? We have broken up and I live alone now, feeling that I should think of myself as Muslim when I feel Bosnian.

In India similarly, as Hindu fundamentalists lay claim to the land and speak of non-Hindus as interlopers, Muslim/Hindu families find themselves the victims of more intensified prejudice.

In Britain, particularly through the years of Conservative rule when 'true' Britishness was linked to ancestry and whiteness – Margaret Thatcher did not want her country 'swamped' by alien cultures – all non-white communities developed a siege mentality. For mixed-race Britons the questions of identity have not receded into irrelevance just because there are so many more of them about. On the contrary, as a growing number of individuals and groups reject the idea of integration and long for purity, when white rejection of non-whites is paid back in kind, the identity issue becomes stronger and simplicity seems more irresistible. Mixed-race individuals do not have the luxury of thinking of themselves in purely personal terms. Their identity exists within a location and connects to how a family sees itself racially and culturally, and, ultimately, the self-definitions of communities and nations.

The politics of rejection

Oona King, a London MP representing constituents in the East End of London, feels strongly that these external forces, while important, should not be allowed to thwart people like herself. She represents Bangladeshis, white working-class people, Somalis and many other people from various backgrounds, most of whom are deeply uncomfortable about miscegenation. Walking around her constituency when writing a piece on her in 1997, I was truly horrified to meet people who held her mixed-race identity against her. She was not a 'real' black. She was a 'half-caste' who was therefore 'nothing'. One person, an old Bangladeshi, even said that she was the product of parents who could not 'control and limit themselves'. Today her popularity has risen massively because she is an excellent MP and more people accept her for what she is but it is still hard for her:

> For me racism is not an academic point. It is all too real. Given my background though I feel that I have to be a bridge builder. My mother is working class, Jewish and from Newcastle. Her grandfather was Hungarian and her grandmother was Irish and Scottish. My father is from Georgia in the US and was a member of the Civil Rights Movement. I have been called nigger, yid, and half-caste. I am multi-ethnic.[2]

In *The Colour of Love*, Anne Montague and I interviewed a number of mixed-race young men and women. One of them was David Upshal, a highly respected television producer who spoke with great candour about the way his identity was a problem for others when he was growing up. He felt a 'typically white boy in brown skin and with black features':

> When I went to school, black kids gave me shit. One kid in my first week said, 'Your mum's white isn't she?' It astonished me that these kids could tell just by looking at me that one of my parents was white. It was the black kids who used to beat me up...I don't ever remember a white kid giving me gyp about my colour...gradually I realised that [people seeing my mother] with me was a clear symbol that she had slept with a black man. I can remember all kinds of comments as a child – comments about how even prostitutes would never sleep with anyone black. I did feel a bit conspicuous walking down the street with my mother...But as time went on I found myself having a great affinity for black things and feeling very profoundly about them.[3]

A rising star, young musician Leigh Stephen Kenny, was similarly unaffected by questions of his identity until it hit him in the face. The son of a mixed-race mother who denied her own roots, never discussing her black father and always straightening her hair, Kenny was brought up in Kent, 'the most racist place back then'. He was ten before he realised that he wasn't white.

> I was playing at the bottom of the garden with one of the neighbour's kids. His dad screamed, 'David! Don't play with him. His mum's a nigger.' I went in and asked my mum what the word meant and it was only then that I found out the truth about my grandfather being black. Until then all I ever wanted to be was a skinhead like all other kids on my street...Coming to terms with being mixed-race along with all the other emotions you have to deal with when you are growing up is awful. I knew mixed-race

kids who grew up in black neighbourhoods who deny their white side and mixed-race guys who grew up on white council estates who are like white council estate boys.

The relationship between his parents was destructive and he witnessed this as a child. As a teenager he had a major breakdown which took him into an institution for a year. It was after meeting a wise Rasta woman who told him to embrace his mixed heritage that Kenny could make sense of his identity. Many of the songs on his records deal with this. Yet his black and white friends still insist on categorising him and his music into black or white.[4]

Akousa, half Irish, half Barbadian, one of the 'mestisse' women interviewed by Jayne Ifekwunigwe, says of her identity:

Gettin' into me late teens, I didn't think about myself because of all these conflicts that were startin' to come up from the past. Also new ones that were comin' in from other communities – black communities – that were really shockin' me. I mean there were times when I wouldn't show me legs. I'd go through summer wearing tights and socks. Cause I thought they were too light and white lookin'. There was a lot of pressure. I remember one day I was leanin' up somewhere and this guy said to me, 'Boy, aren't your legs white.' I just looked in horror and felt really sick and wanted to just run away. I was thinkin' God why didn't you make me a bit darker? . . . Because of what happened in the 70s in terms of the Black Power Movement, especially in this country, if you weren't black like ebony, then you just didn't have a chance basically. [My mum] used to take things in her stride. I kept comin' home and I'd say to her, 'I hate all white people, Tonkers, Honkies or whatever.' There's my mum sittin' there and I just didn't think about it.[5]

The tensions are not only between mixed-race people and the pull towards simple group and national identities. They are also between those two other fundamental needs of life: belonging to a community or communities and the right of every human being to be different and unique. As Maalouf says: 'Mankind itself is made up of special cases. Life is a creator of differences. No "reproduction" is ever identical. Every individual, without exception, possesses a composite identity.'[6] And yet we all need to belong to groups of some sort and we all do appear to have the need for some core and defining identities. In her paper, 'Communities to Conjure With', Jill Olumide puts it well:

. . . the question of ways in which we are required to define ourselves may not always conveniently coincide with the ways we may wish or are able to construct ourselves. This is surely an important matter for the 'mixed-race condition' which is required, at times, to behave like social ectoplasm. That the 'mixed-race condition' continues to look for its own sources of affirmation with an eclectic eye may not be regarded as politically astute, but it does store up some interesting possibilities for the time when it sits down as a collectivity to conjure up its own community. Meanwhile it may be regarded as a community in exile.[7]

For Lorrie, 30, confusion about identity was made more acute because she did not look mixed-race enough:

I look Asian and really am not. I was brought up by my middle-class, Oxford-educated Indian father and French mother to think of myself as me. I remember my mother telling my father not to wear a trilby because West Indians wore them. And my father never talked about his family history. I have this dark skin and dark eyes. When I went to an inner London school Asian kids would talk to me in one of their languages – I used to think it was all one 'Indian' language. I was so embarrassed because I could not understand a word. I didn't know what Eid was or Diwali either and they were all into all this multicultural thing in the seventies. I wasn't a part of them and didn't want to be a part of them. I find their values hypocritical. I feel British above all else. I hate this roots business. I think you can catch an extreme case of identity, language and culture which can lead to some shocking self-righteousness.

Donny Duggan, himself mixed-race, a church minister in Scotland who has an African wife and mixed-race children, says: 'You are not accepted by either side. You are not full-blooded. You are in the middle. I was British with a black skin. I was angry.' His son wanted to take on a white identity but he was seen by others as black. If anything happened in the town, police would look for him. He was abused at school and was taught by his parents to stand up for himself, which landed him in more trouble. Their daughter, Jambi, learnt better to embrace her own particular identity.

I decided to make a path for myself. I see myself as brown in colour. I am special. I am true to myself. I am happy knowing that my experiences have made me a strong person and I know my identity. I am a young Kenyan Scottish woman and nobody can take that away from me. I love Scotland and feel dedicated to it, but deep down inside I do not feel that Scotland wants me.[8]

Lingering histories

Mixed-race people who were born before the sixties have their own horrendous stories to tell about unforgiving white anger at their very existence. The denials of their heritage, abandonment and racism were common.

Lola, a talented painter, was born in Notting Hill Gate in 1958. She was a few months old when the riots erupted during which her father, a Jamaican, lost one eye and, in due course, his mind. He started beating up her mother, Susan, a twenty-year-old from Hampshire whom he had met when she first moved to London to join a secretarial school. From being a couple completely in love they began to hate one another. Susan left and took Lola back to the small English village where she herself was born:

> She, my mother, became a complete racist. She hated my hair and at one time even used whitening cream on my skin – I was only ten – to change my colour. She claimed my father had drugged and raped her and that she had never chosen to be with him. I remember seeing *To Sir With Love* at the cinema and telling my mum that I thought my dad was probably like Sidney Poitier. She slapped me. It was the only time she hit me. She never showed me any pictures of them. Then one day my gran, who was more understanding, secretly showed me a photo of their wedding when they both looked so happy. I never saw my dad again. All my paintings are about that loss of my blood, my life, my identity. I don't see my mother any more. I am an orphan, the product of a marriage nobody wanted, of the fucking multiculturalism dream turned nightmare.

Inner and outer battles over mixed-race identities are still more common than anyone believes, even among young, metropolitan people. Yet these adults were children long after anti-racism became established in urban areas as a force, even if in most of the rest of the country it was perceived as a threat. It is clear from what they say that even for the toughest and most talented it has been incredibly hard for them to come to terms with who they are and to develop a proper sense of self-worth.

Spice Girl Mel B and her sister, actress Danielle Brown, both wanted desperately to be blue-eyed and blonde. Danielle remembers how:

> Every day as a child I'd wake up distraught that I still had frizzy hair and coffee-coloured skin. At school I was called 'brown bread' so I would plaster my face with white powder to look like the other kids. We grew up in a suburb of Leeds and were the only black kids at school. It is only as we got older that we learned to love ourselves for being us.[9]

She went on to add this statement a few weeks later: 'I don't feel like that now. I'm really glad I've got my hair. If I could change my mum and dad to both being black or both being white, I would keep them just the way they are. Even though having a black dad and a white mum has caused me and Mel hassle, it's all been worth it.'[10]

Amita Dhiri, half French, half Ugandan Asian, shot to fame after she landed a plum role in the popular BBC series *This Life*, about young lawyers sharing a house. She grew up in Brighton where she too was called names, 'Paki', 'nig-nog', 'chinky'. Sadly she says she agreed with them 'because I thought I should be white too . . . I used to cry and cry and tell my mother I wished I was blonde and blue-eyed.'[11]

Although this kind of abuse is still common, confidence is growing and in areas which are cosmopolitan, mixed-race families seem to face less raw abuse and burning rejection. Molly Mahamdallie, a white primary school teacher who used to live in the town of St Helens near Liverpool, had a black boyfriend and in 1989 gave birth to their daughter, Stevie Ashton. In a heartbreaking newspaper interview, Molly described what happened after that: 'From the moment she was born, there was racist abuse. I remember trying to work out whether it was because we lived in a small town up North where almost everyone is white or because people took particular offence to mixed-race families. Maybe it was both.' Whatever the source of the hatred, it was everywhere in their lives. Restaurants would not let them in as a family; teenagers would call her baby a 'golliwog'. The couple split up and Molly then married an Asian. Things became even more vicious. Now her home was ransacked and covered in racist graffiti. The family moved to London and Stevie noticed the difference at once:

> I was really happy when we came to London. It isn't peaceful but there are people from all over the world here. Mum and me never stand out when we are walking down the street. It made me feel like I wasn't very different from her after all. I could see other people in mixed-race families and they seemed to be close . . . I like the fact that my mum's white. Some people might feel upset about not having a mum that obviously looks like you and some people think white mums don't understand racism. But not me.[12]

Claiming normality and the endless quest for labels

Why is it still so hard for mixed-race people to be accepted as 'normal'? The reasons are the same all over the world. As Maria Root points out in her book, *Racially Mixed People in America*:

> The presence of racially mixed persons defies the social order predicated upon race, blurs racial and ethnic group boundaries, and challenges generally accepted proscriptions and prescriptions regarding inter-group relations. Furthermore, and perhaps most threatening, the existence of racially mixed persons challenges

long-held notions about the biological, moral and social meanings of race...the increasing presence of multiracial people necessitates that we as a nation ask ourselves questions about our identity: Who are we? How do we see ourselves?'[13]

They are, in other words an affront to distilled and purified identities. So, when Tiger Woods, the great American golfer, said that he was 'Caublinasian', meaning a mixture of Caucasian, black, Native American and Asian, more African Americans than whites were offended.[14] Some sprang up to condemn or to pity him for not wishing to embrace his 'true' African heritage. Internationally it appears there is an obsession with terms and a feeling that all words, are, in the end, inadequate to describe mixed-race people. Jayne Ifekwunigwe, herself the product of a Nigerian father and an Irish, English and Guyanese mother, explores this dilemma in her delicately written book, *Scattered Belongings*: 'In varied cultural and historical contexts, countless terms are employed to name [mixed-race] individuals. "Mixed-race", mixed heritage, mixed parentage, mestizo, mestiza, mulatto, mulatta, creole, coloured, "mixed racial descent", mixed origins, dual heritage, dual parentage, "multiracial", "bi-racial", multiethnic, to the more derogatory half-caste, zebra, half-breed, mongrel, oreo, Heinz Fifty Seven.'[15]

If to hyphenated identities such as Anglo-Indian are added black, hybrid and the many words for different physical mixes in the Caribbean, the US and elsewhere, it becomes clear that the vocabulary which has evolved is itself a mark of confusion and the struggle to accept miscegenation. Medical student David Dean, of Asian and European descent, wrote to me in 1999 arguing persuasively that we should use the term 'compound ethnicity' rather than 'mixed-race' because the term better describes people such as himself.[16] Ifekwunigwe, who has reclaimed 'mestisse' to describe herself, feels that there is an ongoing tension in society between phenotype, the way a person looks, and genotype, their genetic inheritance. She also believes that mixed-race people and mixed-race families must have the right to determine who they feel they are and to change these if and when they wish. People in general are freer than they have ever been to choose their own versions of family life and yet mixed-race people are expected to 'belong' solely on the basis of their looks or genetic make-up.

It is only in the 2001 national census that the British nation will be deemed sufficiently grown up to cope with an official 'mixed-race' category instead of that catch-all niche 'other' which has only served to render this community invisible. This census recognition is symbolic of real progress which has been achieved by individuals and families and some (too few) institutions. But we have to see this as the beginning of a positive process, not the end of it. The battle over terms is not settled. Anne Phoenix has described how some people now prefer 'mixed-parentage' to 'mixed-race' because race is a racist construct. Others have started to use 'dual heritage' but this replicates the idea of two distinct, binary halves.[17] This flux can only be an essential phase which is challenging the authoritarian imposition of labels on people. The Early Years Anti-Racist Network rightly points out:

> There are no terms that are 'right' for ever more. Groups define and redefine themselves, their sense of who they are culturally and politically as preferred terms change. Also within one group one person may like a term which another may not. We have to constantly pay attention to changing definitions and to the reasons why they are changed. People need to discover for themselves who they are and not have terms imposed upon them.[18]

Jeremy Murray, the son of a white Irish mother and a black West Indian father, has been forced to sit on the fence for too long. He says instead of negatively and defensively opting for one side of his heritage, he is now most comfortable thinking of himself as a 'Third Race' which is positively mixed-race.[19] Another mixed-race woman I met said that she used to call herself an 'inbetweeny' and that this made her feel special because it was her own word for herself. This feeling that they are part of a distinct group was strong in many of the interviewees. Others felt passionately 'black'. The arguments for this are well put by the American journalist Lisa Jones:

> My mother is white. And I, as you might or might not have figured out, am black...Are you still staring? Let me guess. My white mother presents a different set of enigmas to you based on your own racial classification. Those of you who are black might find 'evidence' of my white parent to question my racial allegiance. For those of you who are white, evidence of my white lineage might move you to deep-seated feelings of racial superiority. You might wonder why I would choose to identify as 'fully' black when I have the 'saving grace' of a white parent. I realise both sets of responses display an ignorance of our shared cultural and racial history as Americans.[20]

The same passionate arguments are provided by 'black' mixed-race people in Britain.

Research and interpreting change

Anne Wilson's research on mixed-race children, although more than 13 years old, is still one of the most important pieces of work showing the progress that has been made on the issue of identity.

She set out to look at the identity and self-identification of 51 mixed-race children aged between 6 and 9. They were all children who lived with both natural parents, one black (African or Afro-Caribbean) and one white. To cut out variables and get 'clean' results for one small group, Asians and others were not included. Wilson wanted to find out about racial awareness, racial identification and racial preference. Coloured photographs rather than dolls were used. Later, mothers were also inter-viewed. The study, which was multi-layered, did reach very important conclusions:

> If the main findings of this study had to be summarised in a single sentence, it would be that mixed-race children do not necessarily conform to the stereotype of the social misfit, caught between the social worlds of black and white. Not all mixed-race children are torn between the ethnic loyalties of their parents and not all spend their lives trying to make themselves acceptable to one ethnic group. Some interracial families (and some areas) seem conducive to the development of a positive mixed-race identity where the child is content to be both black and white without perceiving a contradiction between the two.[21]

Wilson found that the outcomes were most positive where race was openly discussed within families and school, and when families lived in multiracial areas. And the anecdotal evidence which has gathered over the years would bear this out. Stevie above does have a happier time in London than she did in an all-white area. Ngiao Anya, the six-year-old mixed-race daughter of white mother Henrietta Wilkinson, regrets bitterly the decision her mother made to leave London and move to the country. Ngiao was bright, confident and well liked by her teachers in the metropolis. In an all-white school where she was big for her age, she became withdrawn and inarticulate. Her teachers complained that she was attention seeking. The local doctor assumed she was adopted. She started bed wetting and was bullied endlessly. Wilkinson was told by the school that it was her 'aggressive political stance more appropriate to an inner city ghetto' which was the problem, not the racism her child was facing. They moved to Bristol and Ngiao is thriving.[22]

But you can find purists within cities too. My own mixed-race daughter, who is eight, was made to feel very uncomfortable at the local Church of England primary school. Few parents would talk to us and the silent message was that we were not normal because we were not white Christians. I am a Muslim and this quickly became an unspoken disadvantage for my little girl. We have started sending her to a girls' school with a diverse population and a large number of mixed-race children. My daughter is blooming and no longer feels inadequate. Just like Stevie above, her best friend is another mixed-race girl. It is as if without knowing it they know one another. When she was six, I asked her what colour she thought she was and if she wanted to be white 'like Daddy'. 'No way,' she answered, adding: 'Nobody is white, Mum. He is peach-coloured a little bit like me but I am more brown peach than pink peach. And you are like baked potato.' To her colour is just colour, and like a fastidious painter, what matters is exactitude, the matching of descriptive words to the colour she sees. Of course it is only a matter of time before she begins to understand the symbolic meanings of skin colour and who knows how she will react? And how can we prepare her for that?

David Milner showed in his research on young children and race that at about three-and-a-half to four all children can describe skin colours and attribute different values to them. Clearly my daughter can do the first but not the second, in spite of living in a household where race and culture are constantly and openly discussed. I have no idea whether I should worry that Leila has not absorbed social messages about white and black skins or rejoice that she – at least now – loves and knows her physical self. One of the most interesting studies was one that was carried out in 1992 when black culture was beginning to be seen as cool. A third of white children between 8 and 11 said they wanted to be most like the Afro-Caribbeans in pictures shown to them.[23] The study can be dismissed as a blip but that would be a mistake. I think it reveals that cultural shifts can affect attitudes and this is cause for some limited optimism. But this cultural trend has not reduced the racism faced by young Afro-Caribbeans in this society, and there are still many black and Asian children who end up wishing they were white because of the bullying and exclusion they experience.

Earlier research using dolls or pictures found that the majority of non-white children said white and light dolls were 'nicer' than darker dolls and also that the darker dolls 'looked bad'. Even more worrying was the wishful self-identification. Asked 'Which doll looks like you?' most children said they were like white or coloured dolls. Many of the children became nervous or tearful. Kenneth Clark, one of the most prominent of these researchers, concluded: 'The fact that young Negro children would prefer to be white reflects their knowledge that society prefers white people.'[24] In some of this research, lighter-skinned children were more likely to move themselves towards white than more obviously black children. In others it was the opposite. Since some of this early research, important questions have been raised about the conclusions that were drawn. Are the children choosing the doll as a real preference or are they simply making choices which are based on the understanding that in society darker skin is of lesser value? If it is the latter they could be said to be making a rational decision.[25]

Another study carried out in the USA to examine the identities of mixed-race children where one parent was Japanese or Hispanic revealed that in the case of the former, children were happy to accept the Japanese identity and one reason put forward for this was that the Japanese had a high status in American society.

Milner's research[26] and other studies by social scientists from the UK and the USA appear to show that over the decades, there has been a marked decrease of out-group preference among young non-white children although there is also a body of respectable research which concludes that, well after the Black Power movements, black children were still expressing an unhealthy preference for white dolls.[27] There has been a marked improvement in the way this doll or picture method is used. Instead of using simply black and white dolls, more complex physical types are used so that children can find a closer match.

My daughter Leila is obsessed with blonde Barbie dolls and has a vast number of them. I have offered her the other nationalities but she has not taken them up. Her other dolls are also mostly white except for one black doll she has named 'Brown' and an oriental doll named Mulan. I believe this tells us something about how attractiveness as defined in the still emerging consciousness of my mixed-race daughter is already more on the side of white than black. I then started wondering why I have happily paid out for these dolls without once questioning what was going on or engineering a more multiracial doll population in my home. I can only conclude that my own upbringing – under colonial rule and living among East African Asians with racist attitudes towards Africans and dark skins in general – has poisoned my own aesthetic sense too.

Ground-breaking work on identity was carried out by Barbara Tizzard and Ann Phoenix in the early nineties. Their book, *Black, White or Mixed Race*,[28] came out of specially commissioned research funded by the Department of Health. One of the main – and most controversial – conclusions they reached was that 'a sizeable proportion' of young people reject the idea that they have to see themselves as black just because the black consciousness movement has led to 'a renewed insistence on the "one drop of black blood makes a person black" rule'.[29] People of mixed heritage do not want to deny the white part of their inheritance and some suggest that to do this could be psychologically damaging. Tizzard and Phoenix interviewed 15 to 16-year-olds of both sexes and across the classes. Because of insufficient resources, they concentrated on white/Afro-Caribbean children which is a pity because we have little other than anecdotal evidence about the other mixed-race Britons. The results were significant. Over half the sample used the word 'black' to describe only people who had two African or Afro-Caribbean parents. 49 per cent used it for mixed-race people with one African or Afro-Caribbean parent. Only 12 per cent used it to include Asians and only one interviewee used it to mean anyone 'not white'. 39 per cent said they thought of themselves as black with another 10 per cent saying that they did so in certain situations. 49 per cent said they did not. One girl living with her single white mother said: 'I wouldn't call myself black. I mean, lots of people have said if you are mixed-race, you may as well call yourself black, but I feel that is denying the fact that my mother is white, and I am not going to do that.'[30] Another interviewee said: 'I don't think of myself as black, exactly, I think of myself as half-British, half-Jamaican, though essentially I feel myself to be British because I was born here.' A girl who looked white said: 'Sometimes I think of myself as being English and sometimes I think of myself as being more Afr...well kind of African, it depends on the situation a lot. And sometimes I think of myself as neither really, just being like tanned, a tanned British person.'

Those who did not call themselves black used other terms such as brown or mixed, and coloured, a word which has been anathema to anti-racists for decades but used by 43 per cent of the mixed-race young people interviewed by the authors. I suppose die-hard advocates of 'black' will see these people as unsound and in need of serious re-education or therapy. Those who rejected the term 'coloured' felt passionately that it was wrong to use it. Most of the young people who felt 'black' argued the case for it in terms of history, 'bloodlines' and oppression.

> Defining themselves as 'black' was strongly related to a set of attitudes about racism which were more politicised than those of the young people who did not use the term...they tended to describe racism as coming only from white people...and to believe that if they had been white, both their past and their future lives would have been easier and if they had been black, more difficult.[31]

Interviewees who felt they had their own mixed-race identity were asked whether they would choose one side or the other if there were a serious conflict. Some said 'black' because they were the ones who suffer in society. Two responses quoted below show how hard it is to reduce these identities to a single word.

> I think I would probably go on the black side, but if it has to happen to my mum and my dad as well, no, I think I'd go with my mum on the white side.

> Half the time I think of myself as a white person, but with darker skin, and I sort of forget exactly what colour I am. When I say

'white' I mean the personality, because you'll find like black people have different views on things.

My own research for this book reveals the same complexities. They are not denials of some essential and large truth, but a perfectly understandable and highly intelligent response to lives which cannot be neatly categorised. Maya, a mixed-race teenager with an absent Asian father, calls herself Irish because that is what her mum is: 'Why should I call myself half-Asian when my dad's family hates me for being born? They are so racist about my mum, I have no need to belong to them.' But Bev, who is also a child living with her Irish mother and an absent black father, is the opposite: 'I am proud of being black whatever my dad did. If he rang me tomorrow I'd go with him. He was so handsome. I think he left because whites made him feel bad. I don't get on with my mum.'

A large number of young mixed-race people I met were proudly hybrid and very much at peace with this identity. Zara best expressed this pride and confidence:

I have many MR friends, we call ourselves MR. We love the way we can be both black and white or Asian and white. In my home I dress up all Indian and go to weddings with my Asian mum and I am accepted. They all say I have beautiful skin. But we also do Christmas and I have a white family which adores us. There is no conflict. We are more evolved I think.

But even among the most confident, the road to this comfortable identity is never that easy and the most upbeat young people in the Tizzard–Phoenix study remember all too well the taunts and the racism they faced along the way. A Nigerian girl spoke about how she is 'always different, always out of it'. Others spoke of abuse from white children and the indifference of teachers, who are often too paralysed because they do not think they know the 'right' way to respond. And yet 86 per cent said they no longer wished to be a different colour from the colour they were as teenagers. And one very important fact emerged: *only two interviewees described feelings of confusion normally assumed to afflict most mixed-race people* [my italics].

Family dynamics had a much greater influence on the identities of these young people than the schools they attended. Children who had a positive racial identity were not all living with a non-white parent. 60 per cent of the sample had a positive identity. But nearly 75 per cent of these called themselves 'mixed' rather than 'black'. They were proud of their heritage, saw it as advantageous and felt comfortable in both worlds. 20 per cent of the sample had problems and were still exploring the identity which felt right for them. Another 20 per cent were not confused or unhappy but were not proud either. There was no 'natural' connection between a black identity and inner well-being. Some interviewees felt a sense of dislocation from the existing landscape and this was mainly attributed to the lack of narratives, history, or music which reflected a mixed-race sensibility.[32]

Other studies have revealed positive outcomes too. A qualitative study among biracial adolescents in San Francisco found that the majority were positive about themselves, had learned to negotiate an ethnic identity that chimed with their backgrounds, achieved good peer group relationships and emerged as autonomous individuals comfortable with their sexuality. Twenty-five per cent suffered from problems of low self-esteem and/or immaturity and anxieties. The best adjusted young people appeared to come from intact families with a higher socio-economic status who had been educated in integrated schooling in a mixed neighbourhood. Where the parents confronted issues of mixed-race identities, the children fared better.[33]

But these sensible findings have not yet entered the national discourse on mixed-race identity. There is still too much polarisation and politicisation which passes for debate and most social policy is lagging behind the findings of the substantial and important research described in this chapter.

Complexity and the self

Chapters 1 and 2 demonstrated how researchers have spent decades 'proving' that mixed-race people are confused, lost, marginal and potentially self-damaging or destructive, presumably because they do not have one clean identity. The response to this accumulated unwisdom has been to impose a single identity on those of dual or triple heritage, which feels to me like ignoble surrender.

In his study of how identity is constructed in mixed-race children, Ilan Katz produces both compelling evidence and, by implication, a critique of how such simplistic ideas are damaging. Racial prejudice, he says, consists of three dimensions: psychological, social and cultural. He questions the assumption too frequently asserted that black people are better able to prepare black children for life in a racist society. Can one really divide families into 'black' and 'white' types? What about individuals and the specific nature of families? And how do family dynamics determine the identity of a mixed-race child? Katz spent some time with white mothers of mixed-race infants to study how child development and identity development were related and to record the manifestations of the latter. He wanted to search out the attitudes of white mothers and to study the messages, conscious and unconscious, which were transmitted from mother to infant. Two women were followed, observed, questioned in great depth. Other mothers were researched in less detail. All the mothers thought of themselves as English and had no close social contacts with black people although they had more cosmopolitan lifestyles than their own original families. Some of the women went into relationships with black men in order to break out of the dull reality of English life. Some of the family members had racist views. Broadening their horizons was an important motive for the steps taken by these white women. Racial issues were a central part of the family dynamic. In one family the black father was present and rows were often racialised. In the family where there was a lone white mother, she idealised black culture. Katz concluded that:

> The interviews confirmed that racial identity could not be seen merely as a set of identifications with the 'racial' aspects of the self or of society. It also became apparent that the children did not have a set of racial or cultural 'roots' which were being transmitted by the parents. Each family was negotiating the issues of race and culture in different ways, both within the family and within the extended family and society as a whole.[34]

Katz goes on to reiterate what has been said by a number of important thinkers in recent years including Paul Gilroy, who has argued that anti-racism and racism share the discourse of totality, identity and exclusion:

> Instead of deconstructing racist ideologies and practices, modern anti-racists have simply inverted them...Modernist anti-racism views 'culture' and 'race' in essentialist terms and imposes its own teleology...so black children have a right to their roots and culture which are given to them by 'the black family'. 'The black family' itself is seen as having strengths which have allowed it to survive through the tests of racism.[35]

Katz is critical of some key writers and academics who have invested much time and thought in developing the ideology that mixed-race children must be taught to embrace their black identity as if it were the only sane and proper label for them, if only they knew. He describes the highly regarded work of Nick Banks who has developed a way of ensuring this blackening process. It is called the Cognitive Ebonisation Technique and involves lots of positive black role models and figures of beauty. Banks does accept that it is wrong to impose black identity on a child before he or she is ready to embrace it but strongly believes the following: 'Blackness as a positive aspirational goal to be achieved can also be useful with statements such as "when you understand more about the world, you will like being black" or "when you find out the good things black people have done you will be so happy to be black".'[36]

This seems to be, at best, debatable. Black people have done good and bad and continue to do so. Mandela and Martin Luther King demonstrate the heroic side while the leaders of Rwanda who orchestrated the genocides there show another. Mahatma Gandhi was one kind of leader, Indira Gandhi quite another. Besides, an identity means more than hanging on to the coat tails of heroes. There are appalling black and Asian families and healthy white families and vice versa.

Paul Gilroy (who has personal experience of being in a mixed-race family) finds such discourse unacceptable:

> It is disturbing that what might be called the triumphalist presentation of black family life was part of the wider drift in black political thought towards an implosive obsession with identity as selfhood...As far as social work is concerned, nothing critical could be said about the black family or the tidy forms of pure community that were apparently to be constructed from its simple agglomeration without courting accusations of betrayal.[37]

Qualitative studies such as the one carried out by Katz are important because they remind us that there are several known and unknown factors which go into the making of a human being with self-esteem.

There is a central paradox in the construction of an identity, says the academic Barry Richards: 'To have an "identity" is to feel distinctive and to be able to relate to others different from oneself...Yet, at the same time, there is in our understanding of identity a strong component of sameness...a commonality with others.' We find and reinforce ourselves through relationships with other individuals rather than wholly through our place within a social grouping.[38] Mixed-race families or white mothers of mixed-race children can have subconscious anxieties based on skin colour and race, but then no identities are simple anyway.

Does the label have to be 'black'?

Yet it appears hard even for right-minded people to shift away from the idea that all mixed-race people are black. In *Remember Me*, the authors, who set out to celebrate mixed-race people, describe Oona King as 'black'. The resource manual *Celebrating Identity* (which I have quoted in this book) was produced by people who are from mixed-race families and by those who have long worked in the area of race and identity. Yet they too insist on using the term 'black' for mixed-race people. They believe as do others that such people need to have a 'positive black identity' in order to survive and grow. A white mother of a mixed-race child gives her perfectly understandable reasons for this in the manual:

When my son walks into a shop he is followed around the store like any Black boy of a similar age is followed. I don't believe that any security staff in the store are thinking 'Ah now he is half white so I don't need to check him out.' The stereotype image of young Black males affects my child as much as any other Black child.[39]

On *Woman's Hour* on Radio 4, when discussing the sexual stereo-types of black women, the interviewees kept describing the mixed-race actress Cathy Tyson and Melanie, the mixed-race competitor on *Big Brother*, as 'black'.[40] This is a simplification of the identity of mixed-heritage people and most of those whom I have interviewed over many years would agree that it is important not to make such assumptions. Some mixed-race people feel black; others do not. In neither case can anything be taken for granted and most of the time there has been a long and hard journey to find the label which fits. I do think that identities need to be more than just the labels society heaps on you.

The whole identity issue is going to receive even more attention when the box specifically designed to include mixed-race people appears in the next national census. Many influential people feel strongly that the term ought not to be encouraged. The late Bernie Grant was highly critical when the idea was first tested in a pilot study back in 1996. He said:

A mixed-race category would give the illusion that such people make up a self-sufficient racial or ethnic group. Society sees mixed-race people as black and they are treated as black. They are never accepted as white, so they have no choice. Both my children are mixed-race. They see themselves as black. They have never had a problem with that.[41]

Sybil Phoenix MBE, a phenomenal woman who fostered hundreds of black and mixed-race children in care over the last forty years, is equally convinced that black is what mixed-race children are because that is how they are regarded by society. On a video produced by People In Harmony, a self-help group for mixed-race families, she tells a story of how a white looking mixed-race child in her care came crying to her: 'Tell me I am white she said. All the children at the school say I am white. All three of us are white. I told her you are crying because you are in pain about being black. All three of your fathers is black so you are black.'[42]

Darcus Howe wrote an article in the late nineties also insisting that mixed-race people are black. 'I am a dab hand at bringing up mixed-race children. My daughter Tamara is head of the production department (Factual) at London Weekend Television. Taipha is a freelance researcher. They were brought up with the sound belief that they are black, not mixed, not half anything, just black.' Yet in the same piece Howe describes one family where the mixed-race son of a white woman had become a member of Nation of Islam and now believes his mother to be the devil: 'He refuses to speak to her because she is white.'[43]

Several letters were published by the paper in response to this piece. Three are worth quoting because they illustrate the present-day debates over terminology and identity. Dr Andrew Crowcroft wanted to know: 'Why does Darcus Howe describe his children as black? It must be important for mixed-race children to know and take pride in both of their rich backgrounds. Do the mothers of these children generally submit to his description?' In the same vein, Nick Alexander asked whether such a view is not a 'denial of the white side of the family. Are the mother's genes worthless?' And a mixed-race man from South Africa claimed his own label: 'I was brought up to believe I was neither black nor white; that I am what I am.'[44] It seems curious that none of those who argue so passionately about the black label for children whose mothers are white and whose fathers are black ever consider the implicit sexism of their views. For Maria, who has had three mixed-race children with three black men and is expecting a fourth by yet another, this is all about sexism and power play:

> I have never been able to live with any of these men because I won't take their rubbish that my children are black only. They think they can go around having white baby mothers and then just own the children without paying a penny. I go with black men because they are great in bed and because I know I can have really lovely children. Look at them. One has blue eyes, they are toasty brown, the way I like my toast. And no way are they black.

During the course of researching this book I found many examples of black and Asian men who assumed that their identity would define the children – whatever minimal role they were playing in the upbringing of the child, and white mothers who felt that they had to go along with this in order not to appear racist. Some television documentaries have tackled this issue in recent years. Lionel Robinson was removed from his mother by his father and taken over to the Caribbean at the age of ten. He is light-skinned and could pass for white Mediterranean. But in his heart he says he feels black and only black. Lionel never saw his birth mother again and appears to have no regrets about this.[45]

The fathers think that they are acting in the best interests of the child. Danny was also taken away from his white mother by his Jamaican father when he was just six. He was handed over to an authoritarian uncle in Jamaica and he lived there until he was sixteen when his uncle died and he had to come over. He has had a number of breakdowns and only recently found his mother, now suffering from MS:

I hate my father. I hate my West Indian family who treated me like a slave. Not my cousins, they were good. I don't know how to love my mother but I am happy I found her. Why did she not fight for me? What right did my father have to deny me my mother? If she was not good enough to be my mother, why was she good enough to be his lover? I feel black British but a part of me wants to feel white so that I can feel close to my mother as she sits in that wheelchair.

I talked to Danny's father and he explained why he decided to separate mother and child in the way he did:

Martha's family hated me. They hated all black people. I think she went with me to rebel. I did not want them to get to my son and tell him he was nothing. Martha was too weak to stand up to them. They told her not to bring 'the black bastard baby' to their house so she obeyed. I know I should have brought him up here, but he would have been pulled between us two. We hated one another soon after he was born. I just wanted him to be with people who would not make him hate himself. I didn't know my brother was as bigoted as the rest of them.

Not all white mothers feel this resentment. A large number of them like Teresa Alleyne and Hannah Murray quoted in the next chapter are also convinced that their children are black and proud of it. Donna Alleyne and Lynda Murray both confirmed that they feel happy with their blackness and at ease with their white sides too. Lynda remembers hating her hair when she was young and, like Donna, feels that the black is beautiful movement helped her enormously.[46]

The fight for individuality

If you are not all white, one of the most pernicious effects of living in a racially divided and unequal society is that all sides conspire to rob you of your individuality. You are always representative of one thing or another, never just another unique individual human being. For the artist and broadcaster Clare Gorham, this problem has worsened since the politics of identity erupted on to the social landscape. She was adopted when she was three months old, the second mixed-race child in a family of nine, some 'biological' and others adopted. Her own father, a Nigerian academic, had a relationship with one of his students who became pregnant. He went back home soon after because he had to marry the 'right sort of Nigerian' and because his parents would never have accepted either the mother or the child. Clare loves her adoptive mother:

The fact that I was black and my parents were white didn't bother me at all ... In my twenties I started noticing people looking a bit confused when I introduced mum and dad to them. It was almost as if they were questioning my position. It made me a bit angry because I was so proud of them and proud to be their daughter.

Clare has found her biological mother who explained that she had to give her up because she is not very maternal and because she had to finish her Ph.D. Her 'real' father sent her a bangle from his tribe which she does not wear. She says there is no relationship with either really and that it makes her 'sick' when the woman who gave her birth is called her 'mum'. What Clare feels and expresses most strongly and persuasively however is her sense that she is just Clare. 'I have roots from around the world, but I am me.'[47]

Clare made a film for Channel 4 on this issue and interviewed Nimmy Marsh, a black girl adopted by the Duke and Duchess of Richmond, wealthy people who wanted to make some of their good fortune available to those less fortunate and who are now probably regarded as completely misguided. Their daughter does not think so. Like Clare she is a strong individual who feels confident, proud and, yes, grateful that she had all the advantages she had. The most interesting case in this film was that of two self-defined black sisters who were adopted by a white family in the shires. Jade looks black but feels only herself. She is uninterested in black identity politics:

I have never known this so I don't miss it. I don't have black friends because I went to a white boarding school. I have never had a black boyfriend. Black men don't know how to treat women. They want them to cook, to serve them ... My sister has her hair done in Tottenham. I wouldn't dream of it. It's not my area. I guess that is snobbish.

All this is delivered in a cut-glass accent. One could pathologise Jade and conclude that she has problems with accepting who she is. Or one could say that hers is a perfectly sane response to the life she has lived. Her sister Helen is the exact opposite. She went to a boarding school with pupils of various nationalities and she is proudly black and only goes out with black men. She explains that this is because she wants a black child which presumably means not a white-looking mixed-race one.

On BBC2's *Love in Black and White*,[48] there was another story which revealed this search for individuality, perhaps in this case thrust upon the people involved. Jessica is eight and the daughter of Maureen, a Scottish mother, and a Jamaican British father. They met at a nightclub in Wolverhampton and the father departed as soon as Maureen became pregnant. She had the baby alone, lived through all the objections, racism and sheer bad manners of people who never thought Jessica could be hers and has brought up a wonderfully confident and articulate child. They live in a remote part of Scotland where there are no other black children. Whilst potentially a problem, it is where Maureen was brought up and where she clearly feels happy. When asked if there is anything that Jessica would change about herself, her answer is 'my shoe size'. She is close to her mother and obviously mistrusts her father who has only spoken to her once and then made promises he never kept: 'I don't like him. He's hurt me.' She would like to see him just to know him a little but another side of her is scared that she will be let down again. She says she has been called 'horrible names' in the park, but her mum has taught her to be proud and to remember that these people are 'just jealous'.

In this kind of complicated situation, is it not dangerous to make assumptions about 'black culture' and identity? If this child is content being herself, by what right does anyone interfere in order to inject blame and values?

Hidden identities

Matt is an attractive man in his twenties, with a Jewish father and a mixed-race mother. His identity, or one version of it, confronted him at school where he was called both a 'Yid' and a 'nigger'. His own father has never explained to his children why he has kept them hidden from his Jewish parents. Even now, he says he does not want to talk about this. His wife, meanwhile, is furious about this shameful concealment, even more so because her own mother, a white woman, did not tell her daughter about her father – a Nigerian man – until her daughter was forty-eight. A year after she finally found him, he died. The family is obviously close and far from dysfunctional. Yet there is all this unexplored anger over identity and acknowledgment.

Another example of the painful limbo that people can be left in over their identity is Geraldine Roberts, one of the children looked after by Sybil Phoenix. Her white mother refuses to accept that she gave birth to Geraldine. She is in denial over the birth itself. Geraldine's father died in prison, and as you watch her you feel she is like a ghost roaming the world in search of peace which she will only find if her identity as a mixed-race woman born to a white woman is recognised.

But for every such story of pain there is another one of impressive strength and reclamation. Bisi, an interviewee in Jayne Ifekwunigwe's book is one such example. Born in Ibadan, Nigeria, she is the daughter of a white woman from Newcastle-upon-Tyne and a Nigerian father, both teachers. Bisi came to England to study art and ended up married to an Englishman, something her African side of the family had warned her against. As time has gone on and she has had children Bisi has constructed an identity which means something real to her:

> One gets to a point where one realises that you cannot identify with a white culture. You have to go and seek that black culture from somewhere. If you can't find it you have to synthesise it, which I think many people here have done... it's funny though, when I started relaxing about it and owning that there is a lot of English in me basically... that [I found] yes, there is a lot of English, but there is a lot of African too.[49]

Then there are those who pass for white and either love it or hate it. Mondeo, half Chinese and half black, wants to be a model. He looks like a tanned Leonardo DiCaprio and sees no reason at all why he should bring out the fact that he is not white: 'I am me. I like me. I like it when people think I am Italian, Brazilian, Spanish whatever. This is rainbow country now. Why should these old labels apply? My parents have no contact with their families. They are both in the money business and as a family we feel we are the future. Without any racial baggage.'

Sheila also passes because she has had the shape of her nose altered and wears a light brown wig of straight hair all the time:

> I am white because my mum is white and she is the one who took care of me. I don't want any sign of my dad on me because he was ashamed of me. My mum's quite racist. She thinks that most black people are unattractive. My dad was different she says. He once wrote me a letter asking if we could meet. I think it was after *Secrets and Lies* came out and he was feeling all guilty. I told him to piss off. I don't want this black guy crawling all over my life thank you. After this letter, my mum told me that it was she who told my dad to stay away from me and not ruin my life as a white child.

But Sammy, who can also pass for white, hates what this has meant. He has been rejected by black kids unlike his brother who looks much more like their black mother. 'He dresses like Bob Marley and that, while I look like this boring white trash. I want to look like I feel inside and I feel black, not white, not mixed anything. I feel like transsexuals feel. That I have a body which does not reflect at all what I am inside.'

Vicky Phillips looks white but is the mixed-race child of a West African father and a middle-class English mother:

> I think the experience of being culturally black but perceived as white gives you a very interesting, slightly objective view of what it is to be white and what it is to be black... What I have realised is that being black is not just about a political awareness or choice. It is about being culturally and socially a black African.

There are things about me which I've inherited from generations back, attitudes and habits which the culture has bred. Because a lot of my time in this country has been in London, the equivalent white development and white cultural awareness haven't come to the surface as much as the Sierra Leonean side has. I do have a lot of Caribbean friends, which is strange because Africans and Caribbeans don't tend to mix, but I think it is because like me they are seen as the 'other'. What I realised though is that even after I became intimate with them, there was a point at which they rejected me because I looked white.[50]

In 1990, the *Phil Donahue Show* in the United States tackled this explosive issue. Several guests on the show who looked white said that they liked that because it gave them so many advantages. It was easier to get jobs, a home and loans. In one case the family, which was mixed-race, actively cultivated a white identity. The secret was never openly discussed, but no black children were allowed to come and play and all the family friends were white. The mother of the family later explained that she did it to make sure that none of her family would be killed in racist America. Rock, another of the interviewees, spoke of his discomfort when racists would talk to him about 'niggers', not realising that he was mixed-race. Passing for white may at times make life easier for the people concerned, but as several such interviewees told me, there is also discomfort and a struggle between the person on the inside and on the outside.

White mothers of mixed-race children

There are particular difficulties over identity involving white mothers of mixed-race children. Not only do they have to deal with the confusion following a sudden change in the way they are seen, but more painful and subtle processes of collusion. Sue Norris is a single mum who has learnt to accept that she is called a 'white wog' on the South London estate where she lives. But she cries when she hears the abuse her children face and most bitterly when she finds herself wishing all this had not happened to her:

It is terrible to say this because I am talking about my own children and I love them. But because I am white, if I am alone, I can walk anywhere. I feel free. Nobody bothers. But when the children are with me, I am a prisoner to what people feel about me and the children. And you do want to belong to your own kind. It hurts. It's like that film where you wake up one day and you are black. The first day I went to the nursery all the white mums started getting together and being pals. Then they saw this notice about Diwali and they started to be really rude about 'Pakis' and that and I just froze. I hoped that my daughter wouldn't rush up to me at that point. Once I was walking through a market and I remember thinking, Thank God it is Terry – who is light skinned – who is with me and not the other two who look quite dark. Afterwards I felt terrible about it. Perhaps it's because all parents want their children to look like them and when Terry and I are together we don't look like a mismatch, different coloured socks that should not be together.[51]

When couples are stable, this weariness, fear and lack of security seems less obvious. You get the impression that if the bond between the couple is strong, the abusive and hurtful experiences faced by their children and themselves do not end up being as potent.

Gill Danesh, a Yorkshire woman, went through some dreadful times when she fell in love with Sayeed, an Iranian engineer, and married him. They have twins, a boy and a girl. The girl, Sarah, has dark skin and looks like her father. Matthew, the boy, is white and blue-eyed. Gill has had to fight against all the prejudices that Sue experiences. But she is bold, strong and angry and takes on the bigots, shaming them.

When the children were young, these people would only admire Matthew. I would tell them that they had no right to do that to my other baby and they would apologise. One day when my dad had had too much to drink – the twins were eighteen months old – he suddenly blurted out that I had contaminated my Anglo-Saxon blood by having half-breeds. It felt as if someone was cutting through my heart. If my father who has held my children and cuddled them feels like this, what about others? But you know we are such a strong family and we both love each other so unconditionally, that it really doesn't make that much of a dent after the first few minutes. The pressures on the children worry me though. I am glad my son is white because he won't be picked on. I know it sounds bad, but if he looked Oriental he would have a harder time and no mother wants her child to be hurt. Sarah is essentially a beautiful child – and although it is strange having a child who does not look like you, I cannot now imagine her any other way. And we constantly tell her how lovely she is.[52]

During the course of writing this book, I came across a number of young mixed-race children and adults who, in spite of the many negative experiences of the sort described above, started to take control of their own lives. They embraced whichever identity felt most comfortable and then made it mean something and matter in their own terms. Jane Ifekwunigwe found many such examples in her detailed explorations with a group of mixed-race people in Bristol. One of them, Akousa, is light-skinned which meant much confusion, labelling and rejection in her early life. But as she matures, she more than knows who she is:

I see myself as 'black'. Other people see me as being 'half-caste' as some like to call it . . . [you ask yourself] 'Am I really who I think I am? Who I have decided I am?' All these people are trying to define who you are, tell you that 'you can't be black. Look how light you are!' or 'Your mother's white, so how can you be black?' I think white society has never accepted me. They have seen me as a contamination to their stock. Diseased person, even worse than havin' two black parents, worse than even that. If you come to extermination you would probably go first. Nazi Germany. That's the sort of vibe I get off white people. With black people generally, I know they have accepted me as I am. I have been part of their community. I have been raised within the Caribbean culture . . . I don't consider myself half of anything. I think I have become stronger about who I am. As I get older, I get firmer.[53]

But it is not only by opting for one 'clean' identity that such confidence of the self is acquired. For Shameera, half Pakistani, half Irish, it is her dual heritage that gives her an edge.

I love the way I look. Don't get me wrong, I am not showing off. But I love myself. My green eyes, black hair, smooth brown skin – all come together to make real beauty. So many mixed-race people are stunning looking. Look at Sade or Oona King or Michael Caine's daughter. And I love how it confuses people because they can't put you into a file marked black or white or Pakistani. I would not have had these head turning looks if I had been only Pakistani or only Irish. In fact both sides of the family are always saying how lovely we all are. You know Asians love light skin and eyes. And the Irish side with their white skin think I am really lucky. My cousin is always sticking on fake tan to look like me.

If this chapter shows anything it is that it is foolish to generalise about mixed-race families or to impose strong but false categories on them. Debates about identity and family rights go back to the sixteenth century. What is new however is that we now have a critical mass of young Britons who see themselves as mixed-race and who wish to challenge many of the assumptions that have been made about them for four centuries. They do not wish to be labelled by others. They do not wish to be subsumed by others. Most of all they do not wish to be patronised by those who always seem to know what their needs should be. This is why identity and terminology has become increasingly important when the issue of mixed race is raised.

Chapter 5
Family and Relationships

'I feel uneasy walking down the street with him, or taking public transport. There is a flicker of uneasiness in white men's eyes partly because black men with white women is one of the last great sexual taboos of our times. On the other hand at parties I have been ignored by black women. I am worried about our future children being the target of racism because it's not something I grew up experiencing which will make it harder for me to know how to help them.'
Jo-Ann Goodwin, a freelance journalist, who is married to a Brazilian interviewed in the *Daily Mail* in 1996.

'We have never had any hassle or nasty comments – not at all. We've noticed people looking but I think that's just because they are interested or curious rather than hostile. If you go to London or Brighton, there's lots of mixed couples so it is no longer a big deal.'
Caroline Owusu, black woman who has a white boyfriend, quoted in the *Express*, 1998.

'They are complete cowards. It is disgraceful. But what can you do? I suppose we are a fairly public mixed-race couple so if anyone has a hang up about it we get it.'
Dawn French after she and her husband Lenny Henry were threatened by the Ku Klux Klan in 1991.

'They burnt my hands. See? They scarred my face with a sharp pen. They tried to get me to kill myself by sitting around me and giving me Panadols in my hand. Go, they said, die before you bring shame and marry a Muslim.'
Gurinder, a Sikh, who fell in love with a Muslim in 1996.

'I am a white British woman and I am proud of my mixed-parentage children. I feel I have brought two wonderful people into the world and have unconditional love for my daughters.'
Lisa Smith, People in Harmony Calendar 2000.

Mixed-race families and couples have never had it so good. They are accepted, admired even and considered the most optimistic sign that the modern diversity of Britain is more than a superficial thing. Yet at the same time – and this is one of the complexities of race and society – individuals who follow their hearts also receive the message that they are deviant, wrong, a danger, guilty of base and uncontrolled sexuality and unconcerned about the children produced as a result of desire.

New research carried out by Jacques Janssen, in the Netherlands where 'heterogamy', as the researcher calls it, is still rare, concluded that: 'Homogeneous couples with a Dutch background have significantly lower rates of divorce than average, and mixed couples consisting of two foreigners have higher rates of divorce than average.' The research is not only about racial differences. All significant differences – status, age, education, wealth, religion – decrease stability within relationships. Janssen claims that:

> People might be able to get over different preferences and lack of support by the social environment in the beginning of a relationship or during a honeymoon period. Nevertheless, the expectation here is that after marriage, the lack of a common social background will bring about a higher divorce risk. Also after childbirth, problems due to heterogamy may arise when spouses discuss the raising of their children. Furthermore, even though the marriage partners may be willing to overcome differences and accept the in-law family and respective friends as they are, those family and friends may not be willing to do the same in return. This is beyond the control of the marriage partners and will result in a lack of support towards the marriage.[1]

That social support is more important than people believe, especially during periods of transition within nations when values and lifestyles are in flux. These particular times may be harder in some ways because there is already a major public panic about divorce and the general lack of stability in family life. Such research is vital because there is now an unprecedented number of 'mixed' relationships across the European Union. Divorce laws are different in the various nations which means agreeing to sensible settlements is made all the harder because there is so little common ground between the parties. Patriarchal societies, for example, have very different expectations from those with more egalitarian values. Gina married a Greek sailor whom she met on holiday. Five miserable years later, she fled back to her native Scotland. But she was not allowed to take her son:

> They are so backward I couldn't believe it. They are in the European Union but they behave as if they are living in the sixteenth century. They kept Alex. He was a boy, their son. He

can't even speak English any more. I regret all this so bitterly. And of course my parents think I was wrong to follow lust.

Society loves the rush which takes over when two people fall in love, but not always if the individuals are from different ethnic, religious or racial backgrounds. Most of the couples I interviewed said that many people they knew – from friends to family – assumed that it was lust or physical attraction or even ambition that moved them to gravitate towards such partners. The assumption is that the choice to go with someone racially or ethnically different comes out of something that is too emotional, untamed and intolerably risky. Very few people outside the relationships can see that the reason so many mixed-race couples choose each other is because they are true soul mates, intellectually and emotionally well matched. This is why they take the risks they do. Speaking on a television programme in 1999, the athlete Sharron Davies described how people did not understand that her relationship with her ex-partner, Derek Redmond, the black athlete, arose from the feeling that she had more in common with him than anyone else she had ever been out with.

For Sarita, a devout Hindu married to Chris, an English barrister, these prevailing attitudes do have an effect:

> My parents, who are quite broad minded, still believe, after ten years, that I was too impulsive and that our children will lose out because we could not be sensible and marry our own. And it goes in. His parents were coming out with the same trash, though less directly. This is why I think we are still without children. I am just too scared. What if they are proved right?

Yet mixed-race relationships (and children) are increasing and are here to stay. Between 1980 and 1990 there was an increase of 32 per cent of mixed-race babies. The number of mixed-race babies rose from 70,000 to 287,000.[2] The biggest difficulty facing such relationships, and therefore the children, is not one of inherent pathology or 'maladjustment' or 'deviancy', but of social stigma which exerts outside pressures. In 1996 when I tried to place my daughter in a Catholic primary school, the head said to me on the phone: 'Oh no, Mrs Brown. We don't take mixed kids. They are just mixed up aren't they? They are more trouble than we have time for.' I know about all this and yet I was so shocked I cried.

Although some mixed-race people do challenge such prejudices, many people in mixed relationships often have not talked about 'race' and treat difference as taboo. It is as if they cannot afford to look at negative attitudes so they lock themselves indoors and try to pretend that they do not exist. They believe that love is enough but often it is not enough at all.

Continuing resentment and hatred

Jenny Miller who is black and her white husband David are on constant alert to pre-empt and prevent what may confront them next. They have been spat at; he has been told by strangers that he should be shot. They feel that often people make assumptions that David could not find himself a white women and therefore had to make do with black. As Jenny says:

> People still torment, insult and patronise us although we have become used to it over the years. When we are out as a couple white people see their whiteness getting horribly mixed up with blackness and black people see the blackness disappearing. They are always looking for hidden motives. Neither can accept that we just fell in love like anyone else.[3]

Fiona now has profound mental and emotional problems and is unable to work. Her life has been destroyed by such attitudes. She met Ali, an African Muslim, when they were both university students. He was shy and studious and she was outgoing but unhappy about her size. She is a very attractive large woman with long blonde hair. She had never had any serious boyfriends because 'How could I let them see what my body looked like?' and so when she met Ali she had already decided that she was never going to have sex because she was 'too fat and gross'. Ali thought she was beautiful. African men, he told her, 'liked meat on their women'. Fiona found out the joys of being loved and wanted by a good man. They decided to get married when she was 26, five years after they had met. Ali did not believe in people living together. They told her parents, who were from Suffolk, and they were quite decent about it, but the day before the wedding, Fiona found her mother dead in the bathroom. She had taken an overdose and left a letter which said that she could not bear to see her daughter marrying 'a savage' and that it was all better this way. This was in 1986. Ali fled to Africa and has never been in touch. Fiona talks in such a broken way that it is impossible to quote her, but this is the gist of what she told me. The only further point of contact I had with Fiona – whom I met through a psychotherapist who knew I was working on this book – is a cutting she sent me of the story which broke a few years ago involving an under-age English school girl who married a handsome Turkish man whom she met on holiday. She too thought she was unattractive because she wasn't thin and conventionally beautiful. He thought she was quite lovely and adored her. Fiona obviously related to this deeply.

There has been a spate of stories in recent years where white hostility to mixed-race couples has manifested itself in even more terrifying ways. In June 1994, three white men were found guilty of attempted murder after they attacked a mixed-race couple at a garage in East London. Lynn Woodward who is white was with her black boyfriend, Kenneth Harris. The attackers abused her and called her a 'slut' and then beat up Harris and stabbed him with a screwdriver which pierced the bone in his leg. However the final act of barbarism was yet to come. The men got into Harris's car and drove it over him as he lay on the ground, bleeding and unable to move.[4] In 1998, Sunil Modi, a British Asian scriptwriter, and his white female partner were ambushed by a gang of white men and seriously assaulted. This was in Liverpool, the city with one of the oldest mixed-race populations in the country. The mixed-race McGowan family living in Telford, an area where racism festers but is not on the surface, have fought to open a new investigation into the so-called suicides of two young men in their family who were mysteriously found hanged over a six-month period. The wife of one of these men is white. One Saturday as I was watching her on a display television set in Dixons, on Ealing Broadway in West London, two white men standing next to me started abusing her and calling her a 'nigger's tart' who had it coming. The horrendous experiences of Mal Hussein, an Asian man, and his white partner Linda Livingstone are both unbearable and unbelievable. Since 1991 they have suffered over a thousand attacks on themselves and their shop and home. He has been in hospital and both now suffer from serious depression. The now separated Sharron Davies and Derek Redmond were once sent explosives hidden in a video cassette. The boxer Frank Bruno, his white wife and his mother had to request police protection because they were receiving so many serious threats against their lives. Dawn French and Lenny Henry too have found that fame makes them more, not less vulnerable to this hatred which comes mostly from strangers.

There is a tendency to believe that if you are middle class and living in urban Britain, this kind of resistance to mixed-race relationships is the exception rather than the rule. In a scathing article in the *Observer*, Richard Ellis, the former Africa correspondent of *The Sunday Times*, wrote about how false this view is. He is right. His son, when only eight, went with a relative and other people from different races to play a football match in Kent. They faced so much abuse that five years on he still worries about why 'white people hate black people'. Their white liberal friends have been astonished to hear Ellis's wife Martine telling them that things were harder for them in the UK than in South Africa because there you knew where you stood. As Ellis says:

I would certainly be more welcome in Soweto than my wife would be in Feltham... the statistics stink. The reality stinks. My son is more likely to be stopped, searched, arrested, sent to prison, than his twelve-year-old white cousin. He is more likely to be attacked on the street because of his skin colour. He is more likely to be regarded with suspicion when he walks into a shop. He is less likely to get a bank loan, more likely to be unemployed, less likely to get a promotion should he get a job. How does that make me feel about my fellow white Britons? So angry I can hardly articulate it; and so fed up with benign liberal platitudes every bit as ill-informed and ignorant as a BNP supporter, it makes me feel physically sick.[5]

Sad endings

While writing this book I looked back at some of the first person accounts in *The Colour of Love*. Most were eloquent testimonies, some optimistic, others fearful for the future. I tried to trace what happened to some of these people over the subsequent decade and although a number remain rock solid together, there certainly is no cause for facile cheerfulness.

Several of the couples have broken up, some very bitterly. Their personal pain is compounded by the knowledge that their fight to prove society wrong failed. As one of the disappointed lovers put it: 'All relationships can fail. They do all the fucking time. But when the white lover of a black woman turns out to be a bastard, what you feel is that you have been punished for being a traitor, for being so blind to history. For sleeping with the enemy.'

At times individuals begin to learn – and it is a very painful lesson – that 'adventures' with people from another background have a limited time span and that in the end many people seek the comfort of what they know best. The angry black woman above now only wants black boyfriends: 'When they go wrong, I know it is the man in him and not his colour and a whole history of hate.'

What is so very sad is that even the couples who were enthusiastic and bold have fallen by the wayside for all sorts of other unpredictable reasons. Separations are always messy and hard, but race adds a further dimension, without doubt. The journalist and novelist Shyama Perera was born in Russia of Sri Lankan parents and came to Britain when she was five. Her (now ex-) husband, journalist David Rose, was born to a Jewish family. Shyama and David were expecting their first child when they were interviewed for *The Colour of Love*. Shyama had grown up as a Londoner living in close proximity to all racial groups and confined to none:

My mother had a relationship with the white community that was based on mistrust and fear. I didn't. I was blossoming, an adolescent, I had nice clothes. The boys would pay attention. I knew I was Sri Lankan, but I didn't feel that it made me different. Whereas my mother dressed in a sari, and if she walked across a group of skinheads they'd shout out 'Paki', if I walked past they would whistle at me – the opposite reaction.

So from that early age I had strong views about how you integrated. I was very critical of my mother for not having English friends, I felt that as long as she thought of herself as different, she would always be different.

All my boyfriends were white, apart from one Asian and one Nigerian, but it was never an issue. I never met any Sri Lankans. I wasn't averse to meeting Sri Lankans or Asian men but there really weren't Asian men around who were on the right kind of wavelength for me. I always knew I would marry a white man, although I never thought about it in those terms. I knew when I started going out with David, I knew he was the one.

By that stage my mum was very grateful to get me married; I was getting beyond a marriageable age in her eyes. At first she was worried because he's Jewish and from a very orthodox family but he's not religious. I asked him whether he wanted me to convert to Judaism if he wanted the child brought up Jewish, but he categorically does not. His family are brilliant. They had given up any hope of him marrying a Jewish girl.

David has since left and has a new family. His new partner is white. His two young mixed-race daughters live with their mother who says she is watching with interest how they relate in time to their new white step-brother.

Frank Crichlow who came to Britain from the Caribbean in the fifties and Lucy Addington who was his white partner for many years have also separated after years of sticking together through terrible times, including Frank being accused of drug-dealing in his restaurant, The Mangrove, in Notting Hill Gate. This erupted when Lucy was pregnant with their fourth child and although the police subsequently paid compensation, the Crichlows' lives were turned over for ever. Frank was one of the founders of the Notting Hill Carnival. Ten years ago Lucy said to me:

All our friends, black and white, were such a tremendous support, often in a practical way. I suppose you could look at it as a positive demonstration of how black and white people can get it together in this way in spite of all the racism out there...It makes your relationship very strong. In fact maybe it is more difficult now the pressure is off up to a point...I have no regrets about being with Frank. I have had to find hidden strengths and ways of living and thinking to deflect the stress.

Frank added:

It is important to stress that a lot of white people who are political and involved in community politics do think of themselves differently from the old days. They turn up at meetings and demonstrations – they like to show they are not like the rest. That took off in the sixties in the hippie days. Relationships across the races, like mine and Lucy's, began through that. If you ask me if I felt a sense of guilt or impurity being with a white woman, the answer is no, emphatically no.

Today both couples, who knew what they were doing, who had thought things through, are apart and their children will have to navigate not only all the treacherous waters produced by the storms in the heart which follow parental separation, but they will have all the additional issues of identity and identification to carry as well.

Rejection of mixed-race relationships by non-white Britons

Britain is now a diverse society which is gradually coming to terms with itself. But white and non-white people still fear and resent mixed-race relationships. Baroness Howells, who has been a prominent fighter against racism for decades, recalls how when she married John, her white husband, black people would say behind her back that she was 'black by day and white by night', judgemental comments which, she says, both infuriated and hurt her.[6]

Asians with a very self-protective view of their cultures have been savagely intolerant too. But black resentment is relatively new. In the past, Caribbeans especially embraced mixed-race families with greater ease than some are able to do today. Loanna Morrison, a journalist and a black woman, wrote in *Pride Magazine* in 1994:

> I do find it bizarre that famous and successful black men never settle down with a decent black woman after they become famous. I can understand that as successful blacks they mix with other successful people who are bound to be mostly white. But these guys weren't always famous. They had black girlfriends before. Why can't they drag one or two good black women after them? If they still do have black girlfriends they'll go to bed with them and even have children with them. But they will never marry them. They won't even take them out. I think they are ashamed of black women. They can't take them into polite company because they won't know how to mix.[7]

Ms Morrison herself was once married to a Polish man. At the time she wrote this, she was linked to Andrew Neil, editor and broadcaster, who is from Scotland.

The negative reactions of black women to 'their' men having white partners can be extreme. In 1995, for example, Channel 4 ran a series called *Doing it With You is Taboo* presented by the black journalist Donnu Kogbara. The aim of the programmes appeared to be to titillate, to represent mixed-race relationships as grotesque. In one, three black women raucously discussed their views on why white women were so undesirable. They smelt, said one, because they did not know how to wash their private parts. One black woman said that white women were not as sexy as black women and that she could not understand at all why black 'brothers' went for them. Another claimed that black men prefer white women because they get an easier time, because the women are easily fooled and pliant.

There are explanations why some black women react in this way. For a large number of them, the quest for a good black man who will nurture them and their children has been a disappointing one. Black men are among the groups most discriminated against in this country. In some inner city areas, over 60 per cent of them are unemployed; they are over represented in prisons and often leave school with few qualifications. It has to be said too that a macho gang culture is emerging among some young black men. Add to this the large numbers of black men who choose white partners and the shortage of long-term black partners for black women becomes an even more acute problem.

Jill has lived for a long time with black disapproval because of her marriage to a Nigerian man: 'The English family weren't happy but they were under control, I made sure of that. I have had to cope with outspoken anti-English Nigerians, lawyers, doctors, all sorts who picked on me for ten years.' That combined with abuse from white bigots has made for a challenging life. Her son, now a teenager, is often so provoked that he sometimes feels like reacting physically, because he feels that he is the keeper of his mother's honour.

In 1989, the influential US radical black writer Shahrazad Ali wrote in her book, *The Blackman's Guide to Understanding the Blackwoman*: 'Dating and marrying the white man is another flimsy excuse to get out of the inevitable submitting to the black man – it seems that Black woman and white America are in cahoots with each other against the Black man. This is not the way it is supposed to be.' She goes on to attack the 'unnatural' scenes in movies where black men are seen kissing and making love to white women.[8] I personally believe such ideas to be dangerous because they espouse an essentialist idea of race and culture.

But why do so many obviously thoughtful people find mixed-race relationships so uncomfortable? Eriq LaSalle, the black doctor in the successful hospital series ER, complained that the script reinforced certain assumptions. His relationships with black and mixed-race women had all failed and he was shown to have found real fulfilment with a white woman: 'It sends a message I am not comfortable with,' he told *Hello* magazine in March 1999. This is an interesting divergence from the old criticisms that Hollywood most shies away from white American woman in sexual relationships with black men. On screen mixed-race relationships have always been an affront to white racists. But today they alarm black Americans too. Integration remains as elusive as ever and is arguably harder today in the United States because of increasingly intense anxieties felt by non-whites and whites about cultural annihilation.

For this book I organised a number of group meetings with young black men, all fathers and in relationships with white or black women. This 'focus group' approach produced various insights. Vincent is bitter that anyone should want to sleep with a white person because 'the white man has not yet said sorry for all that he did'. He feels that black women are so flattered to go with white men that they are not as tough on them as they would be on black men. But then, an hour later, he told me that he had a white partner and kids he loves. 'But one day I would love a black wife. My kids are not too white. They have a good colour. But still to have an all-black child is my dream.'

Patrick, a Rastafarian and writer, never goes with white women:

It destroys our values. My grandmother told me when I was five that I should never go with a white woman. Some white women – especially middle-class, nicely brought up ones – they love a bit of black rough. They have spent too long with Mr Square. And they deliberately get pregnant without thinking who will be the role models for the children.

Professor Lola Young has said that in her view:

It is a hot and contentious subject with the black community, with accusations of deserting the race and an underlying anxiety that it will be wiped out. There is a lot of trophy-ism in all relationships, especially connected to celebrities and status. Going with black men is trophy-ism too, the exoticism of otherness. It is also an act of defiance and rebellion.[9]

These deep fears are important to remember, but they cannot excuse inexcusable attitudes. Brother Sulaiyman of the organisation Islamic Action says that such intolerance is spreading. At some 'black' meetings apparently there are some mixed-race adults who stand up and denounce their own white mothers as 'dogs' and 'jackals': 'These are the women who raised them, who cared and looked after them, but the children feel betrayed and don't want to know.' Sulaiyman believes these volatile emotions show that mixed-race relationships have no future.[10]

Many others worry that the melting pot is melting away all traces of blackness. Marcia Williams, an Afro-Caribbean author, takes a very hard line on this subject. In an exchange of views with the black journalist Maurice McLeod, who is in a mixed-race family, she wrote:

Where does this trend to blend come from? Is it an attempt to lose our black selves? As we have been told over and over that we are worthless and problematic? To make the world a melting pot of beige people so that the black and white races die out...You can adopt a culture but a race is something you inherit. It's our lips, our backsides, our hair and eyes...A black-on-black union is so much more spiritually fulfilling for the two people and also their children. We have a duty to keep the bloodline going.

McLeod argues back saying that 'bloodlines are already mixed' and that 'living in a multi-cultural society means accepting our differences and revelling in them.'[11] Often the lived experiences of people such as McLeod are drowned out by criticism. But their views are as valid as anyone else's.

What colour is love?

Some black and Asian people seem to have such strong and at times worrying views about why they prefer white women that it feels treacherous to listen to them. But honest accounts, even brutal ones, are an essential part of this complicated narrative. Terry, 35, and Dee, 33, have been together ever since I first interviewed them in 1990. He is black and she is white, both fitness trainers and very much in love. Terry says:

> I know I will be killed for saying this but I would not go out with a black woman. They always act like they need nobody. They are defensive, demanding. There is nothing feminine about them. My mum hassled my dad till he died. Nothing he did was ever good enough. So what did he do? He had a white mistress secretly. I met her twice. She was not a clever woman or good looking but she gave him love. The best thing about her was that she spoke quietly. Then my mum started picking on me. Dee is sexy, gentle, giving. She has been through hell with her folk but she has never given up on me. There is something delicate about European women, something that turns me on. I like the slim look. Most black women don't have that. I hate bright red lipstick on a black face. And those tight dresses. Dee looks like an angel. She needs no fucking make-up. Maybe because history has been so hard on us, black men and women can't make it together. There is too much shared pain for romance and love. Maybe deep inside I have grown to believe the stories of white beauty and purity. But I am happy with Dee so does it matter?[12]

The irony is of course that as increasing numbers of black women (especially those who are moving up the economic ladder faster than black men) take white partners, black men are getting uneasy that their sisters should be 'shaming the race' in this way. The black broadcaster Henry Bonsu says:

> A few years ago it was common to hear black women say they did not want a mixed-race child. But now they are no longer ruling it out. Women try to find a black partner for longer. They have a strong sense of seeing themselves with a black man and it takes years to shift that. But I think in the next few years we are going to see an avalanche.[13]

I do understand the strength of feeling. Too many men are 'lost' to the white community and too many black women who want to make families with decent black men feel let down by this. There is a history too to take into account. As Chapter 2 shows, the early migrants from the Caribbean were mostly men who within a short time started relationships with white British women. Some had wives and girlfriends back home who did not know about this. When the women arrived there was much emotional turmoil as they dealt with their previously 'hidden' white rivals. Elma is one such woman who is now in her seventies. She is an extraordinary woman with a story which she has kept to herself for many years:

> I came, all tall and proud. You know I was nearly Miss Trinidad once. To find that James, a man of God, had fathered a child with an Irishwoman who had then died.
>
> Can you imagine? I arrived with my wedding dress hand made by my aunt and full of such hope. Well, as if the cold weather and cold people weren't enough, three weeks before the wedding James says he's got this child which we will have to have. The mother died you know. I looked at this baby and just cried. We never did get married. But we stayed together for a few years and I got to love Estella. Of course it was hard when people asked if I was the babyminder. But what was I? With James I understood he was lonely and all that. But he should have told me before and not after I came. He died last year and before that I had forgiven him. The Lord wants that anyway. But I never married. The dress is still there. Do you want to see it?

I was shown the dress, lovingly wrapped in bubble wrap as if it would break. And it was hard not to cry. Another man, Tony, had a relationship with Moira, also an Irishwoman. It is extraordinary how many Irishwomen have had black partners over the last fifty years. One reason for the attraction must come out of a common experience of discrimination. This couple married in 1970 but it was only in 1980, three children later, that he told his family back home in Jamaica about them:

I was stupid. They had no problems at all, at all with it. My father said that we were all mixed anyway in the Caribbean so why bother with all this purity nonsense. Moira became one of ours and the children say they are black Irish which is fine by us. I think I felt guilty for no reason. Yes, I had a fiancée back home but I broke off as soon as I met Moira but to be honest did not tell her the real reason. We were so eager when we arrived here and when we were treated so badly at work and all that, it was important to find love among the whites. I was not proving anything. Only that like in all races, there is good and bad. I could not have had a more caring wife.

There is one fact which should not be lost in all this complexity and that is that whatever new anxieties Afro-Caribbeans may now have about mixed relationships, they have been less disapproving than any other group. Tony, a mixed-race adult living in Liverpool, is umbilically attached to the black community he has known all his life:

They never gave up on me. They told me I was one of their add-on sons, come to make their numbers bigger. They live with who I am. I never have to explain myself. With my white family I am always a guest, tolerated on sufferance. I have read the history and spoken to people. This is always what Caribbean people have done with biracial children. They have humanity.

White mothers and the nurturing of mixed-race children

White mothers of mixed-race children have confusing emotions and reactions to their own lives and to what they have done. Shelly is a very strong woman who has been married to Will, Jamaican British, for forty years. They have one daughter who looks South American. Shelly is delighted:

I did not want a child who looked too black. We live here in Surrey as a typical middle-class family. Race is nothing to do with us. Will is not like other black men. He is like one of us. He just mixes in, not making a fuss about racism and all that rubbish. He is loved in the village because there aren't too many coloureds here. That Stephen Lawrence case, well I think too much fuss was made about it. What about whites who are killed by blacks? And our daughter who was mugged by a black guy? I think we are all human and should stop talking so much about race and that.

Will said nothing and did not want to add his views. He sat reading the *Telegraph* and ignored the conversation. When I asked him what he thought he said: 'Well we are all the same race, the human race.'

Some lone white mothers find themselves in an impossible situation, lonely, unthanked, and one cannot blame them if their children end up in care. But most do not succumb. They are proud and able mothers who try to bring up their children with a sense of both their identities.

Marion is white and a mother of seven, four her own biological children and three adopted mixed-race children. They span from thirty-three to thirteen. She parted from her Nigerian partner just after her fourth child was born. She loves her children fiercely and her pride is palpable as she tells me how one is a Radio 4 producer, another a graphic designer, the third a university researcher and the fourth a performance artist. She warns me not to stay on the phone too long in case something happens in school and her children are trying to reach her. She brought her own children up in Gateshead, Newcastle where there were hardly any people of colour and the schools were all white:

> I brought them up to believe in themselves. Racism, which they do face, is not their fault. The problem is inside the person being racist. I taught them not to look for it but never ever to ignore it when it happened. They were taught – not to fight – but to make their views known. To show that they were not prepared to tolerate this kind of thing. We don't think about race all day long but we do talk about it when the subject comes up. Sometimes it has been hard on my own but you cope because there is no alternative. I have no regrets and I have never regretted having them, not ever, not even secretly. I think it is tragic when women with mixed-race children feel they have to put their children into care which is why I adopted the three young ones.

Marion never claims any of this is easy. One of the girls she has adopted, for example, insists she is 'brown' and is revolting against her own tightly curly hair. Society, says Marion, sees her children as black, which is fine, but she thinks of them as mixed-race, giving equal validity to both sides. What has helped, she says, is the support she has had from her own family who were very anxious before the children arrived, but fell in love with them when they were not a hypothetical fear in their heads but real flesh and blood. Her son, the journalist, says that everything he has achieved comes from the fierce love and support he has always had from his wonderful mother.

Sue Norris is also a brilliant mother with three mixed-race children and an abusive partner long departed. For her it has been more difficult, mainly because her own family has never accepted her children. She herself was adopted and when she traced her birth mother, she was told not to bring her children over to see their grandmother because she found them embarrassing. George, her partner, had become more and more demanding: 'He said black women were better in bed. I remember one day after we had sex, I just cried and cried, saying I wanted to be alone, to sleep without him always inside me. He got up and left. My friends said he was a black bastard. I told them he was just a man.' Her children are all different, some dark and others light. She finds it hard to feel positive about them all the time and is ashamed of the way she lets racists influence how she feels.

In 1992 I wrote an article in the *Guardian* about white women in mixed-race marriages. Audrey Kureishi, mother of Hanif, wrote a letter to the paper in response:

> I was most interested to read 'Love in a Cold Climate'. I can't imagine what the fuss is all about. My husband was born in India, I in Bromley. Sadly my husband, Shanoo, died in November but we did have 37 years of happy marriage. My son, Hanif Kureishi, and daughter, Yasmin, have done very well in life and have many friends. Children find it difficult at school, but then young people can be very cruel; it's not just black children who suffer...[14]

The more modern white mothers of mixed-race children feel just as positive in some ways but are perhaps more aware of the difficulties faced by their children. Sue Funge, who co-runs the training and consultancy company Celebrating Identity, is one such mother. She is a lone parent but says that she is grateful that she has her son to bring up and feels herself to be deeply fortunate to have been given this experience , 'this incredible opportunity'.

The most impressive women I met were those who do not play down the problems they face as white mothers of mixed-race children, but still retain an enormous commitment to their families and the decisions they have made about whom to love and marry. Kay Reece is one such woman. She has been married to Winston for many years and they have two children:

> If you walked into my house you would be able to tell that it is not just a white British house by the pictures, books and things around. We've got a portrait of a black man at a piano which dominates the front room, we've got a painting from Egypt and lots of political things in the kitchen. Things from South Africa for example...If you came and sat with us over dinner, these issues are constantly talked about. I've become a white mother in a black household. As far as you can, while still obviously remaining white, you take on the hurt of racism against your children – initially perhaps you take it on more. It is possible that at some stage when they are teenagers, they will reject me because I am white. I hope it is only a phase, but I have to give them space to do that, however much it hurts. The things you take on are lifelong, you don't realise it until you go into such a

relationship. How can you? But I wouldn't change a thing. I've been with my (Jamaican) husband for 16 years. We have two children and a good relationship, unlike many of our friends who are now getting divorced. However, love is not enough. A mixed relationship is definitely a relationship under pressure and so needs more awareness, because there are changes once you have children (some good and some bad), with the grandparents, relatives and friends. I still do wonder, if somebody is racist to the children and they come home and I'm the only one there, whether they will see me only as white, rather than as their mother. If that happens, I need to be able to give her the right answer for her and for me, to fortify them for the world outside. This is a self-doubt that doesn't occur if you're a black woman in a black family or a white man in a white family. Take, for example, the question of where to go on holiday. We probably would not go to Germany and, while black families also say that they worry about where to go, there is an extra dimension to the venom of racists when they see a mixed couple. This raises two issues about the children's future welfare that it is important for mixed families to think about.[15]

Mixed-race relationships and Asian families, old ways and new responses

With white/Asian marriages, as many interviewees in this book testify, most families still react with bewilderment and hostility. They blame the individuals and then blame themselves or the mother who is the person with the duty to ensure that cultures and religions remain uncontaminated. Again, just as with the Afro-Caribbean community, it is important to understand these reactions without necessarily approving of them. Many Asian families are only just beginning to understand the dynamics of immigration. The assumption was that people could emigrate in order to improve their economic prospects without anything else changing at all. They found instead that family members began to be influenced by the society in which they were living. This does not mean that they all started to dissolve into some hot pot, but that all boundaries became porous and a new British Asian culture started to emerge, as far back as the fifties. Certainly by the sixties and seventies it became ever more difficult to talk about Asian communities as unchanging outposts of the subcontinent. Hanif Kureishi's *Buddha Of Suburbia* and *My Son the Fundamentalist* both concern themselves with these transformations. Baroness Shreela Flather, the first Asian to enter the House of Lords (as a Conservative) has long been married to her white husband. Yet she never appears anywhere in public without her sari, a real statement that it is possible to marry out and adapt to new homelands while still retaining a deep link with your heritage. She seems not to have suffered rejection from her community but for most Asian women it has not been easy. Among those who have wanted to marry out or who have actually done so, there has often been a terrible price to pay. Some have lost all contact with the family and community; others stay on the outside of both while being tolerated superficially.

Yasmina, a Muslim with a Scottish husband, is one of these women.

> After our children were born my parents started accepting this marriage even though Don didn't convert. They were happy that I called the children Reza and Miriam. But there is a glass wall between us. I am an outsider and my sisters speak to each other in Urdu but to me in English as if I have given up my mother tongue. My children are not invited for the main family Eid celebrations but we are asked for dinner later which we eat with knives and forks. Don's family are the same. They treat us well but with polite distance. I had to tell them that it was OK to give our children Christmas presents. None of Don's friends have invited us over, not once.

There are other developments which are important to recognise. More Asian women are marrying white men and in some communities genuine approval is given. Asian women who have moved up the professional and educational ladders do seem, in greater numbers, to be choosing white men. Preeti is fairly representative:

> When I was studying at Manchester University there were a lot of Asian men but I think they are too spoilt by their mums to think that they are kings with ladoos (sweetmeats) in their gobs. I am very ambitious and most Asian men change after marriage. They don't encourage their wives and are scared if we aim too high. With white men, there is no question that you can follow your dreams and be a wife. Maybe I am painting them too perfectly but many of my friends who are married to Asian men have much less scope to work long hours and all that than I do.

Among some Hindu families, parents are themselves becoming keen on a nice English boy with a good job and background because they never demand dowries which have become cripplingly high in some communities. Rohit Patel proudly shows me pictures of two of his daughters who have married out and one who had the traditional wedding with another Patel:

> Once is enough. Even my chest hair turned white giving thousands of pounds for the first one. I don't mind, she is my blood. But I think these customs are stupid and we should stop

them. Paul and Simon they had a proper Hindu wedding with all the nice clothes but no rubbish dowries and hundreds of relatives. Culture? What culture? We have got the culture of the Mercedes Benz and big houses, nothing else.

Some Asian marriage bureaux have started matching 'good' white men with Asian women, sometimes older or divorced women who have the blessings of the family. And even more interestingly white men disillusioned with white feminists are coming into these match-making services to find 'submissive' Asian woman who will give them what they want (curry, housekeeping and sex) without making too many demands.
Martin is one of these men:

I went to this place and paid £500. Still nothing compared to going to Thailand and buying a bride. Summi, is thirty, divorced and great looking. We have been together six months and I have never been happier. You know she massages my feet! She knows how to please and knows that if she does that I am her pussy cat. I was married twice before. White women need to come for lessons here.

Summi smiles wickedly and says:

For every foot massage I get trunkfuls of love, appreciation, as much money as I want to spend and a guy who makes me laugh and doesn't take me for granted. My mother and aunt taught me that if you make a man feel he is the most important thing in your life, he will do anything for you. And whatever feminists think, battling against men just brings out the animal in them.

But we should not forget the inhumane reactions of some Asian families when they find that their children have gone beyond the fences so carefully built around their lives. In one prominent Asian family a son killed himself after running away and marrying someone from another ethnic group. The suicide came soon after he was discovered by his father and uncles. Kasia Myers had an Asian boyfriend, Hardip Samra. They were going to get engaged when he was beaten up by a gang of Asian men who disapproved of this relationship. He lost consciousness and his face was severely bruised. Samra's family closed rank and in March 2000 Myers said, 'I don't think we will get married now. I think there will be pressure on him from the Indian community.'[16]
I met Amina a few years ago. She had been in a relationship with a Polish man and had a child by him. Her family rejected her and then he left and has never been in touch. Her mother told her they would have her back as long as she put her baby up for adoption. When I met her she was not sure what she would do but she knew she could no longer live so isolated a life.

Arguably the worst of these cases is the ongoing saga of Jack and Zena. These young people, a white working-class man and Muslim girl from the north, have been married and on the run from her family for over seven years. Zena's family wants nothing less than her death and they have hired bounty hunters – Asian men who charge hundreds of pounds for this service – to find Zena. Jack's mother's house has been ransacked and she has been threatened because she will not reveal where her son is. In their own written account of this story which cannot be read without rage, John McCarthy writes in the preface:

It is very hard to believe that this is happening in Britain today. But it is and the story raises important questions about how we move on as a multiracial society. How can a family be free to plan to kill a daughter and the man she loves while the establishment appears unable or unwilling to work for a resolution? It is too simple to say that her family must just be made to drop their threats. Their actions come out of a cultural tradition that needs to be better understood before it can be reformed...It is a tragic irony that it is Jack and Zena, the victims of this awful culture clash, who are the shining light of race relations in this country...Zena remains a devout Muslim, with a commitment to her family and community. Jack remains proud of his wife's different background and traditions and is keen to understand them as she is to understand his.[17]

In many Asian women's refuges you find young women who have fled from their families whom they love, in order to escape forced marriages. According to a number of workers in these agencies, these women then end up with white or black men because they have no other option. Sometimes they are in love. Sometimes they don't know any better and go off with violent or under-educated men. If the relationships break up, the girls end up on the streets. They are truly social outcasts.

As we have seen already, some of the worst reactions from Asian families arise when Asian women pick black men as partners. Bali Kaur was beaten with a belt and thrown out of her home when her Sikh family found out about her black boyfriend Patrick. Her father will not allow anyone in the family to speak to his daughter who is 'dead' in his eyes. As he said to me ten years ago: 'I was like a mad lion when I saw her with that monkey. They are animals. They don't know how to work, to make good lives. They are not like Asians.' Her mother wept for years, missing her only daughter:

She is my life. My dream was to get her married, like all Asian mothers, to have a big wedding with gold and all that. She phoned and her father put the phone down. A mother loves her daughter too much. She made a mistake. But my husband is a hard man. How can I die without seeing her? He has even destroyed her pictures, even baby ones. We should not have left Punjab.

Bali is prematurely grey and now living alone, working as a social worker. She never again saw her mother who has since died. The guilt killed her love for Patrick who is married to another Asian woman. She says Asians are the most intolerant people in the world and that she is 'ashamed of the hypocrisy – not even another Asian religion is good enough'.

Yet Bali was comparatively lucky. Seventeen-year-old Gurdev Sohal, a Sikh girl, was in love with Geno Alseed, a West Indian. Soon after her family found out, she hanged herself. At the inquest a counsellor at the college where Gurdev was studying said that the young girl had sought help from her because she felt she was under intolerable pressure: 'She said that when she admitted seeing the boy, her father had stood on a chair, hung up a piece of cloth and invited her to put her head in the noose.'[18]

Inter-faith relationships

As religious identity becomes more important to people there are new issues to tackle concerning the dynamics of inter-faith families. Sometimes, simply in order to make life easy, one partner converts. At other times, the conversion is the result of a change in values. Patricia converted to Islam before she married Aziz, a Muslim doctor:

I went to mosque for months before I decided on the conversion. I was worried about not being able to drink and giving up bacon and covering myself and all that. It all sounds silly now. I don't miss any of it. I have more respect for myself. Aziz had to get permission from the religious leader and his family. If they had not been persuaded this could not have happened. Our children know that they are mixed-race but one religion and that makes them feel whole, not two halves.

For Flora, Islam has given her more than a husband and family:

I was a waitress in a nightclub. I smoked, drank, did drugs. Men were in and out of my life, my flat, my body. I had to have them to tell myself I was something. Then I met Tazdin. He was the accountant in the club. We became friends and I realised he saw me as a person, not just a sexy woman. He and I talked differently, about the world and life. I fell in love with him and converted. I started wearing the hijab and living like a good Muslim person. I love it. It has been fifteen years and I have missed nothing. I have an Open University degree and I feel self-respect.

It is not clear that other kinds of inter-faith relationships have resolved these tensions. There are a million Catholic-Protestant marriages on the mainland of the UK. The pressures to bring up the children as Catholics still prevail and can have a subtle influence on families, even those who do not think religion is important. Catholicism does not always easily co-exist with 'partner' faiths.

But this mutually respectful co-existence is what Derek Barnes and his wife Rohini have chosen in deciding to keep their different faiths. Rohini is a devout Hindu and her husband is a Church of England vicar. Derek explained:

> Soon after we met my colleagues started putting pressure on me and said it would be better if she converted. That's the assumption, particularly among the evangelical wing of the Christian church. We decided that we'd keep our separate faiths; we never saw them as two watertight compartments but ones that would flow into each other. So Rohini would come to church and play the part of the vicar's wife and I'd go to the Hindu temple and all the major festivals...

Rohini's family were upset for the first few months but now they have accepted the choices made by the couple. She found it hard when people said to her that the only way to God was through Christ, but love and mutual respect has seen them through these times and the two children are free to choose the religion with which they feel most comfortable. So far it is Hinduism which is winning, Derek thinks because their Indian identity is so strong through living in Southall.

Sexual fantasies

There is a further issue in mixed-race relationships which is so dangerous that most people do not talk openly about it. This is the question of how much racial and sexual stereotypes and fantasies play a part in pushing people into mixed-race relationships. The rise in mail-order brides and the lure of the slavish Eastern maiden in these post-feminist times does seem real enough. A number of white men are convinced that in order to be treated as real men, they have to go elsewhere, to those places where feminism is not even a whisper inside the heads of women. Terro, a pub owner from Leeds, is alarmingly clear about this:

> No man can keep it up with a woman who thinks she is better than him. Nature made us aggressive, conquering. We need to have the softness and obedience of women to be real men. Only Asian woman – Chinese, Japanese, Indian, Javanese – know how to do this so I have had three wives from those parts and when I

have finished, I send them away with a grand in their pockets and you know what? They are grateful.

Stephen Komlosy, who is married to the black singer Patti Boulaye, knows the power of that other fantasy – the sexy black woman:

> Men do find her terribly attractive, especially white men. I know it's there, but I don't react to it; in fact I am immune to it. It is lust, I suppose. Part of it comes from the fact that Patti is very attractive, but as a black woman maybe she evokes some folk memories of slavery, of black women being available, of being forced...Some funny things have happened. I was once standing watching Patti on stage and the man standing next to me, turned to me and said: 'I would really like to give her one.' I turned to him and said: 'I frequently do.' I didn't say anything else and it suddenly dawned on him who I was and he apologised.[19]

The most taboo fantasy of all still is that of the black man with a large penis. White women attracted to black men are always suspected of being drawn by this myth and at times black men themselves believe that they are especially good lovers. Bad is a bouncer in a nightclub: 'Have you ever been with a black man? No? Scared or what? You have had no sex until you have been with a black man, sister. They are all gagging for it. We have the equipment and the know-how. That is why white guys want to kill us. They know they have no chance with us around.'

Beauty, a mixed-race prostitute in London, says she plays to the fantasies that her clients have built up about certain racial and ethnic 'types'. 'I am half Indian and half black Caribbean. So for those who want a sex slave, I dress up as an Arabian princess and play that. They go away very happy. Those who want the dominating wild black woman who will bite their flesh off can have that too.'

These views may offend, but they are very much a part of the sex industry which often plays on and plays out fantasies. You only have to look at the advertisements put up by sex workers in phone boxes to see how both clients and prostitutes are attracted by sexual and racial stereotypes. These are not only restricted to the (often sordid) world of commercial sex. In several books where ordinary people are asked about their sexual fantasies, the same stereotypes appear.[20]

Gay couples

One group of people who have never been researched in this area are mixed-race gay couples and what follows is nowhere near enough. I spoke to a dozen of them in London and found that this small sample fell into two camps: the super-confident who see themselves as progressives and people free of hidebound prejudices of all sorts, and those who are frightened and feel burdened by their sexuality. Raj is a handsome Indian who has only had white lovers. He is now HIV positive and has dropped all contact with his close-knit community in Coventry:

> I have to have white lovers. If I ever went with an Asian everyone would know and there would be hell to pay, not only for me but my younger sisters. At times with my white lovers I feel I'm just a bit of the other. They often cannot treat me as an equal. It is quite imperialist. You know, like they have got their own Arab boy to bugger.

Soni feels even more trapped:

> I wish I had never been born. I am always with whites and doing things that all my upbringing teaches me is corrupt and wrong. Have I sold out? Have I become too white? My dream? To have a nice Asian partner and get the blessings of my parents. The moon would turn green before that can happen.

Some of the happiest mixed-race couples I know are gay. They seem to have developed an understanding because they know all about discrimination on several fronts. There is that deep awareness which comes out of a shared history of exclusion and the result can be long-term stability and a relationship which is supportive and strong where there is no need to explain things all the time.

Perhaps the best known mixed-race gay relationship in this country is the one between Lord Alli and Charlie Parsons. They have been together a long time and with Bob Geldof set up the successful television company Planet 24, which makes programmes for young adults. They are rich, urbane, popular and powerful and a symbol of modernity. Shahida is a lesbian who is very much part of this new gay elite: 'My partner is Italian and we run our own design store. It is small, select, very expensive and most of the customers are mixed-race gay couples. For us, breaking taboos is no longer an issue. We live as free spirits.'

But Sujata and Irene believe this is nonsense. Their lives are invaded by doubt, torment and abuse. They could not rent a place together for months because they said they were a couple. Some of the landlords were Asian and some white: 'They look at us and see double impurity. First mixed-race sex and then same-sex sex. I have seen looks in the eyes of Patels and others which told us that they would prefer us dead. One of these people said we were worse than prostitutes.'

Step families

A relatively new phenomenon but nevertheless a very important one is the emergence of mixed-race step families. My impression – but this is not a sociological fact – is that the most common pattern is where black or Asian women with mixed-race children form new relationships with white men who are themselves single or living apart from their children from a previous relationship. The old enemy – the white man – becomes the person who replaces black and Asian fathers, at least in the day-to-day upbringing of the mixed-race children. The actor Mark Wingett from the television series *The Bill*, who adopted the eleven-year-old Jamaican-born son of his black partner Sharon, said in 1991 that the two of them were 'the best thing in his life'.

My husband Colin helped to bring up my son Ari, who was ten when his Asian father left us for an English woman. The dynamics of this are enormously complicated. On top of all the usual divided loyalties that divorce brings, there are racial loyalties to deal with too. Freddie has been such a stepfather to three mixed-race children, now all at university:

It was really hard at times. Their dad was unemployed for years, not through any fault of his own. I had a big house, my own business and money which could give the boys a good life. The eldest hated me for years and said that he felt polluted living with a white man. The other two have found it easier to love me without guilt, but they do say that their father is the only one who lost out. I agree but he never was a family man from what I know. I felt worried when I had to take charge. They must have thought I was acting like a big white bwana. But they didn't know how scared I was.

But what happens when non-white men or women take on the role of step-parent to white children? When Pat Fleming married her husband Karl in the fifties her white children suddenly found themselves victims of racial abuse. Pat nearly gave up: 'I considered breaking up with him. But I so wanted to be with him that I couldn't. I also thought that the children would have an advantage being in a family with a black step-father. They would learn that we were all the same under the colour. They would have a close-up view of that.'[21]

One of the most tragic examples of how difficult it is to do this was Jan Martin Pasalbessi, a forty-eight-year-old man originally from Indonesia. His white partner died in 1994 leaving her daughter, Christina, then twelve-years-old. As a stepfather Jan was devoted to Christina, but some people in the Welsh community in which they lived would not accept this unusual family. In 2000, when Christina was bullied and physically attacked by white gangs, her stepfather took her to the hospital and in the grounds he was set upon and killed by, it is thought, a racist gang.[22]

Then there is that other fairly common scenario: a white mother with mixed-race children making a new life with a white man. Here, the problems are often very acute and a number of the children have ended up in care. Moira was seven when her mother began living with Brian, a builder with a bad temper:

He hated us. He was abusive, verbally most of the time. We were 'niggers', savages. He didn't let us eat at the table with him. And once in a while he would throw things at us. I ran away from home when I was 13 and never went back. I see mum, who is on her own, and she is very sorry that she put us through this. But she was lonely and my dad had let her down so I can't blame her.

Anna is a stepmother to two Asian children whose mother died when they were young:

The extended family treats me more and more like a danger to these kids. It was fine when they were young and I had a good job so could buy them nice things. But I made the decision not to have children of my own so that there wouldn't be further complications. And now as the kids – who really love me – are growing up, I am being told that their culture is more important than mine. I am furious. We have decided to leave the Midlands and move to London so that we can live our own lives in peace. Ramesh, my husband, is helpless, torn between so many sides.

But for every such tragic example, you find stories where newly formed mixed-race step families do manage to make things work.

Anisa took her Asian daughter with her when she left her husband to go off with Don, a Trinidadian:

I can't tell you what a wonderful father he has been to my Ayisha. You know when she was born, her own father was so disappointed that she was a girl. There were long faces and misery. Don treats her like a princess. He calls her that. There is nothing he won't do for her. The other day she – now thirteen – asked him to adopt her. But he thinks that that would break all chances of a link with her father which he doesn't think is right. Her father has seen her twice in the last eight years.

The depth of these relationships can be astounding. There was a moving letter in the *Guardian* written by Alan Mountain, a white man who was describing the murder of the mixed-race son of his partner: 'I feel the pain of Doreen Lawrence. Eighteen months ago, my partner's son was killed by a thug who was burgling his home.

Scott was young man of mixed race with a warm caring nature and an enjoyment of his mixed race ... '[23]

These bonds are genuine and need to be better acknowledged but perhaps a good deal more thinking also needs to go into the dynamics of mixed-race step families.

Fiction and fact

Currently there is very little representation of these relationships in books, films, or the theatre. From time to time television picks up the theme in soap operas and dramas but the storylines are fleeting, shallow and rarely move beyond the obvious idea of star-crossed lovers or forced marriages. Increasingly, too, relationships are shown where colour difference exists but is not at all an issue. This is both good and unfortunate because it gives an illusion of normality. Most (not all) people interviewed for this book would not be so glibly positive. But novels are beginning to catch up. *The Map of Love* by Ahdaf Soueif, the British Egyptian novelist, was short-listed for the Booker prize.[24] This big, sweeping book is based around two mixed-race relationships between white women and Egyptian men, a hundred years apart. What you learn from this novel, what so many of us have learnt in our own lives, is that love is, in the end, a political act, especially when individuals come from separate worlds. Many of us recognise how the act of loving someone who is from the ruling race implicates you in the undermining of all that you are, your family, your nation, your personal and political past. In an interview with me Soueif spoke about her own sense of being a divided self as she negotiates her life in a mixed-race relationship and as a mother of two sons who are both British and Egyptian: 'I long for Egypt. I feel more and more that I am in this place but not of it. Fifteen years ago I might have said I was both Arab and English. Now I feel an anxiety that I am not in Egypt more often.' In *The Map of Love*, Omar, one of the main characters, tells his American lover Isabel that he is Egyptian, Palestinian and American, adding 'I have no problem with identity.' She thinks he is lucky. He thinks the opposite.

Another remarkable book, *Admiring Silence*,[25] also manages, with superb skill and sensitivity, to dig underneath the usual clichés around these relationships. Its author is the Zanzibari writer Abdulrazak Gurnah who has lived and worked in Britain for decades and understands perfectly how love between the races is often the testing of love between nations. The narrator is a cynical and dejected teacher who came over from Zanzibar and stayed on after he met a white middle-class woman who loved the fact that he was such an outsider, such a mysterious man with strange stories to tell about even stranger places, to keep bored imperialist Englanders happily amused. In one of the most telling lines in this novel, the hero says: 'After all these years I can't get over the feeling of being alien in England, of being a foreigner. Sometimes I think what I feel for England is disappointed love.' This is what ER Braithwaite expressed too in the fifties in *To Sir With Love*, referred to in Chapter 2. In *Admiring Silence* the unnamed hero fails to tell his own family back home about his wife or his teenage daughter from whom he has always felt detached. Then one day he decides he has to go to Zanzibar:

> The truth was I had not written home about Amelia and the other truth was that I had not written home about Emma either...I did not know how to tell Emma about this – I still haven't...To my mother Emma would be something disreputable. Now we have lost you, she has stolen you away from us, and so on. God, home, history, culture would all come into it, boom doom blah bah. As if I was not already lost and stolen and shipwrecked and mangled beyond recognition anyway.[26]

Confused feelings of guilt, shame, pride, defiance and love bubble up in the hearts of many in these relationships. The easy going, untroubled mixing which is joyfully described in Zadie Smith's book *White Teeth* is far less common and still perhaps an impossible idyll because even as the world becomes more alike, it also becomes more obstinately tribal. Younger generations, especially in urban areas, are at ease with diversity because that is what life is. But at the same time, it is among the young that you find deep resistance to cross-racial relationships.

An extraordinary first novel, *From Caucasia With Love* by the American writer Danzy Senna, looks at these issues through the eyes of children.[27] Two sisters, both mixed-race, with an African-American father who is increasingly obsessed with black power politics and a white middle-class mother, unstable and easily led into revolutionary zeal, try to make sense of their lives as the parents separate. One looks more like the father and the other more 'white'. As they grow into teenage the 'white' one learns how everyone, including her father, can only see what she looks like and not what she is:

> ...[my father] never had much to say to me. In fact, he never seemed to see me at all. Cole was my father's special one...her existence comforted him. She was proof that his blackness hadn't been completely blanched. By his four years at Harvard. By my mother's blue-blood family wedding reception in the back of the big rotting house on Fayerweather Street. By so many years of standing stiffly in corners, listening to those sweatered two-haired preppies talk about the negro problem, nursing their vermouth, glancing at him with so much incredulity in their eyes.[28]

Then one day this distance is institutionalised. When she is with her father in the public gardens, lying on his stomach (a rare moment of real contact made possible only because her 'black' sister, his favourite, is not with them), the police are called by a suspicious elderly white couple who think the girl is a kidnap and abuse victim. The police do not believe they are father and daughter, not when he shows them pictures of the two sisters in his wallet, not even when he produces an identification card which confirms he is a professor at Boston University.

Replanting roots

Your children are your children of course but how many of us are honest enough to debate with ourselves, where nobody can hear, whether it matters what they look like, especially if they are mixed-race? I wonder if my daughter would feel such a part of me if she didn't have my colouring. Jim never recovered from the shock of having a daughter who did not look white:

> I have always found black women wild, sexy and unpredictable. I have had a number of one-night stands with them and long-term relationships too. You have no idea how good they are in bed. White women are boring by comparison and I would never even think about an Asian with all those hang ups about sex. So I married one. And we had a daughter. But I couldn't accept that my daughter was more black than white. I was jealous and I didn't want her to act like a tart and be looked at in that way by guys, the way I looked at her mum.

The marriage broke up and Jim has not seen his daughter for ten years.

But do black and Asian people also have hidden anxieties about the physical appearance of their own mixed-race children? I have met black mothers of mixed-race children who ruin the hair of their young children by trying to frizz it and make it look more 'African'. In the Asian community, the reactions are even more complicated. If the Asian partner marries white, the children are often light-skinned which makes them instantly more attractive than darker skinned people. If the partner is black, on the other hand, the community regards them as brutish and ugly. In many cases the parent who is Asian spends the rest of his or her life pushing the children back into a simple Asian identity. One of the most moving examples of this was on a series of programmes broadcast on Channel 4 in September 2000.

Tarsan Singh, then a Sikh without a turban, saw a beautiful young white woman, Nancy, in Huddersfield in the fifties. He fell instantly in love, followed her for weeks, shyly spoke to her, broke down her resistance, took her to the cinema seven days a week (the only place they could meet safely), learnt what courting was and eventually won her heart. Her family, Yorkshire, working class and Christian, did what they could to stop this. The couple married anyway although to this day Nancy, now a grandmother, becomes tearful when she remembers that she did not have a white church wedding. She converted to Sikhism and brought her two daughters up within that faith. She finds it a 'nice gentle' religion although she does still do her 'English prayers, although the church, the backbone of my life is gone'. Tarsan's father did not speak to him for forty years and only now when he is a hundred years old can he show his son some affection. Tarsan says his wife had to convert because 'she really can't be anything else. It would have been difficult for us to survive if she had not converted.' The sentiments behind this statement are startling enough (why should anyone have to convert?), but the most extraordinary part of this story comes later.

They have two daughters, and both parents have insisted that they should marry Sikhs and have arranged marriages. Nancy is more committed to this than Tarsan. The first daughter was married too young and took this to be her fate. Nancy arranged this marriage. Her daughter seems happy enough and has a teenage daughter herself who refuses to follow these ways. The second daughter refused an arranged marriage and chose her own husband, also a Sikh. Tarsan refused to attend the wedding and Nancy still has terrible regrets about this. Like the father in the film *East is East*, Tarsan was making amends and trying to purify himself by compelling his daughters to re-enter the traditions against which he had himself has chosen to rebel.[29]

The same series told the story of Carol, a Catholic, and her childhood sweetheart Russell, an Orthodox Jew. They were not allowed to marry by his parents and went their separate ways, marrying other people from their own communities. Both had children too. Then they met at an old school reunion and: 'It all came back. We couldn't help it. Religion had torn us apart before. It was not going to do it again.' Abandoning their children and partners to set up home together, they are now expecting their first child. Both claim that their identities remain secure. But Carol wants her daughter to marry in church and to be Christian, and Russell wants his daughter to marry a Jew.

Ruth, who feels 'very Jewish', married Robert, an atheist Gentile. As a mother she can pass her Jewishness on and this is what she is doing. They had a registry office wedding which lacked the splendour of the wedding organised for her sister who married someone from within the Jewish faith. Many of Ruth's acquaintances did not attend the wedding because they could not accept the marriage. Ruth's father would not speak to the bridegroom and refused to smile for photos. Robert's parents remain distant too. Ruth says: 'They are cold people who are never warm to me and they are not to my children. I dislike them intensely.' Her brother-in-law refused to be godfather to her daughter because he could not bear to step inside a synagogue: 'When Robert told me this, I was devastated and hurt beyond belief...It makes me angry because I want them to tell me directly what they think. I want to be able to stand up and talk to these people and argue for myself.' And yet after all this Ruth ends the interview saying: 'I would like my children to marry Jewish. In a strange way I now realise what my parents must have felt like.'[30]

A useful guide has now been published by Rabbi Jonathan Romaine and the Reform Synagogues of Great Britain. It says:

> This pamphlet does not signify approval of mixed-faith marriage – to be honest, ministers of virtually all religions regard marrying within one's faith as the best option. However it does recognise the fact that a substantial number of Jews today are marrying outside of the Jewish community...and that this seems an increasing trend. Rather than deny or simply decry this situation, many rabbis feel that it is important to come to grips with it and also to care for the thousands of Jews already in mixed-faith marriages.[31]

Most people who fall in love with someone from another racial or ethnic background do not allow themselves to think about what happens when the children are born, or the pressures of making family life work, or what happens when you die outside the narrow confines of your community. The Shah family in Cornwall managed these challenges and came through. Abid Shah, a Muslim, and his English wife Parveen (who converted to Islam) lived in this mostly white neighbourhood for forty-two happy years. He then died and as there is no mosque in Cornwall they had to ask an imam to come from London and perform the burial ceremony. Parveen thought it was wonderful to hear the sounds of Allahu Akbar, God is Great, ringing across the Cornish landscape. She says that since the funeral she has become more interested in Islam. But Abid, who ran a small studio taking family photographs, was also mourned in the local church, where he was known affectionately as 'our Mr Shah'. A satisfying compromise was achieved in this case.[32]

Other people often find that such issues can be unexpectedly difficult. What happens when a baby is born and you want a ritual which makes sense to both sides? And how will you be buried? Are there priests, imams and rabbis who will be prepared to share the task? One of the thoughts which wakes me and my English husband up at night is the fear that when one of us dies, our families and communities will reclaim us back from the lives we tried to lead and the values which mattered to us. I am a Muslim and of course that must be partially reflected at my funeral. But I am a mother of a mixed-race daughter whose father is English and I believe that all roads lead to one God and that is what I would choose to be the main thrust of whatever ceremonies are arranged.

Others feel differently. They believe that after death there needs to be a return to origins. For some people, as they age, feelings of fear and guilt haunt them, telling them that they did wrong by stepping out. Manju is a Hindu doctor who married her English husband in the seventies:

> As I get older, I am getting more afraid that I am nobody and that I will be punished. So I have a little shrine in our home and have started doing puja and all that. My sons go to public schools and one is in a choir. They think I have gone mad and often laugh at me saying I am becoming like that guru in *Goodness Gracious Me*. I was so happy to be free of all that superstitious rubbish in my community, statues of Khrishna drinking milk and all that. But after my fiftieth birthday I find it is all changing. Maybe people are right. You can't change your roots. If you do, you die.

Obviously there are people who do not long to return to 'roots' at all. They understand the nature of the lives they have chosen and seem ever more determined to resist the calls, inner and outer, to abandon their ideals. Elizabeth Ahmed was born and brought up in Scotland. Her father, who was Scottish, was considered unusual because he married an Englishwoman. Elizabeth had a 'good' Christian upbringing. She worked as a social worker in the international field. She married Nasir Ahmed in her late thirties. Nasir grew up in Calcutta and East Pakistan – now Bangladesh. Politically active since early days, he has lived in Europe all his life. Born into a Muslim family, he has first-hand experience of other religions and believes that a sense of personal moral spirituality is essential:

> I have always had a deep commitment to the universality of human beings, and I still do. Maybe that is why I see these things in a different way. A question I do ask myself is: have I made any transition at all in cultural terms by moving here or getting married to Elizabeth? I began to think in more cosmopolitan terms long before I came here. From the word go, my life has been so mixed up that I don't think I am located in any culture in that narrow sense. I would not fulfil those cultural norms even if I had married within my community, because of my life history. I suppose I have been a kind of rebel all my life. Perhaps it says something about me that I will always link up with the opposite group to the one I am expected to belong to. During the Hindu-Muslim riots I joined the Hindu relief centre, with my Muslim

name. Everyone used to say, 'You must be bloody crazy, they will kill you.' I am still alive.

He died just four years after he told me this, but his embracing of diversity, without any apology, is what keeps him so alive for Elizabeth:

That was what was so extraordinary about Nasir. From the age of twelve, he was politically involved. People here go on marches and that sort of thing, but not to the extent that Nasir described to me. He can still get quite passionately angry with the British and with other injustices. I had been to India in the sixties before I met Nasir, which was a very different scene. One of my sisters was out there as a missionary, which I really rather shudder about now. I went by boat. That was a fantastic experience because there was a boat load of Indians who had been here for five years, returning home with great expectations. I found them fascinating – their traditions and the way they thought about themselves, their commitment to their families and their country; quite intense feelings.

I didn't have that imperial arrogance because of the missionary influence, I think. When we got married, I remember someone saying I should be more worried that he was a psychotherapist than that he is an Indian.

Maybe that is what has happened – we have dissolved away a very tight sense of belonging to one part of the world, and that gives us many more options in terms of an identity. Perhaps it works better if people with these international outlooks, people not too culture-bound, marry across. That doesn't mean you think alike all the time. You are constantly surprised about the alliances you feel. The Gulf War brought out strong feelings in Nasir and in me. Nasir became quite strongly anti-American and anti-British. I often don't know how he is going to react. That is the difference between marrying the boy next door and marrying Nasir Ahmed. On a whole range of issues, I just don't know. That can be very exciting in a way. The children are like that too, very open about every issue and not tied to certain predictable positions because of who they are. They feel like Londoners. Not British, not Indian, not white, not black – New Londoners.

Hypersensitivity

There is a real danger that mixed-race couples themselves are too tuned in to the possibility that there will be slights and rejections and that a little more ease might reduce the sense that society treats them as aliens. This is an important point and one that is hard to verify. But most of the families I spoke to were indeed very alive to and conscious of how they might be seen and treated, by strangers and close ones.

I am too. I wonder afterwards if I have been fair to regard all upsetting remarks as racially loaded. My best friend lives in the United States and like me is a Ugandan Asian. She is married to an American who is ethnically Jewish. Two of their children look mixed-race and have brown skin and dark hair. The third has red hair and very 'white' features. When she took him out as a baby people would ask if she was the babysitter. Similar experiences have been described to me by scores of mixed-race people. But could it be that these questions are more innocent than they appear? That there is no hidden message, only a perfectly normal assumption that most children do look a bit like their parents and as yet society has not grown used to the idea that families come in all colours and shapes.

Dynamics within these relationships need to be better understood too. Maybe it is the sense that many in the wider community do not accept the 'normality' of such relationships, maybe it is history and racial inequality, but there is no doubt in my mind that the inner workings of these relationships are more complex than people ever imagine. I have learnt much during my ten-year marriage to Mr Brown. I can see that people like us can develop an unreal and unhelpful sense that we are warriors for a cause. You can only do your best. Things are harder across the divide and it would be foolish to deny that. On the other hand, maybe these are just normal pressures which always acquire a racial or cultural hue needlessly. Several interviewees expressed fears that these pressures would one day force their partners to escape into conformity. Manju feels that even in a good relationship, there are constant struggles:

> I have had a good life and a happy one. But I am more fatigued today than I would have been if I had been a good girl and married another Hindu. There would not have had to be this constant struggle for meaning, these unending thoughts on the right way and the too much talking all the time about who we are and who we want to be.

Baroness Ros Howells and her husband John still have very different responses to the world around them, many years after their marriage. John says she's 'constantly on the look out' for conscious and unconscious racism while he is quite oblivious to it. Ros on the other hand feels that 'John is not prepared to put up with racism but he isn't prepared to see it either.'[33] I have felt this chasm at times too in my own marriage. White people, on the whole, even when they are very open and sensitive, often cannot sense the real slights, the unspoken rejections and exclusion that so many non-white people experience. It may be that guilt and the burden of their own whiteness in this situation makes them want to retreat into not wishing to know.

A new world

Many of the young mixed-race people and mixed-race couples interviewed for this book felt this sense of belonging to a wide, modern and dynamic world. I met a group of these people at a wine bar in central London. Arnie, mixed-race, and his mixed-race girlfriend Sophie are both models:

> What's all this shit man? Just ignore all these idiots. They know nothing. We are the future. We're cool. We're it. We don't think race and all that shit. Look around you. Can you see how many mixed-race couples there are at this place? They are the majority. Is anyone looking? Does anyone care? We get asked to the best parties in town and sorry, lady, but nobody is sitting there making sure I don't get in because I am a half-breed.

In one sense Arnie is absolutely right. There is no problem among some sections of British society. I live in Ealing where a quarter of the population is non-white. Everywhere you go you see mixed-race families and couples unselfconsciously going about their business. Large British cities have developed an easy hybridity which is envied and much discussed around the world, especially in the European Union and the United States, where for different reasons there is much discomfort with cross-racial sexuality. It is important that this good story is told and reflected because it makes many of us feel good and on the winning side, an important thing for a growing group of people who have been denied self-esteem for far too long.

Viv wrote me a passionate letter in 1999 saying that the way we still discussed mixed-race families was part of the problem:

> ...opportunities are being lost as long as the media restrict their focus on black and white citizens. The reality is that there are hundreds of thousands of young and middle-aged people who are of mixed race. They are living in London, in the big northern cities and are minorities in small rural communities throughout the United Kingdom...mixed-race young people are getting on and living, for better or worse, as British citizens, facing and challenging attitudes where these are outdated and providing their peers with the opportunity to live with them in non-racist friendship...[young people I meet] tell me that things will improve as their multiethnic generation move to centre stage and when earlier generations with their outdated views on the world pass on. These young people are speaking as the confident representatives of multiethnic Britain...I am convinced that

significant numbers of devoted grandparents black, white and mixed-race, would respond to an invitation to present their challenge to the British population which seems stuck between the past and the future.[34]

Chris Cleverly, one of the youngest barristers to have his own chambers and a successful television style guru, is a perfect symbol of this new breed of mixed-race Britons. He was brought up in Essex at a time when such alliances were rare and yet the family emerged self-assured and proud:

This is who I am. This is who we are. There is really little to discuss about what if and whether. I am grateful to my parents for the way they have brought me up, I know at times it was very hard for them. I don't want to be anything other than what I am. I feel comfortable in many worlds and this is a tremendous advantage in the work that I do.[35]

This strategy of making mixed-race children super-confident and skilled is one that is clearly used by many parents, often because they want to prove the Jeremiahs wrong. Sheah, a Nigerian who has been married to a white Briton since the sixties, explained why this was very important:

Anticipating that people always expect mixed-race children to go wrong, my wife and I made sure that our five children were more than 300 per cent with regards to their behaviour, their dress. I said to them I want you to be very very very good because I couldn't take any chances with what society would get up to. I wanted them to hold up their heads high, to achieve great things so that nobody could point an accusing finger and say 'What do you expect? They are mixed-race children.'[36]

Following this interview in a Radio 4 programme which I presented, I had over a hundred letters from mixed-race people writing about their extraordinary experiences. Some could be characters in a novel. With one couple, the white husband was much older than the black wife. They explained that she had decided to marry his son many years ago, but the white family objected violently. So they waited. Then suddenly the son was killed in an accident. The process of mourning brought the widower father and the girlfriend together and they married in due course. They have named their son after the young man who died leaving them both bereft. Another case was of an elderly couple in the Midlands who were serious Seventh Day Adventists. They too thought mixed-race children had to be more than perfect and said that they had brought theirs up to be 'better than the best'. At the end of the interview I asked if I could meet the children. No, I was told quietly. They had died in a fire which they believe was started by racists.

In the past few years, I have come to understand that the complexities of mixed-race relationships and households carry on through life. Behind optimism there is always the shadow of terrible pessimism. Just when people think they have steered their lives well and are safe, things come up to shock them out of that feeling of security. One of the most outrageous examples of how these insecurities can be heightened was a case of deportation in 1999 when Kiki, a Nigerian woman who had lived almost all of her life in this country and was happily married to Chris Gill, a white Briton, was deported back to Nigeria, a country she barely knew. She had failed to comply with some immigration requirement when she was in her teens and her marriage was forcibly split up by the state. Such experiences made couples wary, even those who felt good about themselves and what they had done. Glen, an Englishman from Dagenham who had had nothing to do with non-white people until he was eighteen, found himself in love with Ishi, an East African Asian woman. They have been happily married for 27 years, yet neither believes the rainbow nation has arrived, or that it will soon. As Glen says: 'The country has come a long way and there has been a huge change in attitudes. But society at large, there the attitudes will take a hugely long time.' His wife agrees:

This dream will take a long time to come true. I still have black friends who will not have relationships with white people and Asian friends who want arranged marriages with their own. White people have their own problems. We have a long way to go. It will not happen in this lifetime. Not even the next generation, I don't think.[37]

Chapter 6
Social Policy

'I will not have you using terms like "mixed-race". In this department, the children are black if they are not white. That is all there is to say about their identity. If a white child says he is not white, would you correct him? So if a half-African child says he is not black, I just correct him.'
A white social worker in a deprived London borough, interviewed for this book.

'We do a lot of multicultural work. We have books with black and Asian families and Chinese and that. But you know what? I never thought of the mixed kids as different till you talked to me about your book. I am going to do something about this.'
A deputy-head teacher in Birmingham, interviewed for this book.

'I am not a nigger. I am white. These carers know nothing. They say my dad was black. But I never saw him and if he was would I look like this? Look at my skin, it's peach. They are saying this to put me down, to tell me I am a nigger.'
A mixed-race teenager in care.

'When I read the adoption guidelines of experts like the British Agencies for Counselling and Fostering, headed by Felicity Collier, I get worried. BAAF, the umbrella group for local authorities and voluntary bodies is putting the emphasis on race when it comes to finding permanent homes for youngsters in care. My first concern here is the unashamed racism of such a statement. To my mind, it essentially advocates apartheid...I know we live in a racist society and that we have to acknowledge that reality, but I don't think the answer is to strengthen that reality by increasing segregation.'
Ishraga Lloyd, a young mixed-race adult who was brought up by her white mother after her Sudanese father was killed in a car crash. She wrote this in an article for People in Harmony.

'You know I never even knew Homa was half-caste. I mean she doesn't look it does she? She looks like one of us. I

mean normal. I have black children, white children, all sorts, and to me they have no colour. They are all the same.'
An interview in 1999 with the foster mother of a nine-year-old child whose father (long gone) is Iranian and whose mother is Scottish.

Mixed-race families are not only increasing in number, but also becoming less invisible, more assertive and complex. If it is senseless (and it is) to talk about 'the white community' or 'the black or Asian community', creative grand narratives around a presumed community of mixed-race people is even more so, although I have little doubt that one day there will be a political alliance of mixed-race Britons which will give them more influence and self-determination of the sort that Jill Olumide described in the chapter on identity.[1] By definition these are the people who, by their actions or existence, defy community, ethnic and racial boundaries. For me, the most depressing part of this rich, varied and fascinating journey through the lives of mixed-race people was the way institutions and professionals still fail to understand this. Evidence is emerging of some effort to improve services to 'ethnic minorities' but that progress has not reached mixed-race people who are still neglected or classified within a broad non-white category. Some professionals do this through indifference; others because they are unable to see the world without clean classification and most because this is the official policy they have been instructed to follow. Most worrying are the people – many very powerful – who deliberately refuse to acknowledge the rights and life experiences of mixed-race people because they are committed to certain ideological positions, some fiercely colour blind, others equally fiercely colour coded. My research was carried out in 1998 and early 1999. Sian Peer wrote her report on mixed-race identities in 2000 and concluded: 'Whilst most professionals intimate that young mixed people will have problems on account of their identity, seldom have we made any attempt to establish whether this is a reality for those who are affected by our presumptions.'[2]

There are issues beyond identity, perhaps even more crucial. It is becoming clear that while many families are doing fine, a substantial number of such families are in crisis and a disproportionate number of mixed-race children are coming into care. The Department of Health accepts this although there are no national statistics available. There are no national statistics on the numbers of black, Asian and mixed-race children in the public care system or on Child Protection Registers. However, reliable small-scale studies indicate that mixed-race children are among the groups over-represented in care. Certainly a large number of teenagers in care are of mixed-race or Afro-Caribbean origins. High numbers of mixed-race children are entering the care system, often at a younger age than average, and spend longer periods in care.[3] A number of academics confirm these findings although because most use the term 'black' some of the time, it is hard to extract the figures and stories of mixed-race children. There is a dearth of data too on the outcomes for these children. It is imperative to find out the specific causes and nature of any problems and provide support networks that are relevant. The issue is sensitive and potentially controversial, and could rebound unless it is handled well.

In 1998, I organised a seminar at the Institute for Public Policy Research to start this process. We invited ordinary families, policy makers, practitioners, government representatives, academics and grassroots organisations to come together and raise some important debates which many felt had been silenced for too long. Our hope was that the relevant bodies would take note and would be prepared to develop separate and suitable policies and practices to empower mixed-race people. Three years on, most institutions carry on with little specific attention to this population.

The failure of institutions

One of the conclusions reached by those attending the seminar was that it is not only individuals in society who impact on mixed-race families. There has been a massive institutional neglect of the needs of this group.

Organisations like the British Agencies for Adoption and Fostering (BAAF) are attempting to deal with the issues but there appear to be many constraints on how much rethinking they can allow themselves, partly because of justified fears of a media onslaught. It has to be said that some of their policies have been non-negotiable for far too long. There was a time when race and ethnicity 'rights' needed perhaps to be overstated in order to wake agencies and institutions up and get them to see the world in colour. As Ratna Dutt of the REU (formerly the Race Equality Unit) told me when I interviewed her in 1999: 'We needed to have an up-front position in order to force things to change.' But in this new century institutions must start to evaluate more systematically the many policies which have been in place since the eighties, or even the late seventies. All sorts of subtle factors need to be taken into account when it comes to mixed-race individuals and families and it is time that these people became subjects in their own lives and not objects for others, however well meaning.

The policies discussed here go well beyond the usual hot issues of adoption and fostering. There are today more family-help organisations than ever before, partly because the government is so concerned about lone parenthood and the high rates of divorce in this country. Not one of the marriage guidance providers I spoke to had given the issues of race, ethnicity and religion any thought.

Nick Banks believes that the responses may go beyond simple neglect and ignorance. In his own research with social workers he found: 'Mixed relationships are sometimes regarded as ideologically flawed and "politically" undesirable in social work assessments of family functioning by both white and black social workers. This, in itself, can determine a negative outcome.'[4]

I believe the same attitudes are found in family counselling services. Some professionals think race is a red herring; others think it is better to treat everyone in the same way, thereby showing that they do not understand the simple truth that treating people in the same way is completely different from providing a fair and equal service. When mixed-race families are in crisis, as is evident in other parts of this book, race is the third person in the marriage, the invisible force in teenage problems, the other inner demon behind emotional problems such as alcoholism and breakdowns.

Ally is black and a serious alcoholic who is destroying his body and knows it. He has been unemployed for seven years, ever since he was laid off when his company restructured. He was forty then. He thinks racism stopped him getting another job. Five years ago he started drinking to forget. He says that he is black and unwanted in his land of birth. Pat, his Scottish wife, loves him but will not accept what she says are his 'excuses'. Their only daughter, who is sixteen, sides with her father because she too has suffered racist bullying in school. Father and daughter increasingly treat Pat as the white enemy within and she is now threatening divorce. They did try a marriage counselling service but came away very disillusioned. 'They know nothing about race. They are white, middle-class do-gooders who can do us no good,' says Ally. Pat is angry for other reasons. 'This woman called Prunella or something, all posh and expensive, looked down on me, I think. I could see it in her eyes that she thought I was no good because I am with a man who has no job and who doesn't sound like Trevor Macdonald. You see I don't think it is race, but class.'

Yet Cheryl Walters, the Head of Policy and Research for Parentline Plus, the national helpline for families in crisis, told me that very few 'ethnic minorities' use their services and that some 'have a fantasy that what is happening to them is about race when in reality it is about relationship difficulties'. She did accept after some discussion that race could be a part of the trouble but it was obvious from talking to Walters and others that these kinds of organisations which provide essential services have not even started to discuss mixed-race families. They seriously need to examine the way they are responding to mixed-race couples and families with emotional problems and to start appropriate training courses. The numbers of broken and step-families which are mixed-race are going up and they have a right to high-quality counselling.

However, there is a wider issue here than just the needs of mixed-race families. Even in the year 2000, overall, public services and the voluntary sector could cater better for the complex, multiethnic population of the United Kingdom. Ravinder Barn, one of our key experts in this area, concluded: 'Although Britain is a multiracial and multicultural society, there is much evidence of the failure of public services to adequately address the needs of users from different minority ethnic groups. This is also true for minority ethnic families and children who are in contact with social services departments.'[5] Within this general malaise, mixed-race families become an invisible and unrecognised minority within a minority and their voices are mostly never heard.

There is so much more we need to know. Do black parents of mixed-race children not refer themselves to social services (which is the case as far as we know) because they do not trust the professionals? Can child abuse be 'excused' for cultural reasons? Do we still have an obligation to push a norm which says that there should be no physical punishment of children? And how does all this impact on mixed-race families with gender battles and cultural struggles going on within families?

The Children Act of 1989 placed a statutory obligation on local authorities in England and Wales to take into account the specific racial and ethnic identities of families and children. Similar laws exist in Scotland. But there is a terrifying lack of information and little or no tracking. BAAF has ensured that it is not all a jungle of ignorance. Lynda Ince's study *Making it Alone* is invaluable because it does more than just take a snapshot. There are some important case studies which track down from a crisis. A mixed-race young offender describing his time in care and his pain over his identity allows us to understand better how much these things matter.[6] Some local authorities have their own systems (and there are problems with these which I discuss later in this chapter) but as Barn et al point out, 'the information is not collected centrally'. One black manager from a metropolitan area told these researchers: 'I would suspect that we have probably got some children inappropriately placed... one of the problems we have is the complete lack of management information. The team couldn't tell me how many placements they made last month, or how many we have in care today or where they are.'[7]

In common with other people examining this issue my impression was that relevant service providers had too much to do already, that there was too much paperwork, too little reward, too many new and batty initiatives and too little will to change anything. I was discouraged to discover that the social service departments I contacted were clueless, uninterested in this project, defensive and determined not to help. After many months three authorities agreed that this was a legitimate area of research and they should allow me access to mixed-race children in their care. We signed many contracts but only one arranged for the access we had agreed on and that was because I befriended one black social worker who felt strongly that mixed-race children were being subsumed and neglected. I met five children, all of whom were furious or disturbed about their identities. In one authority I had to go to the Director of Social Services who promised me the earth. This was nine months after I had asked for and they had agreed to help. I only managed to interview one child and the key worker who was supposed to be there forgot to attend, so I had to do the interview stranger to stranger. A number of children I managed to interview in the end were located informally through word of mouth. BAAF, the National Fostering Care association, the REU and National Newpin, a voluntary organisation to help families in crises, were all more accommodating and helpful. But most other family counselling services I contacted never responded, nor did most of the schools I wrote to. The only way I was able to access schools and teachers was through activist mixed-race families.

Sian Peer had similar experiences. She wrote to over 30 statutory and community groups. Most were unwilling to contribute to the study. She sent out 100 letters to professional organisations and received 14 replies. After several interviews she found many treated mixed-race children as white or ignored ethnicity altogether. In individual cases where children had problems with identity and were desperate to belong, social workers did not seem to know how to deal with the problems. She concluded: 'Professional workers seemed indifferent to considering 'mixed race' as an issue [and] the response is ad hoc with no strategic overview or policy when working with this group.'[8]

Hanging on to a label

In my research I found that where there was some commitment to 'ethnicity' as an important aspect of life, it quickly became clear that almost all the agencies and authorities concerned and most academics working in this area had made the assumption that the word 'black' (often written with a capital letter) was what should be used to describe mixed-race people. The reasons given, if any, were:

- A bit of black made you black, ie the one drop rule.
- Racism. If mixed-race people are treated as badly as black people then you were black.
- Calling a mixed-race child anything other than black was, by implication, saying that black was 'wrong' or deficient in some way.
- Radical policy makers had instructed this.

Some of the most aware experts on mixed-race families – without whom we would know even less than we do – do themselves insist on using the term 'black' or 'Black' instead of mixed-race. Some use both the identity term 'black' with 'Black' in the political sense meaning all non-white groups and individuals. The Department of Health framework document already referred to, produced in the spring of 2000, says: '[In this document] Black refers to children and families of Asian, African and Caribbean origin including children of dual heritage.'[9] The REU uses the term as a positive choice as do most local authorities and voluntary organisations. A report by the NSPCC assessing services to multiethnic populations uses 'black' as an umbrella term which means that valuable information on mixed-race Britons is not available.[10]

Why? Has anyone involved in this document recently checked with British Asians, Muslims, mixed-race people, Chinese, Vietnamese, Turkish and others if the word 'black' fits? Many of us are absolutely comfortable with this as one of our identities, but even same race people are now breaking out of a single label. I am black, Asian, Muslim, female, in a mixed-race household, ethnically Indo-Pakistani, African (because I was born and brought up there) and finally and most importantly a Londoner. It seems to be either extraordinarily naïve or presumptuous to assert such a blanket term for all non-white people. Ratna Dutt at the REU has strong views on why this is right: 'We need to be much more sensitive than we have ever been and different people are at different levels of understanding. "Black" is used as a political term and to ask children to describe themselves before they have developed a political position is wrong. It is wrong to ask the question.'[11]

Culture does not stand still for any ethnic group and it is that flux, change, adaptation which interacts with personal histories and character to make what we call an individual identity. Cultures within a single family over generations are profoundly different; they are dynamic and reactive. Yet a number of key documents and books make the assumption that there is a black culture which a mixed-race child must be fed, and it is my opinion that this is not only unhelpful, but unwise in the extreme. As Stuart Hall said:

> Cultural identity . . . is a matter of 'becoming' as well as 'being'. It belongs to the future as much as to the past. It is not something that already exists, transcending place, time, history and culture . . . far from being grounded in a mere 'recovery' of the past which is waiting to be found and which, when found, will secure our sense of ourselves into eternity.[12]

In Chapter 4, the complexity of identity was dealt with in some detail. Why have so few experts caught up with this complexity?

Then there are those crucial practical issues of language, ritual and belief. If children are placed solely on the basis of their 'blackness', there will be massive failures of hopes and adjustment. BAAF itself has produced some very good, simple and clear guidelines on the importance of race, religion, culture and language,[13] but these sit uneasily with other heavy guidelines on why these children should be seen and treated as 'black'.[14] A sensitively written Commission for Racial Equality policy paper called for the placing of mixed-race children with mixed-race families but then went on to say that if this were not possible the child should be placed with a family which is closest in background to that of the 'ethnic minority' parent. There is no discussion of the kind of rejections that the child could face within such families nor why this is self-evidently sensible or necessary.[15]

In her qualitative study, which is more recent confirmation of the conclusions reached by Anne Phoenix and Barbara Tizzard (see Chapter 4), Sian Peer found the following:

- The most favoured term used by mixed-race young people in her sample, was, in fact, 'mixed-race'. 36 per cent used this although in some situations some did identify with the term 'black'.
- 14 per cent used 'half-caste.'
- 10 per cent used 'black' as the main label.
- 17 per cent described a geographical connection usually with a Caribbean island.
- There was no correlation between the regular use of the term 'black' and living with a black parent.[16]

Inexplicably, a number of these blanket impositions seem to have arisen out of the best of intentions and have been triggered off by many of those who have spent their lives challenging old prejudices and who have been passionately committed to anti-racism. After the intensive research carried out for this book, I have to conclude that it is still remarkably difficult to persuade policy makers in key positions that mixed-race children are different from single-race children and that theirs is an identity which needs to be recognised. There is an irony here. As has been shown already, in the United States during the worst days of slavery, segregation and institutionalised racism, white supremacists used the 'one drop' rule to categorise mixed-race people as black and therefore deny them any rights. A single drop of black blood made a person uncompromisingly black. Similar rules destroyed the lives of people in South Africa. There were unspeakably tragic stories in both countries when mixed-race people tried to pass for white (because they could and knew that by doing so their lives could avoid the cruelty and injustice meted out to black people) and when those who believed they were white because the family history had been kept hidden were then denounced as black. With such a history it is indeed curious that so many black and white professionals decided – without any credible consultation with those affected, like those who had direct experience of being in mixed-race relationships and their children – that one drop of black blood made you black.

More subtle reasons have also been given for why 'mixed-race' is problematic and these too need to be taken into account. Advocates of the term 'black' for mixed-race people say that if there are no races in the way the Eugenicists believed, why talk of 'mixed-race'? And how does that term encapsulate ethnicity? But one could argue that the umbrella term 'black' also denies ethnic and religious diversity so why is that more acceptable? And to 'prepare' a mixed-race child for racism which may or may not come seems a very negative approach to child rearing. Several of the mixed-race people I interviewed said they had never felt rejected. They were perfectly well-adjusted people who had other quests and needs but were certainly not prepared to be bound by a social framework entirely based on racial difference and racial inequality. Nick Banks has done some invaluable work in this area but his assertion that the term 'black' reintegrates a divided self[17] leaves open the obvious counter-argument, ie what about the white side which is thereby banished? This is one half of the child's inheritance and often represented by the mother who, in a large number of cases, has been the sole carer.

In the eighties, a very powerful and vocal alliance was built up between leading local politicians such as Linda Bellos, then leader of Lambeth council, the Association of Black Social Workers and Allied Professionals (ABSWAP), the GLC, David Divine, a mixed-race senior social worker, and others. They felt strongly and perhaps understandably that the black community was in some way losing its children because they were not seen as black: 'The most valuable resource of any ethnic group are its children...The Black community cannot possibly maintain any dignity in this country if their children are taken away from their parents and reared exclusively by another race.'[18] Many interviewees in this book said that they felt under pressure to conform to the idea that they were black even if they did not feel black and some indicated that social workers did not pay enough attention to the feelings of their white parent even when that parent was the primary carer. Rosemary is one of those who feels let down by the system:

> I had to put my son into care because I couldn't cope with all the hassle I was getting from my own mum, the neighbours, the black kids who picked on him. I was drinking too much and giving Sean

a really hard time. So I rang Social and asked them to take him off my hands for a few months. They were really good at the start. But now they tell me he is staying with a black foster family miles away, in London. They could only get white families near here in Northampton. I can't see him as much as I want and he is getting ruder about white people.

But there is never one truth in this fraught area of social policy. There were other interviewees who did feel that in care – especially when they were placed with colour-blind foster parents – their non-white identity was ignored and neglected. These individuals are still very angry about this 'lost' identity and a number of them end up seeking to rediscover their 'ethnic' selves, often completely turning their backs on their white heritage. Sometimes the same dynamics come into play with relationships between people of different ethnicities.

Rory is half Asian and half Caribbean. He was put into care after his black father, who was bringing him up on his own, fell seriously ill. His Asian mother has had no contact with him and has since had an arranged marriage and two children. She has let it be known that she is happy in her new life and that her husband would divorce her if he knew about Rory. Rory looks Asian and while in care other Asian kids assumed he was. But he has decided that he 'hates' his Asian side so much that he is black and only black. He claims that few within the care system ever accepted this or do now that he is an adult. He has been arrested twice for 'Paki-bashing' and imprisoned once.

We know now, through the pioneering research carried out by Ravinder Barn, Ruth Sinclair and Dionne Ferdinand in three authorities, that mixed-race children in care have not always been matched with families who reflect their own ethnicity and race.[19] In one of the authorities I was researching it took me three months to persuade the social services department to give me an accurate ethnic background of the children in their care homes. Initially I was told that these children were 'black'. The list which was eventually produced included an Armenian–Irish mix, and a Polish–Caribbean mix. The mixed-race group was bigger proportionately than any other non-white groups and the large variety was not even being discussed let alone catered for in other ways.

In another area, after much debate and discussion, the authority agreed to carry out a survey. Only 10 per cent of the children chose to call themselves 'black'. All the rest used other ways to describe themselves because they were from a variety of backgrounds. How can it be expected that a child whose parents are Chinese and Indian – a real case in this authority – will automatically call herself 'black'? Bob Purkiss rightly says:

Some people argue that since British society only sees mixed-race people as black, and because these people experience racial discrimination, they should identify themselves as black. However it is equally important that mixed-race people (particularly young people) are allowed to explore and acknowledge both the black and white sides of their heritage, including their long histories in this country. Too many at present feel forced to deny parts of their heritage.[20]

These conversations are not merely about language. They reflect the very complicated struggles over identities. I met white mothers of mixed-race children who had the most confusing encounters with the outside world. One, a young lone mother, had a child who could pass for white and was told by her middle-aged white no-nonsense midwife that she was 'lucky' to have such a pretty baby who looked just like her and that she was 'surprised' that the father was black. The mother thinks her child is black and wants the world to accept this.

A Sikh/Caribbean teenager was placed with an African foster family who could do nothing for her need to understand who she was. On the form she was 'black' and so was the family. She ended up back in care and then tried to run away several times. She never did find a family which 'fitted' and it is only recently, through therapy and finding herself a black/Asian mentor, that she feels a little more settled.

Two little half-sisters in care would have been split up by social workers because one had a Jamaican father so it was assumed she should go to a 'black' family while the other, whose father was white, should be placed with a white family. The mother had to go to court to stop this.[21] I met Chris, a bright and ambitious Anglo-Indian young woman in care who refuses to go to any family because she has had such terrible experiences, especially with 'traditional' Asian foster families who have all tried to make her more Asian than she feels.

Toykin Okitikpi, lecturer in social work at Brunel University, believes that these views of identity in the end become tyrannical. In a perceptive paper about the over representation of mixed-race children in the care system Okitikpi says: 'I argue that the way children's identities have been (mis)handled is a contributory factor to the difficulties, pain and damage these children experience. I am encouraging a return to the debate about how the children should be classified and for social-work educators not to be defensive or afraid of getting involved in the discussion.'[22] This, he says, is the kind of black nationalism which has been powerfully critiqued by Paul Gilroy, Stuart Hall and others. It is living down to an essentialism, a denial of individuality, in my view one of the most pernicious effects of racism. Even more damaging is the fervent belief that the right identity for the child must be black: 'The embrace into the Black fold initiates a magic political trans-formation in which the mixed-race child, the 'other', becomes de facto 'Black'. This is achieved at a cost and the price the child must pay to achieve a 'successful' transformation is in effect the rejection of a crucial and presumably reaffirming part of their identity.'[23]

The basis for this is not unsound. White culture dominates and is ubiquitous. There is no need to reinforce that. But there is in all of us an inner life and an outer life with connections between the two which need to be robust and healthy. If one parent is white or Asian the psychological links between the child and that parent need to be as strong as those between the child and the black parent. It is only when you have a strong sense of self, of confidence built by nurturing and caring adults, that you can operate successfully in the world outside. The self is not enhanced by the deliberate amputation of one side of the parental heritage. By zealously overcompensating for historical injustices perhaps more harm than good is being done by people who have real commitment to the children. Fissures can be created within families. What makes this dogma even more dangerous is the reality that many mixed-race children with a black father live with their lone white mothers. Okitikpi rightly observes that what was meant to be an instrument for the liberation of racially oppressed children has become a straightjacket and is leading to bad judgements:

> These children are being asked in effect to decide to which side of the colour line they belong. In some cases they are asked to demonstrate their allegiance through the adoption of a particular lifestyle with all the social and cultural identifiers that purport to go with it. The result is an idealisation of a particular parent (usually the absent Black father) over and above the present parent, in most cases the White mother. This has an obvious effect upon family relations.

And since so many Asians do not see themselves as black even though they are the victims of racism – sometimes more extremely than Afro-Caribbeans – there is a body of opinion which feels that the black identity is cutting out the Asian identity. So am I saying that the black identity should not be encouraged? Not at all. However, I believe blind and simplistic dogma is dangerous when we are dealing with human character and that there must be a deeper understanding of identity and needs and real choices for those who are living the mixed-race life. Moreover, as has been repeatedly stressed in this book, nobody has only one defining identity, a coat which we can wear for all seasons. Sadly many social workers and academics of all backgrounds have now latched on to this ideology of blackness and will not be swayed or persuaded to think again. Marie has first-hand experience of this:

> Tony, my son, he's eighteen. His dad left when he was six and is now in prison for a violent attack on a shopkeeper. When he was fifteen, he got together with another half-caste boy who was into rap and drugs and all that. He said he was black and that Tone should be too. That's when the trouble started. He started drugs, called me trash, a tart, and said that I had driven out his dad because I am prejudiced. He hit me with a chair and I had to send him into care. His key worker told me I had to let go so he could be black properly. I tell you I nearly hit her. I have worked like a dog cleaning offices and that so I could give him a good life. His black dad is a pimp. I'm not saying they are all like that, I'm not, honest. But I get fed up with black is good and all that. My neighbour, Shirley, she's black and we are mates. But my son is my son and not his.

A young man I interviewed for *The Colour of Love* had the same background as Tony and he too had similar problems with his white mother and did end up in care for six months before returning home, but he tried to understand the emotional pain which was responsible for this:

> My father was adamant I was black and my mother would tell me I was not black, but that I was brown, usually behind my father's back. I was isolated and confused and still am really. But after he left I think my mother's sense of betrayal was terrible. A lot of women in this situation feel unpleasantly reminded of the men when they look at their children and of course it is unfair that they have been left to do the hard work.

Barn et al describe a case where a mixed-race child with a white mother was placed with a black family with not very encouraging results. His mother said: 'He doesn't want to live with black people because he's never lived with black people. He gets on better with white people, he doesn't know the culture of black people.' What worked in the end was finding a key worker who was black himself but who treated the young man primarily as an individual.[24]

The Department of Health guidelines stress that 'black' children with one white parent 'should not be pathologised as having identity problems or identity conflicts. Many children of dual heritage have a very positive and integrated racial identity.'[25] The document goes on to make another profound point which seems to be neglected in this same document in the way mixed-race children are officially labelled and processed: 'Individual identity is the internal model which allows each person to have a perception of themselves as an individual and social being. We are all members of numerous social groupings, but we are also distinct in our own individuality from any other member of a given group to which we belong, despite some areas of similarity.'[26]

Many of the mixed-race people who have or have had problems in their life are only seeking the right to this individuality and to a kind of normality.

Mixed-race children in institutional care

My research in inner London and outer London, plus the interviews I carried out with children and families in the Midlands, has convinced me that mixed-race children are not receiving appropriate attention and interventions. Their specific emotional needs are often neglected. Their identities are either ignored – 'they are all children and I treat them all the same' – or these days subsumed under the 'black' identity or 'educated' in that direction whatever the wishes and needs of the child. In my view, after the age of eight, the specific choices of that child need to be respected. This cannot be stressed enough. We have a stream of good regulations and policies but it is still relatively rare to see these activated into good practice which takes on board the views of the child.

Pioneering initiatives still base good practice on the belief that black is best. Ravinder Barn is convinced that unless mixed-race children are placed with black carers or parents, there is a significant disconnection which could impact on the self-esteem and self-awareness of mixed-race children. In her study, *Black Children in the Public Care System*, Barn concluded that children placed within their own locality, in residential homes staffed by black and white workers, were able to maintain a healthy sense of their racial and ethnic identity and good links with the family and the community. Mixed-race children who were sent to white rural areas with primarily white staff were alienated.[27] But I would argue that just as it is vital for the children to have access to carers who are not all white, it is equally important that they encounter all sorts of other diversity as part of their life experience. If an Asian/White child had only ever had Afro-Caribbean carers and social workers, the deprivation would be as great as if the child had only ever encountered white professionals. Although the dominant pattern of relationships at present is that of Afro-Caribbean men and white women, new groups are coming into the picture and they are ill served by policies which are really catering to one kind of mixed-race group.

Minds need to open up. Recent research shows that white families can successfully cater for these children provided they are well informed and aware and that placing an 'ethnic minority' child with just any 'ethnic minority' family can lead to failures.[28] Earlier research by June Thoburn showed that mixed-race young adults who had been successfully adopted by white families could see the point of racial mixing but most said that they would not have wanted any other kind of family for themselves.[29] Pat Verity of the National Foster Care Association told me that they too were giving careful consideration to foster parents of all backgrounds who had competencies which could help mixed-race children, although she admitted that the process is just beginning. Both BAAF and NFCA have posters showing mixed-race families. Beverley Prevatt Goldstein, an influential lecturer and trainer, first accepts and affirms that 'Each black child with a white parent is equally complex and multifaceted. We are not "one vat of homogenised chocolate milk", easily digested and understood.'[30]

But this genuine progress is still hampered by old assumptions. In the same article, Goldstein asserts that the only way a mixed-race child can be himself or herself is through embracing the black identity, especially if they are with a white parent. She goes on to 'prove' that to reject this 'truth' is somehow to collude in the racist belief that there is something wrong with being black. Quoting an American writer she asserts that the choice is between '... actively or passively siding with the power of European supremacy, ownership and cultural domination – and actively siding with the promotion, nurturing and survival of African peoples and other people of colour.'[31]

I am not dismissing these ideas but questioning some of the arguments. I don't agree, for example, that one element of the black identity is based on the 'fact' that there is a shared 'experience of oppression based on skin colour [which is] a reality for the majority of black children with a white parent'. What about black oppressors in the school playgrounds and in the international political arena? What about class? How do we know that the majority of these children are oppressed by whites? My research shows that there is anecdotal evidence that some are but just as much evidence that others are not oppressed and that some are oppressed by black people. Many of those who espouse the 'black' identity do not adequately deal with the whole range of family, cultural and religious differences which are not even understood at their most basic levels and which are more important than any of the political battles which have been fought for far too long. And what about unsuitable black parents, foster carers and adoptive carers?

In the end, I agree wholeheartedly with Derek Kirkton, lecturer in Social Work, who writes in a paper on these issues:

The two positions afforded seem to be those of political extremism (black nationalist, anti-racist) or invisibility. Particularly for white workers, the latter may be linked to a notion of 'silent majority', fearful of being branded racist by opposing the zealots. Greater involvement of social workers in debate and research on race and adoption would help to move beyond some of the stereotyping and superficiality...collectively social workers have many important tales to tell and this should be facilitated. Again, encouragement of ethnic diversity would be important to build a more rounded picture of perceptions from within social work.[32]

In a useful essay, Nick Banks suggests ways that social workers and others involved with children of colour can increase their awareness of racism and other issues. He feels – and I agree – that identity issues should never be presumed and do at times require activating. Unlike him, though, I do not believe that mixed-race children should be directed towards their 'blackness'. He gives a fascinating example of a 14-year-old child, Nargis, whose white mother died when she was eight and who has never seen her Pakistani father. She gave up her Muslim name and started calling herself 'Susan'. Both parental families had rejected her, one because she was illegitimate and the other because she was not white. She ended up with a white working-class foster family which gave her security. She said she did not want to go to a South Asian family. To insist on an ethnic matching would have been completely wrong in this case. Banks suggests that what was required was intensive counselling which would include bereavement work leading to explorations of how the child sees herself.[33] Such tailor-made approaches make sense as long as they are open and do not seek to direct the children in subtle ways.

Adoption and fostering

The two areas of social policy where this reluctance to accept complex identities has had a profound effect are fostering and adoption. There have been countless stories of alleged and actual bad adoption decisions. In 1997, a mixed-race family was denied a white baby they had fostered. The child had epilepsy and had had to be weaned off heroin when a few weeks old. One reason given was that the child would stand out racially when out with the family.[34] Another case involved a white foster mother who had fostered a mixed-race child from the age of six days. At seventeen months the child was removed from her; her application for adoption was denied although an official report claimed she was a very good parent. The reason given was that the woman was white. [35] There may of course be other reasons for these decisions which have to remain confidential. Nevertheless, leaving media hysteria aside, there can be little doubt that fundamentalist views on identity have sometimes prevailed and that in some cases mixed-race children have been kept within institutions in preference to placements within white families because a belief has taken hold that these children will suffer a loss of identity if they are not with 'black' families.

I have looked through the BAAF newsletter *Be My Parent* and it is clear that there is some shift taking place in the kind of parents asked for in the case of mixed-race children, but 'blackness' is privileged above all other identities which I think is worrying. Here are just two typical examples. A twelve-year-old boy is the child of a white/Asian mother and a Caribbean father. He needs, so says the advert, a 'family with at least one black parent'. Why not an Asian parent? Or a mixed-race parent? Maybe in the end the system is flexible, but at this point a family such as ours, white and Asian mix, would not even bother to apply. Two other children, step-siblings, have between them a background which includes Irish, Turkish, Lebanese and Nigerian. Here again the condition is that at least one parent should be 'black'.[36]

Marie Macey echoes this concern in an excellent new booklet on transracial adoption:

> In the literature on transracial adoption, ethnicity is confused with race and is treated as a fixed and static feature of individuals and social groups. This means that considerable effort is often spent in searching for an 'appropriate match' between babies and families in order to ensure that infants' non-existent 'cultural needs' are met. Conversely, it is not uncommon for social workers to place black children with black families which have totally different ethnic and cultural characteristics.[37]

She gives some shocking examples of these misplacements including two English/Pakistani boys who were Christian but who were placed with a devoutly Muslim Pakistani family. There is no evidence that the people making these decisions are doing so without thinking about the best interests of the children, but bad decisions are nevertheless being made.

It needs to be stressed too that these practices came into being in reaction against the dominant ideas which governed decisions until well into the sixties. During this period, not only was there no attention paid to race, but pride was taken in the fact that child-care services were colour blind. The fact that many more black children were left in care because white couples would not foster or adopt them was ignored. Instead a belief grew that a little more energy devoted to finding white middle-class parents would help these children. The British Adoption Project was instituted in 1965 to find such families for black children. Placing black and mixed-race children with white families was considered a progressive step. It was bringing together the races and creating an integrated society. And the parents themselves thought they were doing something positive to help children as well as enhancing their own lives. I spoke to a number of these parents who described how they felt then and how they feel now. One of these parents wept when being interviewed for this book:

> My own children were away. I had love and a home to give. We adopted Sammy, whose mum was Irish and father African, when he was just three and today he is a successful lawyer. We did it to give back something and suddenly people were accusing us of stealing black children and destroying their cultures. We became the enemy from being the good guys. It affected Sammy. He was a teenager when these ideas were in the media and for a few years it was terrible with him. He hated me. Then one day we had this big fight and I told him that I was like his own mother who was white. He was as white as he was black and both were important. He didn't speak to me for days and then one day just came down and said he was sorry. I can see that he did not get his black culture from us. But he got other things.

The pressure to increase adoptions came in the seventies after policy research revealed that a large number of children, particularly children of colour, were waiting years in care. The pace and rate of transracial adoption increased and little attention was paid to racial or ethnic matching or even to whether white families understood either. Young people who had had these colour-blind experiences began to speak out. In the mid-seventies, initiatives to encourage more black families to adopt were having a little success recruiting such families. As time went on, a small but vocal number of radical black social workers started to describe the white adopters as people who were 'exploiting' black and mixed-race children by 'taking' them to meet their own needs by pathologising black families.[38]

In 1985, a very powerful video produced by the group Black and in Care showed a number of young people telling their unhappy stories of being brought up 'white'. The Association of Black Social Workers and Allied Professionals led by John Small gave evidence to a select committee and asserted that transracial adoptions were a new 'slave trade'. All this had an effect on policies and practice. Not only were same race adoptions to become the norm, but mixed-race children were to be treated as 'black'. As late as 1990, there was a much publicised case of a child who looked white and had a white mother, who was placed with a white foster family which wanted to adopt the child with the approval of the birth mother. Liverpool council decided that the child should go to a black family because she had a black great-grandfather. Only legal threats stopped this from happening.[39] It is important to remember that we had a right-wing government at the time which loathed anti-racist initiatives, so it is possible that some anti-racist professionals felt compelled to take uncompromising positions in response.

The outcomes of a significant number of these placements were, as Katz says, 'remarkably successful.'[40] Research carried out in 1983 by Gill and Jackson revealed that if one looked at relationships within the family and the peer group, at self-esteem and behaviour disorders, only a tiny minority of transracially adopted children had significant problems.[41] They did, however, see themselves as 'white in all but colour', which is not healthy.

In the United States, in the late 1980s, a report came to the startling conclusion that: 'Among pre-school children, transracially adopted children have been reported to develop a concept of blackness and of themselves that is more positive than that of black children adopted by black parents.'[42]

In 1993, other researchers found that mixed-race children adopted by Caucasians had levels of ethnic identity and evaluations of black people which were similar to or better than black children living in black families.[43] Frances Wardle, author of a recently published American how-to book on parenting mixed-race children asserts:

> The research is very clear about the success of transracial adoption. Minority children raised in White homes are as successful as same race children and birth children, and if these children are exposed to aspects of their cultural and national heritage in a constant, positive and meaningful way, they develop a strong pride in their cultural and racial heritage. Research also indicates transracially adopted children grow up with more acceptance and tolerance for people of different racial and ethnic backgrounds.[44]

But such evidence has not been heard through the loud arguments which have arisen in both countries. Many social work practitioners (some black or mixed-race themselves) have ferociously challenged these findings and have argued that transracially adopted children are damaged because black children grow up with a sense of themselves which separates them from black communities and that this can result in isolation, in the adopting of 'white attitudes' and of deep and terrible confusion. Generalisations like these cropped up in various journals and at conferences particularly during the eighties:

> All black children in Britain are constantly at risk of having their self-esteem eroded by the image of themselves as black in a society where white culture and white values predominate. For the black child brought up in a white family, this risk is increased because there are no black role models immediately available,

and no black family members on hand to deal with negative experiences the child may undergo.[45]

Hardly any of this comment was based on empirical evidence although there was plenty of anecdotal material from young mixed adults who described their struggles when they lived as children in white families and often in all-white areas where they would be the only 'coloured' children. One such person, a mixed-race television researcher, told me:

> I grew up in Norfolk with really snooty white parents. They had, you know, napkin rings and a whole pile of prejudices against the poor, immigrants and neighbours with old cars. They never showed their real feelings to anyone because it was important to be polite. I just felt like an alien in that house. I am emotional, I shout and sing and dance. They are half dead. And though they sent me to a private school and I have done very well, I felt that I grew up like an orphan. I often wonder how I might have been in a house with someone like Lenny Henry. You know he has an adopted mixed-race daughter. I think she is the luckiest girl in the world.

Some case studies in the NSPCC report[46] mentioned above showed clearly that the missing 'blackness' was yearned for by some mixed-race children in care. These testimonies are invaluable because they do reveal that colour-blind placement policies can and do have negative outcomes for mixed-race children. Substitute white families who know nothing about race and cultural diversity cannot adequately meet their needs. But this does not mean that only black families will do. Anti-racist white couples and mixed-race families living in multiracial areas have been shown to be good and nurturing parents to mixed-race children.

The same people who advocate that, when matching children to foster families or adoptive families, the nearest match should be obtained when and if possible, then refuse to accept that, for a mixed-race child who grew up with a white mother (many of whom are racially and culturally aware), the best match may be with another such woman. I have never once seen a campaign to recruit white mothers who have brought up healthy and happy mixed-race children to put themselves forward as foster carers or adopters. Black and Asian women with partners outside their own groups also have much to offer if we could break out of this simplistic analysis of what mixed-race children must have whatever their own demands, and surely, in a child-centred world, their choices should matter more than they do at present. Furthermore, in being so ideologically committed to the idea that black parenting is by definition flawless, there are risks that bad, abusive and inadequate 'black' foster and adoptive parents will be accepted because it will look good on monitoring forms. In 2001, these questions were asked when a young African girl was abused and then killed by her adoptive aunt and her boyfriend. The girl was on the at risk register and several adults in the various professions failed her. Concern was expressed that not enough intervention was forthcoming because this was a black family.

The imperative to find black foster and adoptive parents can outweigh other important considerations too. Look at this leaflet produced in Bradford in 1994:

> Black children need you; they need black families. You do not need to have any special qualifications; you do not need to be a house owner; you do not need to have a spare bedroom; you do not need to be married; you do not need to be in employment. What you do need to have is – soul; patience; understanding; energy; love and time to spare.[47]

I think it is questionable whether a child should be placed with a family where there is no employment, or adequate housing but a lot of 'soul'.

There is, at times, a genuine need to redress the balance between what mixed-race children think they are and what they are. And like Marie Macey, I do not believe that we should return to the times when mixed-race children were always and only placed with white middle-class parents. But we do need much more flexibility, openness and greater attention paid to empirical data which has shown that the enormous and generalised damage that is presumed when mixed-race children are brought up by good white adoptive parents is not validated. We need to make, as Macey says, 'a realistic assessment of possibilities and alternatives when making decisions on child placement'.

Ten years ago I interviewed a white middle-class woman who had adopted a mixed-race child and was coping with external hostility and internal family problems because the child had many emotional difficulties. Her own children and husband found it hard to cope but she stayed committed and used her middle-class power to arrange for special teachers and other help for the child. He is now at university. She argues and he agrees that with a black family, the police and others would have used social control methods to 'handle' his anti-social behaviour and through no fault of theirs the black family would not have had the clout to prevent this.

More follow-through data is required to show how many transracial or same-race fosterings or adoptions break down, forcing the child to return to care even more convinced of his or her worthlessness and the harshness of the world. In the important study by Barn, Sinclair and Ferdinand, which has already been quoted extensively in this book, researchers found that for 60 per cent of the children in their sample there were no proper care plans.

Too many times black, Asian and mixed-race children have emergency placements which means that there is little scope for proper assessments of need. BAAF director Felicity Collier points out in the foreword the 'lack of clear policy and guidance at a strategic level, particularly with regards to the placement needs of children of mixed parentage.'[48]

Having a more open mind about adoptive and foster parents is not the same as saying that identity is not important. Nine of the mixed-race children in care I interviewed revealed disturbing confusion about the identities of their parents and, by implication, themselves. Janie was fifteen and mixed-race with a black father and white mother. She was not in touch with either. When the child was seven she was taken into care because she was being sexually abused by her mother's white boyfriend. After some time she went to live with her father, a jazz musician and his mother, a Jamaican. But after a racial attack he became brain-damaged. Janie ended up in care again and started to self-harm. She looks white and says there is nothing to connect her with her black family. She wants to meet her mother but the woman has asked for an injunction to stop this from happening even though she has not seen the child for ten years. Apparently she does not want her partner to know that she has been with a black man. Two of the foster families with whom Janie was placed were considered 'black'. One was West African and the other Sikh. She never fitted in and came back into a children's home which she loves and where she can be herself. It is obvious that children such as Janie need help so that they don't deny their black heritage. But this would need to happen through a long, slow and proper psychotherapeutic process, not through a key worker telling her to behave more black.

Another pair of half-siblings, one nine and the other eleven, were even more lost. Both have the same Asian mother, but one has a white and the other a black father, both now out of the picture. The mother is pregnant and unable to cope. They lied about their lives constantly and I was told later that they were in a special school with psychologists and therapists helping them come to terms with terrible physical abuse inflicted by the mother. Both children were in denial over their Asian backgrounds although the younger one did say that although her mother was 'English' she went to a temple in Southall sometimes.

On the whole, the consensus to emerge from those interviewed for this book is that social services and relevant agencies have not really understood the needs of this community. We now have a critical mass of young Britons who see themselves as mixed-race and who wish to challenge many of the assumptions that have been made about them for four centuries.

Lone parenting

It is white women who have most readily crossed racial, sexual and ethnic boundaries for love and desire. The number carries on growing. More of these white women have first-hand experience of having and bringing up mixed-race children than any other group. A large number of them are lone parents. And like all parents, there are some who have only a destructive impact on their children and others who are strong and constant. Yet in all the emotional debates, fire and fury over the identities and lives of mixed-race children, white mothers have been ignored, neglected and even tacitly blamed for just being. Far too many of them have been too anxious and nervous to object to the world talking about their children without talking to them first or checking what they, as mothers, feel. Neither white nor non-white Britons have bothered to show the basic respect to these women that is their right. Inadequate and abusive white mothers must, of course, be assessed objectively. But I found a certain amount of antagonism amongst experts that I had not expected. Some powerful people told me that white mothers whose children had entered care had proved themselves unable to mother. Claire, a mother of two mixed-race children, is now training to be a psychologist:

> I am doing this course so I can understand the damage that both racists and politically correct blacks have done to our children. The first lot wishes they weren't born; the second wants to snatch them away from their mothers, the most important person in a child's life, and to deny us rights. I may not be a very good anti-racist, but I am a damn good mother. I know many black mothers who can talk forever about racist police but they knock their children about.

According to the mixed-race television producer David Upshal, however, there are some hidden tensions and a lack of awareness in this situation which can lead white lone mothers to do the wrong thing without even knowing it. I first interviewed him in 1990 when he described how he was brought up by a white mother, the daughter of a farmer, who met his Nigerian father in Bournemouth in the early sixties. After many unhappy scenes with her family, the couple married but split up when David was eight, in part because of the racism they faced as a family. David told me that he had not seen his father since he was ten. He felt that this was a deliberate decision by his mother who was worried that her only son would be taken away to Africa. He grew up with a mother who was obviously hurt by what life had doled out to her but also had complicated views about race. She was anti-Asian (some Kenyan Asian shopkeepers were overtly prejudiced towards her and her son) and shared Mrs Thatcher's fears that these aliens would swamp British culture. All this affected her relationship with her son who said:

> I did feel I was a liability to my mum. I wonder sometimes if she'd have been happier or better off with a white kid. I'm part of a relationship and a situation which is a source of unhappiness and bitterness. We've never talked about that at all. I'm not terribly close to my mum. I don't see her very often.

The sad thing was that his mother – who obviously loved her son – could not see that he was growing up feeling more and more black and this identity grew stronger when he went to Oxford where it was cool to be black or gay. By keeping her son disconnected from his black father, his mother simply intensified this identity: '[developing a black identity] made me miss my father like hell . . . I would miss him culturally. I just felt a kind of yearning. I knew there was more to my heritage than World War 1 and Henry VIII and I wasn't getting it.'

Some time after this interview, David did in fact find his father and his family, a development which was extraordinarily important both for him and for his father who had spent years trying to make contact. This example shows how important it is for white mothers of mixed-race children not to try too hard to lay a total claim on their identity and personal life. Many mixed-race children who are denied the black side of their heritage can become damaged and thus far I agree with those who argue this case. My disagreement with them is on the remedy. If you re-appropriate a mixed-race child and claim him or her as just 'black' you are reproducing the problem that you are trying to solve. White people denying a child's blackness are wrong as are black people denying a child's whiteness. Initiatives to support such mothers are still inadequate.

Many white single mothers are still likely to be regarded as feckless and immoral and if there is a black-looking child in the pram, the silent (or at times not so silent) social disapproval is greater. As with other lone mothers, stress and economic hardship is common, but when the situation becomes racialised, additional problems arise. Timmini is white and has two mixed-race children by the same Caribbean father, now on to his third family with yet another white woman:

> They all say I am a slag and no good and deserve this because I went with a black guy who is no good, I now know it. They don't speak to me or my kids on the estate. But look around and there are as many white baby fathers, but no one talks about them in this horrible way.

Some fathers do maintain contact and make sure that the child is included within the extended family at weekends and during holidays. Most mothers welcome this but only if there is other kinds of support, especially financial. Timmini says:

> The children are half black and will be treated as black so I want them to know the granny and the yams and all that. But not if Trevor does nothing for the kids. He doesn't pay them a penny. Says he's unemployed so why is his next woman having a baby? He never looks after them when I want him to. What are my kids learning about the culture of black men, eh?

Nearly half of these mothers and children have no contact with the father and 66 per cent have no contact with anyone in the non-white community.

Research shows that 50 per cent of these women choose another black man in their next relationship though 14 per cent do go on to a white partner. Many in the former group make this choice because they are worried about the impact of a white partner on the lives of mixed-race children. In Sian Peer's research sample, she found that 40 per cent of the mothers of mixed-race children were lone parents and that 75 per cent of these were white. A large number of these white women put their children into care voluntarily because they simply cannot handle the pressure. As Peer says: 'A large number of voluntary referrals may result from the general feeling of non-competence engendered within single parents, compounded by the attitudes of white workers [social workers] towards illegitimacy, inadequate parenting, racial/cultural factors and single parenting.'[49]

Ravinder Barn carried out a study of 134 mixed-parentage children and found that the majority had white mothers over the age of 26 who were on benefits.[50] Most had never been married; others were separated or divorced. The majority of the fathers were also unemployed; the others were concentrated in manual jobs. Most had referred themselves to social services and problems in family relationships was one main cause given. Barn warns, rightly, that caution is needed to prevent further pathologisation of these white mothers. But it is even more important that these findings are not kept hidden because that surely will end up helping nobody. In an earlier study, Barn again found a high incidence of self-referral, with the following reasons given: the most common cause was relationship problems, followed by parental neglect and inadequacy, and then behavioural problems in the child and physical abuse. The mother's mental health played a significant part in outcomes. Sexual abuse came way down the list. Comparative research is needed to find out why black mothers in this position have lower rates of entry into the care system and to establish more comprehensive information on the experiences of the white mothers and their relationship with the agencies. Few appear to have suitable support networks.

Research carried out in the US shows that white mothers are more likely physically to abuse their mixed-race babies than are black mothers.[51] In another crucial piece of qualitative research, Nick Banks found that white mothers showed symptoms of depression caused by the relationship with the father or by behavioural problems of some of the children. They felt under attack, were anxious and during the therapy sessions the women 'confessed' that they had not considered enough the consequences of having a 'black' child. He writes, 'Many white people will be threatened by both the unconscious and conscious thought of the woman allowing herself to be touched by a black person with whom the group cannot relate to as more than a black 'object'.[52]

Once the black partner had gone, the sense of loss of family and other networks could be profound. I found though that in many cases, once the children arrived, white grandparents did melt and some kind of reunion was possible in a number of cases, but then the family became more 'white' and excluding of 'black'. Banks found that new relationships with white men became fraught because of the child and comparisons of white and black sexual prowess. For black women with mixed-race children, similar dilemmas exist. Some women found it hard to find new attachments with children who looked too 'black' and all of these needed to be dealt with in the therapeutic situation. Banks also recommends – I think very usefully – that therapists and social workers working with the woman need to check their own attitudes towards them and mixed-race relationships, just to make sure that there are no hidden, counter-transference dynamics.[53]

The worst case that I have heard of which shows how white mothers of mixed-race children can be treated by professionals was highlighted by People in Harmony in 1999. Linda, a white Australian woman, had a child with her British Asian boyfriend. The baby would not stop crying, and so like any other worried parents, they took him to hospital for a check-up. The doctor found several fractures and staff became suspicious that this was a case of child abuse. Again there was nothing out of the ordinary in this response. For its safety, the baby was taken into care. Soon after this, the couple spilt up and each applied for custody of the child, who was, by this time, with foster parents. While this battle was going on, doctors discovered that the child had a rare bone disease and that this was what caused the fractures. The accusation of abuse now lifted, the Asian father of the child withdrew his application for custody. His own family were not supportive, partly because the child was mixed-race. But the authorities did not unite mother and baby. They kept interrogating Linda on her race and culture awareness and there was a suggestion that the child would be put up for adoption by an Asian family. Linda was told that this was because not enough Asian people lived in Australia. After several months during which both parents had to fight these official attitudes, Linda was allowed to take home her child.

Racial harassment

I met a number of white women whose black and Asian partners were no longer with them. Some banded together or formed friendships with black lone mothers for mutual support. I met a large number, too, who were painfully isolated, angry and frightened. Their children were called 'niggers' or 'Pakis' and they were racially abused too. Peer found that 80 per cent of her sample had been racially abused.

Sue Norris in *The Colour of Love*[54] told me:

Since George left, life has been so difficult. Nobody respects me or understands how people like me feel. There were some skinheads the other day – scum, you know – and one of them kicked my little boy, Matthew, and when I screamed they just laughed and said, 'Look, one white wog and three bloody black wogs.' But you can't just hide them or be ashamed of them. You have to be proud of them. I wanted to blame their dad because he should be here more, to do his thing about black culture.

The extraordinary thing is that most local authorities do not accept that a white person can be the victim of anti-black racism. Strict monitoring forms do not have a category for 'white but seen as black'. Vera, a white mother living in North-west London, has been attacked so brutally by her racist white neighbours that she has ended up in hospital: 'But the Council won't say it's racism, because I am white. I am treated like my black neighbours, but they have had a new flat and I haven't. I think Housing thinks it is a trick so I can move.'

The Leicestershire constabulary initiated an innovative project to deal with this problem after it became clear that, between 1995 and 1997, after Asians, white victims of racial harassment were the biggest group and that 46 per cent of these were victimised because they were in mixed-race families.[55] Among the typical case studies was one which involved a white mother with two mixed-race children who had had stones thrown at them, racist name calling, excrement on their car and other incidents. The police redesigned their ethnic monitoring form to include mixed-race families and white women in these families. They also launched a publicity campaign to inform people of this change. This is still all too rare. Too many white and non-white people working in the public and voluntary sector are convinced that only black people can be victims of racism and that only white people can be racist.

Some of these lone white mothers end up with racist attitudes themselves as they cope with their problems and feel abandoned. Sometimes they communicate these to the children. But far more do their best not to let this happen. In a moving book about mixed-race young adults in Canada,[56] two testimonies show the two sides clearly:

> I love my mother. I hate her racism. I can't separate the two, the racism, the love, the hate.

> When you say you did not give me a black identity, I say to you, 'Give yourself a break. Don't you think you had enough to do?' You gave me a mother's love and I grew up strong and secure and proud to be me. I learnt black pride later, so did you.

Some white lone mothers – the minority – have good relations with the fathers of their children who feel attached to the extended black family. On the whole, middle-class white women with middle-class black, Asian or Chinese men are strong, secure and very happy to be in their situations. Emma is one of these: 'Look at us. Imagine what my life would be like with an English stockbroker. I left my husband for Barry because Barry is African, a man with emotions, not a stuffed shirt. Look at the children. I want to cry when I see how lovely they are. Regrets? You must be joking.'

But if there was a break up, then many of the same dynamics, albeit in a more subtle form, revealed themselves. Ira, a Jewish mother of a mixed-race child, is a lecturer:

> You don't think about any of this when you are in love, pregnant, blissful. Then you have this unique child who looks like nobody and you love it to bits. When divorce happens though you see all that blackness which you want to rub off because it hurts to see it and because you realise that this thing never works and your parents were right after all.

The future

During the course of my study, the following areas have emerged as needing further consideration and research leading to relevant policy development.

Open debate

There is a need for an open, ongoing debate on many of the issues covered in this book. The discussions need to be carried out without rancour and recrimination and without defensiveness. Taboo subjects need to be opened up. These include the racism experienced by children of mixed parentage from their own white family members and the large number of black men who are absent fathers in mixed-race families.

Changing the terminology

Terminology has been fixed by policy makers while in reality people most affected have moved on. The view was expressed by many of my interviewees that it is important to listen to children of mixed parentage, to know what they call themselves, just as white and black young people know what to call themselves. However, from the many discussions I had, it was clear that there is no reason to assume that there will be consensus about terminology.

Ethnic monitoring

Ethnic monitoring is a blunt tool. Some thought needs to be given to how this practice can be used to provide a better picture of mixed-race people, their identity, age and geographical distribution. Categories for monitoring must not, however, be confused with identity categories, which have to be devised by people of mixed parentage themselves and about which there is no easy agreement. Thus, while it is important to keep debating the categories devised for monitoring (particularly to ensure that people of mixed parentage are not obscured in 'Other' categories), these should be tailored to the specific purposes for which they are to be used and are, thus, likely to change over time and be different for different purposes.

Transracial adoption

This is perhaps one of the most live issues in this area. Some people consider that children of 'mixed parentage' could be placed with white, black or mixed families without any of these placements necessarily being transracial (since all these families occur 'naturally' for children of mixed parentage). Transracial adopters want to be supported and not made to feel guilty. For those who have been transracially adopted, some said they wanted greater professional help so they can learn to 'own' their identities. Some people felt that, on balance, children of mixed parentage should not be placed with white families who have no experience of racism and may not have black friends. None of the debates so far have been based on adequate independent empirical evidence.

The significance of geographical location

Mixed-parentage families living in areas of the country which are mainly white may be more at risk of harassment than if they lived in more mixed areas. There are clear implications for housing and racial harassment policies.

National counselling and marriage guidance services which are sensitive to mixed relationships and 'mixed parentage'.

After interviewing all the major agencies it is clear that there is no understanding of how race plays a part in marital breakdown and problems for children. A totally colour and culture blind approach – which is what we have at present – is of little use to many of the communities who make up this nation. Training is clearly needed and is a priority.

Research

There is a pressing need for more research on the identities of people in mixed relationships and the lives of mixed families living in a range of circumstances. People responsible for children in schools, in therapeutic services and in the public care system also need to be aware of the identities of children of mixed parentage. More research on mixed parentage children in the public care system and on the reasons for family breakdown in mixed households of various social classes is also needed. What are the pressures that lead to proportionally more children of mixed-parentage with lone white mothers entering the public care system than other children? Why is there a shortage of 'mixed' adoptive families?

Racial harassment and racism

At present there is too narrow an understanding of racism and how it affects various people. The experiences of mixed families and lone white mothers of mixed-parentage children too often fall outside the simple rule book approach taken by various agencies. Social workers, police forces and those working in education and local authority housing all need to take policy decisions about how to deal with this issue.

Education

We do not know enough about how children of mixed parentage fare in education. How many excluded children are actually mixed-race for example? How does the curriculum address their needs? There is a dearth of materials showing mixed-race families as normal. These children are not black. They are mixed-race and they do not feel that their lives are 'covered' by books and other material which show black and Asian families. There is some anecdotal evidence that bullying against these children comes from all groups, yet there is no specific guidance available on this. In a small number of nursery schools and primary schools, some identity work is being done, but this is ad hoc and entirely dependent on individuals and circumstances. Alice Sawyer, a psychotherapist, describes one model which she tried and tested and which seems to me to have real potential. She suggests that the focus should be the personal identity of each child, whatever the background. This would reduce the risk of making mixed-race children feel self-conscious in a negative way or feel 'picked on' and made to feel that they are creatures apart. Sawyer's suggested process involves the parents and nursery workers and, by being more descriptive than prescriptive, I can see how useful it could be for mixed-race children.[57]

Teaching packs which overtly tackle the history and achievements of mixed-race people and which also include difficult discussion topics for young adults would be very useful too. Frances Wardle suggests that teachers should:

> ... explore their feelings about biracial and biethnic children; they must examine their reactions to these children and their parents. Do they feel interracial relationships are somehow unnatural and unhealthy? Are they uneasy around these families? Do they insist that the child is black even when parents choose to raise them as biracial? And most importantly, does she automatically conclude that any problem the child has is due to his mixed-race status?[58]

Attitudes to mixed-race families

We need to acknowledge that these attitudes can be very negative and that all communities are responsible for the victimisation of mixed-race people. Leaders need to take some responsibility in challenging these attitudes. Why are we so silent when some communities violate their children's basic human rights in order to keep them within the fold when we decry white racism against mixed-race people? Perhaps here too there is a need for some public debate to deal with the 'fear of disappearance' which so many minority groups genuinely feel.

Conclusion

I have come to the end of my long journey in which I have tried to understand and describe mixed-race Britons, their lives and aspirations and the responses of society and policy makers. We need many more people to make many more such journeys so that in a decade or so we too can have a body of writing which gives a fuller picture of these rich and complex global citizens. The future looks full of possibilities and dangers. As this group grows, some people will experience greater acceptance and others may well be faced with stronger objections from people who feel that 'pure' ancestries are being polluted at a faster rate than before. In the twenty-first century, national, cultural and personal identities have become central issues. These pre-occupations will undoubtedly impact on mixed-race Britons, who, in turn, should be empowered to influence the discourse and policies. They will no longer be prepared to be defined by others and will seek to be described and catered for on their own terms. Politicians, policy makers, practitioners and researchers are currently very attentive to the importance and dynamics of family life. All of them will need to incorporate the needs of mixed-race families. And finally, the way mixed-race people are treated in this society will be a test of how well modern Britain is promoting the values of equality, diversity and respect.

Notes

Introduction

1. Clifford S. Hill, *How Colour Prejudiced is Britain?*, Gollancz, London, 1965.
2. In *Britain's Slave Trade*, Channel 4, 3 October 1999.
3. See *The Battle of Britain*, Demos, 1995.
4. In Part 1. Poem first published in 1701.
5. 'Mixed and Matched', *Observer*, 9 January 2000.
6. *Guardian*, 18 December 2000.
7. Interview with Stephanie Merritt in the *Observer*, 16 January 2000.
8. Paper given at a seminar on mixed-race Britons, Institute For Public Policy Research, 20 March 1998.
9. Anne Wilson, *Mixed Race Children: A Study of Identity*, Allen & Unwin, London, 1987, v.
10. Anne Wilson, *op. cit.*, vi.
11. Madeleine Ashtiani, People in Harmony Newsletter, Issue 24, April 2000, 1–2.
12. Yasmin Alibhai-Brown and Anne Montague, Virago Press, London, 1992.
13. Susan Benson, *Ambiguous Ethnicity: Interracial Families in London*, Cambridge University Press, Cambridge, 1981, 21.
14. Tony Parsons, *Arena*, Spring 1991.
15. Beth Day, *Sexual Life Between Blacks and Whites*, Collins, 1974, 8.
16. *Sun*, 10 September 1990.
17. *New Moon*, the Jewish arts and listings monthly, May 1991.
18. Ashtiani, *op. cit.*, 2.
19. *Mixed Race Relationships in the UK: An Annotated Bibliography of Sources*, Bibliographies in Ethnic Relations, No. 14, June 1996, 1.
20. See Chapter 6, 'The "half-caste" Pathology', in Paul Rich, *Race and Empire*, Cambridge University Press, 1986, 120–45.
21. See the introduction in Yasmin Alibhai-Brown and Anne Montague, *The Colour of Love*, Virago Press, London, 1992.
22. *Guardian*, 22 May 1997.

Chapter 1 History up to 1900

1. David Livingstone, *Narratives of an Expedition to the Zambezi*, London, 1865, 416.

2. Fernando Henriques, *Children of Conflict: A Study of Interracial Sex and Marriage*, Dutton, New York, 1975, xii. I have taken much of the material on early history which follows from this very well written and researched book.
3. Zia Sardar, Ashish Nandy and Merryl Wynn Davies, *Barbaric Others: A Manifesto on Western Racism*, Pluto Press, 1993, 38–9.
4. Kenneth Ballhatchet, *Race, Sex and Class Under the Raj*, Weidenfeld and Nicolson, 1980, vii.
5. See Ronald Hyam, *Britain's Imperial Century, 1885–1914; A Study of Empire and Expansion*, London, 1976.
6. Book II, ix.
7. *Anthologia Palatina*, 5, 210.
8. Satire VI, 599.
9. Story appears in *Antiquities of the Jews*, Book 11, Chapter 10.
10. In Henriques, *op. cit.*, 13.
11. See the *Cambridge History of Islam*, 1970.
12. Canto 28.
13. For a fuller and erudite exposition of this, see Chapter 2 in Ziauddin Sardar and Merryl Wyn Davies, *Distorted Imagination*, Grey Seal, 1990.
14. Penguin, 1997, 54.
15. In Henriques, *op. cit.*, 16.
16. In C R Boxer, *Race Relations in the Portuguese Colonial Empire 1415–1825*, Oxford, 1963, 60–1.
17. This meant mixed-race.
18. This meant the product of a European father and mixed-race mother.
19. In C R Boxer, *op. cit.*, 63.
20. *The Financial Times Weekend*, 22 July 2000.
21. Quoted in Susan Benson, *op. cit.*
22. Read Peter Fryer's brilliant *Staying Power*, Pluto, 1884, for an account of this.
23. Published in 1657.
24. *Titus Andronicus*, Act IV.
25. Rana Kabbani, *Imperial Fictions: Europe's Myth of Orient*, Pandora, 1986, 20.
26. Ben Okri wrote a compelling analysis of the play in his essay 'Leaping Out of Shakespeare's Terror', in Kwesi Owusu, ed, *Storms of the Heart*, Camden Press, 1998.
27. I am indebted to Kabbani for much of the analysis in this section of the book.
28. See Peter Fryer, *op. cit.*, 68–9
29. Edward Long, *Candid Reflections*, London, 1772.
30. *Memoirs and Anecdotes of Philip Thicknesse*, 1778, 102.
31. 'Blacks in Eighteenth Century Art and Society', in Kwesi Owusu, ed, *op. cit.*

32. Several of these stories appear in Peter Fryer, *op. cit.*
33. *Bath Journal*, 7 December 1789.
34. Colonial Office, Dispatches and Reports, Series No Co, 267/233, 1 August 1883.
35. *Captain Cook's Voyages*, Everyman, 1906, 38.
36. In J Ritson, ed, *Ancient English Metrical Romances*, 1802.
37. MS Bodley 3938, published in J Ritson, ed, *op. cit.*
38. First published in 1822.
39. Kabbani, *op. cit.*, 5–6.
40. *Cobbett's Weekly Political Register*, Vol. 24, Col. 935.
41. Paperback edition, Los Angeles, 1966.
42. For an excellent analysis of this see Kenan Malik, *The Meaning of Race*, Chapter 3, 'The Making of the Discourse on Race', Macmillan, 1996.
43. Reprinted in 1962, London.
44. Personal communication, Dr Anthony Grayling, author of a new biography of William Hazlitt.
45. See *London Labour and the London Poor*, Griffin, Bohn and Co, 1861, Vol. 1 and Vol. IV.
46. Rozina Visram, *Ayahs, Lascars and Princes*, Pluto Press, 1986.
47. *Daily Graphic*, 30th October 2000.
48. Asher and Martin Hoyles, *Remember Me*, Hansib, 1999.
49. Directors papers, East India Company, 6 April 1687, para 8.
50. VG Kiernan, *The Lords of Mankind*, The Cresset Library, 1969, 57.
51. For a full account of this, see Ballhatchet, *op. cit.*
52. Quoted by Ballhatchet, *op. cit.*, 117.
53. Curzon to Hamilton letters, India Office Library, MSS Eur, f111, 15 November 1901.
54. For further details see Chapter 5 in Ballhatchet, *op. cit.*
55. From Colonial Office papers, quoted by Henriques, *op. cit.*, 93.
56. Henriques, *op. cit.*, 95.
57. RG Ragatz, *The Fall of the Planter Class in the British Caribbean, 1763–1833*, 2nd ed, NY, 1963, 5.
58. Vol. 2, London, 1801.
59. See Chapter 3 in Henriques, *op. cit.*
60. *An Abstract of the Evidence Delivered before a Select Committee of the House of Commons on the Abolition of the Slave Trade*, London, 1791, 73.
61. John Stewart, *An Account of Jamaica and its Inhabitants*, London, 1823, 173–174.
62. Jean Rhys, *Wide Sargasso Sea*, first published by Andre Deutsch, 1966.
63. Mrs Flannigan, *Antigua and the Antiguans*, London, 1944, Vol. 11, 165.
64. Anthony Trollope, *The West Indies and the Spanish Main*, London, 1859, 73.

65. Ann Maury, *Memoirs of a Huguenot Family*, NY, 1872, 349–50.
66. WEB Du Bois, *Darkwater. Voices from Within the Veil*, New York, 1969, 16.
67. Archive material, quoted by Henriques, *op. cit.*, 70.

Chapter 2 History after 1900

1. WEB Dubois, *The Souls of Black Folk*, 1903, in *The Three Negro Classics*, Avon Books, NY, 1965, 102.
2. Adolf Hitler, *Mein Kampf*, translated by R Mannheim, Pimlico, 1992, 259.
3. C Dover quoted by Phoenix and Tizzard, *op.cit*, 21.
4. JA Rogers, *Sex and Race*, Vol. 111, Helga Rogers, Florida, 1944, 32.
5. R Park, 'Human Migration and the Marginal Man', *American Journal of Sociology*, 33(1928), 881–93.
6. E Stonequist, *The Marginal Man: A Study of Personality and Culture*, Russell and Russell, 1937.
7. I am indebted to Christine Chambers, Sue Funge, Gail Harris and Cynthia Williams for this information which appears in their manual *Celebrating Identity*, Trentham Books, 1996.
8. Broadcast in April 2000.
9. Conrad wrote from the end of the nineteenth century into the twentieth century. *Heart of Darkness* was published in the twentieth century.
10. Interviewed in the *Daily Mail*, 4 August 1980.
11. *Along this Way*, London, 1941, 80.
12. Beth Day, *Sexual Life Between Blacks and Whites*, Collins, London, 1974, 23.
13. Quoted by Henriques, *op. cit*, 27.
14. Frantz Fanon, *Black Skins, White Masks*, Pluto, 1968, 63.
15. Eldridge Cleaver, *Soul on Ice*, Dell, New York, 1970, 159.
16. WEB Dubois, *The Souls of Black People*, Bedford Books, Boston, 1997, 36.
17. Paul B Rich, *Race and Empire in British Politics*, Cambridge University Press, Cambridge, 1986, 121.
18. The *Liverpool Echo*, 10 June 1919.
19. The *Manchester Guardian*, 17 June 1919.
20. *The Times*, 14 June 1919.
21. *Ambiguous Ethnicity: Interracial Families in London*, Cambridge, 1981, 6.
22. In Rich, *op. cit.*, 129.
23. *Ibid.*, 138.
24. Interviewed for *Beyond Black and White*, BBC, Summer 1998.
25. Fletcher Report, p 20, full reference below.
26. Muriel Fletcher, *An Investigation into the Colour Problem in*

Liverpool and Other Ports, published in 1930 by the Liverpool Association for the Welfare of Half-Caste Children.

27. Peggy Ashcroft spoke candidly about this on an interview for BBC2 in 1987.

28. S Collins, *Coloured Minorities in Britain*, Lutterworth Press, 1957.

29. Quoted in Rozina Visram, *Ayahs, Lascars and Princes, op. cit.*, 117 and 261.

30. David Omissi, *Voices from the Great War*, Macmillan, 1999, 113–14 and 119.

31. *Ibid.*, 39.

32. *A Report on the Kitchener Indian Hospital, Brighton*, Colonel Bruce Seton, IOR, MSS EUR F143/82.

33. *The Colour of Love, op. cit.*, 66–9.

34. In Ben Bousquet and Colin Douglas, *West Indian Women at War*, 64.

35. Cabinet Papers, 13 October 1942.

36. In Yasmin Alibhai-Brown and Anne Montague, *op. cit.*, 71–2.

37. See report in the *Independent*, July 8 2000.

38. In Yasmin–Alibhai-Brown and Anne Montague, *op. cit.*, 95–100.

39. In *Beyond Black and White, op. cit.*

40. In Yasmin Alibhai-Brown and Anne Montague, *op. cit.*

41. See Yasmin Alibhai-Brown, *Who Do We Think We Are?*, Penguin, 2000, 56. There is a whole chapter which deals with immigration.

42. Kenan Malik, *The Meaning of Race, op. cit.*, 19.

43. BBC TV, 21 May 1958.

44. S Patterson, *Dark Strangers*, Tavistock, 1963.

45. *English Churchman*, 10 April 1964; quoted in Susan Benson, *Ambiguous Ethnicity*.

46. For details see Yasmin Alibhai-Brown, *Who Do We Think We Are?, op. cit.* and Andrew Geddes, *The Politics of Immigration and Race*, Baseline Books, 1996, 56.

47. The *Sunday People*, 11 June 1962.

48. Susan Benson, *Ambiguous Ethnicity, op. cit.*, 150.

49. *The Listener*, 2 November 1978.

50. All these and other characters are well researched and described in *Remember Me*, by Asher and Martin Hoyles, Hansib, 1999.

Chapter 3 The Current Landscape

1. Lisa Jones, *Bulletproof Diva*, Penguin, 1994, 59.

2. *Ethnic Intermarriage in Britain*, OPCS Trends, No. 40, 1985.

3. In Tizzard and Phoenix, *op. cit.*, 13.

4. Reported in the *Guardian*, 24 May 1989.

5. Reported in *Today*, 7 March 1991.
6. See Charlie Owen, 'Using the Labour Force Survey to Estimate Britain's Ethnic Minority Populations', in *Population Trends* 72 (1993) 18–23.
7. Tariq Modood, Richard Berthoud et al, *Diversity and Disadvantage, Ethnic Minorities in Britain*, 1997.
8. John Haskey, 'Population Review: (8) The Ethnic Minority and Overseas-born Populations of Great Britain', *Population Trends* 88, Summer (1997).
9. Charlie Owen, '"Mixed Race" in Official Statistics', paper presented at the IPPR seminar on mixed race, 1998.
10. Owen, *op.cit.*
11. Asher and Martin Hoyles, *op.cit.*, 17–18.
12. See my *True Colours*, Institute for Public Policy Research, 1999.
13. Survey evidence presented in Yasmin Alibhai-Brown, *True Colours: Public Attitudes to Multiculturalism and the Role of Government*, IPPR, 1999.
14. See the survey evidence in my book, *True Colours*, IPPR, 1999.
15. See the press coverage on 30 August 2000.
16. See my column in the *Independent*, 13 February 2001.
17. I describe the depth of this prejudice in *No Place Like Home*, Virago Press, London, 1994.
18. Interviewed for a BBC2 programme, in 1993, based on Yasmin Alibhai-Brown and Anne Montague's *The Colour of Love, op. cit.*
19. For an excellent dissection of this issue see Valerie Smith, 'Split Affinities: The Case of Interracial Rape', in M Hirsch and E Fox Keller, eds, *Conflicts in Feminism*, Routledge, 1992, 271–87.
20. Theresa Wobbe, 'Gender Relations and Racial Violence', in Helma Lutz, Anne Phoenix and Nira Yuval-Davis, *Crossfires: Nationalism, Racism and Gender in Europe*, eds, Pluto, 1995, 89–90.
21. 'Celebratory Discourses and Racialised Practices', paper given at a seminar, *Rethinking Mixed Race Families and Mixed Parentage*, organised by the Institute for Public Policy Research for the European Year Against Racism, seminar report published 1999, 16.
22. Paper given at the IPPR seminar, *op. cit.*
23. Paper given at the IPPR seminar, *op. cit.*

Chapter 4 Identity

1. Amin Maalouf, *On Identity*, The Harvill Press, 2000, 29.
2. Interview with the author in June 1997.
3. Yasmin Alibhai-Brown and Anne Montague, *The Colour of Love*, Virago Press, London, 1992, 241–2.

4. Interviewed by Peter Akinti in the magazine *Untold*, April 2000, 30–3.
5. J Ifekwunigwe in *Soundings*, Stuart Hall et al, eds, Lawrence and Wishart, Issue 5, Spring 1997, 103.
6. Maalouf, *op. cit.*, 17.
7. Jill Olumide, *People in Harmony*, undated, 13.
8. Reported in the *Scotsman*, 5 August 1996.
9. The *Sunday People*, 8 February 1998.
10. Quoted in Asher and Martin Hoyles, *op. cit.*, 18.
11. The *Mail on Sunday*, 8 February 1998.
12. Interviewed by Kate Hilpern in the *Independent*, 30 August 1999.
13. Maria Root, *op. cit.*, 3.
14. He said this on the *Oprah Winfrey Show* in April 1997.
15. J Ifekwunigwe, *Scattered Belongings*, Routledge, 1999, 16.
16. David Dean published his ideas in the *British Medical Journal*, 13 February 1999.
17. See Anne Phoenix's two papers in the seminar report, *Rethinking Mixed Race Families and Mixed Race Parentage*, Institute of Public Policy Research, 1997.
18. *The Best of Both Worlds: Celebrating Mixed Parentage*, 1995, 11.
19. Interviewed in *Love in Black and White*, BBC2.
20. Lisa Jones, *op. cit.*, 29.
21. Anne Wilson, *Mixed Race Children; A Study of Identity*, Allen and Unwin, 1987, 176.
22. The *Guardian*, 9 February 2000.
23. 'Ethnic Preferences and Perceptions among Asian and White British Middle School Children', *Social Development*, 1(1) (1992).
24. Kenneth Clark, *Prejudice and Your Child*, Beacon Press, Boston, 1955, 72.
25. There is a full discussion of this by James Jacobs in 'Identity Development in Biracial Children', in Maria Root, ed, *Racially Mixed Children*, Sage, 1992.
26. David Milner, *Children and Race*, Harmondsworth, Penguin, 1975.
27. For details of these look in Anne Wilson's book, *op. cit.*
28. Barbara Tizzard and Anne Phoenix, *Black, White or Mixed Race*, Routledge, 1993.
29. *Ibid.*, 3.
30. *Ibid.*, 47.
31. *Ibid.*, 53.
32. See the concluding chapter in this Tizzard and Phoenix study.
33. Jewelle Taylor Gibbs and Alice M Hines, *Negotiating Ethnic Identity, Issues for Black-White Biracial Adolescents* in

Racially Mixed People in America, *op. cit.*, 223–39.
34. Ilan Katz, *The Construction of Racial Identity in Children of Mixed Parentage; Mixed Metaphors*, Jessica Kingsley, 1996, 179.
35. *Ibid.*, 189.
36. Nick Banks, 'Some Considerations of "Racial" Identification and Self-esteem when Working with Mixed Ethnicity Children and Their Mothers as Social Service Clients', *Social Services Research*, 3 (1992).
37. Foreword in Ivor Gaber and Jane Aldridge, eds, *In the Best Interests of the Child*, Free Association Books, 1994, xi.
38. See Barry Richard's brilliant essay, 'What is Identity?' in Ivor Gaber and Jane Aldridge, eds, *In the Best Interests of the Child*, Free Association Books, 1994.
39. The manual is compiled by Christine Chambers, Sue Funge, Gail Harris and Cynthia Williams and published by Trentham Books, 1996, 4.
40. 27 October 2000.
41. The *Guardian*, 9 December 1996.
42. *Caste In Half*, 1998.
43. *The Sunday Times*, 11 August 1996.
44. *The Sunday Times*, 25 August 1996.
45. In *Caste in Half*, 1998.
46. In *Love in Black and White*, BBC2.
47. In the *Independent*, 14 February 2000 and the Channel 4 film, *The Colour of Love*, 16 February 2000.
48. In *Love in Black and White*, BBC2.
49. J Ifekwunigwe, *Scattered Belongings*, *op. cit.*, 147–9. This whole transcribed interview is well worth reading to understand how this confidence came into being.
50. Yasmin Alibhai-Brown and Anne Montague, *The Colour of Love*, *op. cit.*, 274.
51. Yasmin Alibhai-Brown and Anne Montague, *The Colour of Love*, *op. cit.*, 222.
52. Yasmin Alibhai-Brown and Anne Montague, *The Colour of Love*, *op. cit.*, 217.
53. J Ifekwunigwe, *Scattered Belongings*, *op. cit.*, 112–13

Chapter 5 Family and Relationships

1. Jacques Janssen, 'Mixed Divorce? And Why?', paper presented by Janssen of University of Nijmegen University, the Netherlands, at a conference at the University of York, 14 April 2000.
2. OPCS figures published in July 1990 and reported in the *Daily Mail* on 5 July 1990.
3. In *Today*, 7 March 1991.

4. Described by Jo-Anne Goodwin in the *Guardian*, 2 July 1994.

5. The *Observer*, 20 March 2000.

6. In *Love in Black and White*, BBC2.

7. In the *Daily Mail*, 4 March 1994.

8. Quoted at length by Jo Anne Goodwin, the *Guardian*, op. cit.

9. In *The Sunday Times*, 19 July 1998.

10. In the *Guardian*, 2 July 1994.

11. The *Guardian*, 12 November 1998.

12. I interviewed Terry and Dee for *The Colour Of Love* and checked these ideas with them for this book. Nothing had changed in terms of how Terry saw things although Dee was more worried about racism than before.

13. In the *Independent*, 15 August 1998.

14. The *Guardian*, 13 December 1992.

15. From two separate interviews with me, the *Guardian*, 6 February 1992 and *The Colour of Love, op. cit.*

16. Story and pictures in the *Guardian*, 1 March 2000.

17. *Jack and Zena, A True Story of Love and Danger*, Victor Gollancz, 1997.

18. Reported in the *Daily Telegraph*, 7 September 1990.

19. Yasmin Alibhai-Brown and Anne Montague, *The Colour of Love, op. cit.*, 23–4.

20. See the various collections put together by the American, Nancy Friday. Her books became bestsellers in the 80s.

21. In *Love in Black and White*, BBC2.

22. See 'Are We A Tolerant Nation?', in *The Reader's Digest*, November 2000.

23. 29 February 2000.

24. Ahdaf Soueif, *The Map of Love*, Bloomsbury, London, 1999.

25. Abdulrazak Gurnah, *Admiring Silence*, Penguin, 1996.

26. Abdulrazak Gurnah, *op. cit.*, 89.

27. Danzy Senna, *From Caucasia With Love*, Bloomsbury, London, 2000.

28. Danzy Senna, *op. cit.*, 56–7.

29. *Marrying Out*, Channel 4, Programme 1.

30. Yasmin Alibhai-Brown and Anne Montague, *The Colour of Love, op. cit.* 1992, 182–91.

31. Rabbi Jonathan Romaine, *I'm Jewish My Partner Isn't*, January 1993.

32. *Marrying Out*, Channel 4, Programme 3.

33. In *Love in Black and White*, BBC2.

34. Letter written to me in March 1999 following *Beyond Black and White*, Radio 4, March 1999, which I presented.

35. Personal communication, June 1999.

36. Radio 4, *Beyond Black and White*, March 1999.

37. Radio 4, *Beyond Black and White, op. cit.*

Chapter 6 Social Policy

1. See end note 7, Chapter 4.
2. S Peer, *Negotiating Identity*, 4.
3. Ravinder Barn, 'White Mothers, Mixed Parentage Children and Child Welfare', *British Journal of Social Work* 29 (1999) 269–84.
4. Paper given at the IPPR seminar, *op. cit.*
5. Ravinder Barn, Ruth Sinclair and Dionne Ferdinand, *Acting On Principle: An Examination of Race and Ethnicity in Social Services Provision for Children and Families*, BAAF and the Commission for Racial Equality, 1997, 1.
6. Lynda Ince, *Making it Alone*, BAAF, 1998.
7. Barn et al, *Acting on Principle, op. cit.*, 65.
8. S Peer, *op. cit.*, 76.
9. *Assessment Framework; Assessing Children in Need and their Families, Practice Guidance*, Department of Health (DoH).
10. Adele Jones and Jabeer Butt, *Taking the Initiative*, 1995.
11. Interview with me in 1999.
12. Stuart Hall, 'Cultural Identity and Diaspora', in J Rutherford, ed, *Identity: Community, Culture, Difference*, Lawrence and Wishart, 1990, 225.
13. See BAAF, Practice Note 26.
14. See BAAF, Practice Note 13.
15. *Adopting a Better Policy*, CRE,1990.
16. Peer, *op. cit.*, 19.
17. See Nick Banks 'Mixed up Kid', *Social Work Today* 24 (1992) 3, 12–13 and his 'Some Considerations of "Racial" Identification and Self-esteem when Working with Mixed Ethnicity Children and Their Mothers as Social Service Clients', Social Services Research, 3 1992.
18. ABSWAP submission to the House of Commons Select Committee on Adoption, 1983.
19. Barn et al, *Acting on Principle*, 1997, *op. cit.*
20. Paper given at the IPPR seminar. *op. cit.*
21. See reports in the *Manchester Evening News*, 8 November 1996.
22. T Okitikpi, 'Mixed Race Children', *Issues in Social Work Education*, 19 (1998), 93–106.
23. T Okitikpi, *op. cit.*, 111.
24. Barn et al, *Acting on Principle, op. cit.*, 71.
25. DoH, *op. cit.*, 46.
26. DoH, *op. cit.*, 43.
27. Ravinder Barn, *Black and In Care*, BAAF, 1993.
28. June Thoburn *et al*, *Permanent Family Placement for Children of Ethnic Minority Origin*, Jessica Kingsley, 2000.
29. Reported in the *Independent*, 31 May 1998.
30. B Prevatt Goldstein, 'Black Children with One White Parent', in *Seminar Papers*, BAAF, 1995/1996, 57.

31. *Ibid.*, 61.
32. Derek Kirkton, *'Race', Identity and the Politics of Adoption*, Centre for Adoption and Identity Studies, University of East London, 1995, 28.
33. 'Direct Identity Work', in Ravinder Barn, ed, *Working With Black Children and Adolescents in Need*, BAAF, 1999, 18–34.
34. See press reports of 28 September 1997.
35. See the Law pages of the *Independent*, 4 September 1998.
36. Both cases are in Issue 51, April 1999.
37. Marie Macey, *Transracial Adoption: What's the Problem?*, People in Harmony, 1998, 15.
38. See for example John Small's 'The Crisis in Adoption', in the *Journal of Psychiatry*, Spring, 1982.
39. See *The Times*, 17 March 1990.
40. Ilan Katz, *The Construction of Racial Identity in Children of Mixed Parentage, Mixed Metaphors, op. cit.*, 4.
41. O Gill and B Jackson, *Adoption and Race: Black, Asian and Mixed-race Children in White Families*, Batsford Academic and Educational, 1983 .
42. 'Transracial Adoption and the Development of Identity at Age Eight', *Child Welfare* 66 (1) (1987), 45–55.
43. See Marie Macey, *op. cit.*, 23.
44. Frances Wardle, *Tomorrow's Children*, Center for the Study of Biracial Children, Denver, 1999, 49.
45. A Mullender and D Miller, 'The Ebony Group: Black Children in White Foster Homes', *Adoption and Fostering* 9 (1) (1990), 33–40.
46. Adele Jones and Jabeer Butt, *op. cit.*
47. City of Bradford Metropolitan Council, 1994.
48. Barn et al, *Acting on Principle, op. cit.*, iv.
49. Peer, *Negotiating Identity, op. cit.*, 49.
50. Ravinder Barn, *Single White Mothers with Black Children, op. cit.*, 29.
51. B Needell, *Preliminary data analysis on biracial children in foster care in California*, unpublished paper discussed by Barn 1999, *op. cit.*
52. Nick Banks, 'Single White Mothers with Black Children in Therapy', *Clinical Child Psychology and Psychiatry*, 1 (1) (1996), 20.
53. Nick Banks, *Single White Mothers with Black Children in Therapy, op. cit.*
54. Yasmin Alibhai-Brown and Anne Montague, *The Colour of Love, op. cit.*, 21–3.
55. Paper delivered by Inspector June Webb at the IPPR seminar, *op. cit.*
56. C Camper, *Miscegenation Blues: The Voices of Mixed Race*

Women, Sister Vision, 1994.
57. Alice Sawyer, 'Identity Project on "Myself"', in *Working With Black Children and Adolescents in Care*, BAAF, 34–48.
58. F. Wardle, *Tomorrow's Children*, op. cit., 58.